D0204913

CAMPAIGN FOR PRESIDENT

The Managers Look at '88

Susan Estrich   Ronald H. Brown   Judy Woodruff

David Gergen   Frank Fahrenkopf   Roger Ailes

Linda Wertheimer   Lee Atwater   Susan Estrich

CAMPAIGN FOR PRESIDENT

The Managers Look at '88

Edited by
DAVID R. RUNKEL

The Institute of Politics
John F. Kennedy School of Government
Harvard University

Auburn House Publishing Company
Dover, Massachusetts

Library of Congress Cataloging in Publication Data

Campaign for president : the managers look at '88 / edited by David R. Runkel.

    p. cm.

  Includes index.

  ISBN 0-86569-194-0

  1. Presidents—United States—Election—1988—Congresses.
2. Electioneering—United States—Congresses. 3. United States—Politics and government—1981–1989. I. Runkel, David R.

E880.C363   1989

324.973'0927—dc20   89-6767
                                        CIP

Printed in the United States of America

CONTENTS

THE PARTICIPANTS

Roger Ailes, the Bush campaign
Lee Atwater, the Bush campaign
Robert Beckel, consultant
Paul Brountas, the Dukakis campaign
Ronald Brown, the Jackson campaign
William Carrick, the Gephardt campaign
Susan Casey, the Hart campaign
John Corrigan, the Dukakis campaign
E. J. Dionne, *The New York Times*
Frederick DuVal, the Babbitt campaign
Larry Eichel, *The Philadelphia Inquirer*
Susan Estrich, the Dukakis campaign
Frank Fahrenkopf, the Republican National Committee
Howard Fineman, *Newsweek*
Edward Fouhy, the Commission on Presidential Debates
David Gergen, *U.S. News and World Report*
Richard Hatcher, the Jackson campaign
Allan B. Hubbard, the DuPont campaign
William Lacy, the Dole campaign
Daniel Mariaschin, the Haig campaign
J. Frederick Martin, the Gore campaign
Terry Michael, the Simon campaign
Martin Nolan, *The Boston Globe*
R. Marc Nuttle, the Robertson campaign
Martin Plissner, CBS
A. Matthew Reese, political consultant

Timothy Ridley, the Biden campaign

Edward Rodgers, the Bush campaign

Edward Rollins, the Kemp campaign

Paul Taylor, *The Washington Post*

Linda Wertheimer, National Public Radio

Judy Woodruff, "The MacNeil-Lehrer NewsHour"

Graham Allison, dean, John F. Kennedy School of Government, Harvard University

Milton Gwirtzman, Senior Advisory Board member, Institute of Politics, Harvard University

David Runkel, deputy director, Institute of Politics, Harvard University

Shirley Williams, John F. Kennedy School of Government, former Member of Parliament, Great Britain

INTRODUCTION

The 1988 election year, the first in 20 years without a sitting President in the race, has been roundly criticized. Many have said that it started too soon, that it was too long on negative advertising and too short on discussion of the problems and challenges facing the country, and that the press was too intrusive in the political process.

Only 50 percent of the eligible voters participated—the lowest voter turnout since immediately after women were added to the pool of eligible voters. Some attribute the lack of interest to revulsion by the electorate to the conduct of the campaign, while others contend it was just a further expression of the inwardness of the "me" generation of the 1980s. One of the campaign decision makers said the challenge facing campaigns in the future was to make "politics as interesting as sex."

While the public may not have been as interested in politics as in the past, the professional politicians leaped into the 1988 campaign with both feet. Fifteen persons officially entered the race, while numerous others considered running, only to decide against it. An estimated $500 million was spent in the candidate exploration stage, the primaries, and the general election. Hundreds of thousands of persons participated in the process by working full time or part time on campaigns, volunteering, hosting candidates in their homes, or donating money to one of more of the candidates.

This book offers an analysis of the campaign from the viewpoint of those persons who actually made campaign decisions. The major part of the book is a verbatim transcript of discussions about the campaign by party leaders and persons who held top management positions in each of the announced campaigns. These discussions took place during a three-day meeting, December 2–4, 1988, sponsored by the Institute of Politics at the John F. Kennedy School of Government, Harvard University.

The session, the fifth of its type held by the Institute, was organized around the major issues in the campaign—not the issues facing the country, but the issues facing the candidates and their campaigns as the presidential race unfolded.

On the opening night, each of the campaigns was given time to outline why their candidate entered the contest and to review the initial strategy in light of the candidate's perceived strengths and weaknesses. The evening began with comments by Al Hubbard, manager of the campaign of former Delaware Governor Pete du Pont, the first candidate to formally enter the race. He announced on September 17, 1986, some 26 months in advance of the November 1988 balloting. It ended with remarks by Bill Lacy of the Bob Dole campaign, the last entry who announced November 10, 1987.

In between, Lee Atwater, manager of Vice President Bush's victorious campaign, spoke of his "lifeboat" strategy of winning elections, and Susan Estrich from the campaign of Massachusetts Governor Michael Dukakis told of the joys of winning the primary season and the heartache of losing the general election.

Saturday's sessions dealt with "Character Cops at Work"; "Campaign Organization"; "The Message: Advertising, Sound Bites, and Reporting Polls"; and "Money and the Campaign." On Sunday the general election campaign strategy, vice presidential candidate selection, the conventions, and the debates were discussed.

The conference closed with the decision makers offering recommendations for improvements in the election and campaign process, highlighted by Roger Ailes' "reform" speech and Jack Corrigan's call for changes in federal campaign laws.

The Institute, political scientists who study campaigns, and the general public are indebted to the campaigns for support of this conference and this book. In particular, we are indebted to the participants for their time and their candor in discussing numerous difficult decision-making periods, from the Gary Hart episode to a heated exchange over the role of the Willie Horton case in the general election. We are also grateful to the diverse group of persons who declared their candidacies in 1988, without whom we would not have had anything to discuss.

It is our hope that this book will contribute not only to a better understanding of the political process but also to improved campaign practices in the future. From these discussions, it is clear that the Congress needs to take a look at campaign laws, including the finance regulations and the provisions providing taxpayer support for the presidential election campaign. The political parties must review their rules and regulations with regard to delegate selection, and the professional campaign consultants need to take a hard look at the practices of the trade. Finally, the press's role in the political process needs to be studied by the television networks and the major daily newspapers and news magazines covering politics, in light of their traditional role of informing the general public about those persons seeking the highest office in the nation, the challenges facing the country, and the policies advanced by the candidates.

This conference could not have been held without the advice and participation of numerous persons, including Kennedy School Dean Graham Allison and a group of journalists and political consultants who were informal advisers to the Institute in the conference planning and conduct of the sessions. This group includes Bob Beckel, a media observer and manager of the 1984 Walter Mondale campaign; E.J. Dionne of *The New York Times;* Larry Eichel of *The Philadelphia Inquirer;* Howard Fineman of *Newsweek;* Ed Fouhy, a veteran broadcast news executive and 1988 Institute Fellow; David Gergen of *U.S. News and World Report;* Martin Nolan, editorial page editor of *The Boston Globe;* Matt Reese, veteran political consultant and 1988 Institute Fellow; Paul Taylor of *The Washington Post;* Linda Wertheimer of National Public Radio; and Judy Woodruff of the Public Broadcasting System's "MacNeil-Lehrer NewsHour."

Special thanks are due to the extraordinary staff of the Institute which handled the logistics of the conference, most notably Karri Copman, our conference coordinator. Providing valued advice were Institute Associate Director Terry Donovan and Heather Campion, the dean's public events coordinator. Assisting in the program were two Harvard students, Greg Anderson and David Grazman, who were part-time assistants to the Institute, as well as a strong, interested, and energetic contingent from the Institute's Student Advisory Committee.

In addition, Dick Thornburgh, the Institute director who was on leave to serve as Attorney General of the United States, took a personal interest in this conference before his departure and was a trusted and valuable informal consultant throughout the process.

January 3, 1989 DAVID RUNKEL

CAMPAIGN FOR PRESIDENT

The Managers Look at '88

Chapter 1

CAMPAIGN STRATEGIES

The Campaign Decision Makers meeting, sponsored by the Institute of Politics of Harvard's John F. Kennedy School of Government, opened on December 2, 1988, with Martin Nolan of The Boston Globe *presiding as moderator.*

Martin Nolan: We begin with a general discussion of campaign tactics and strategy. Each campaign will be given time to discuss the strengths and weaknesses of the candidate and to outline initial campaign strategy. We will proceed in the order of the candidates' official entry into the race. The Pete du Pont campaign was the first out of the block.

Allan B. Hubbard: When he was thinking about running, Pete obviously thought about George Bush and whether he could be beaten. Pete concluded that if Bush ran on his resumé and on loyalty to the President, as opposed to commitment to the President, there was a shot that someone else could beat him. And Pete felt that if someone else beat George Bush, he could be in a position to be the alternative to whoever it was who beat George Bush.

He thought there was a reasonable chance someone could beat George Bush in Iowa and New Hampshire, and he felt that if Bush were defeated in both Iowa and New Hampshire, he would be mortally wounded and would not be a viable candidate after that point. Pete himself felt that he didn't have the resources to win in either Iowa or New Hampshire—certainly not in Iowa—but thought he did have the resources and the ability to come in a strong third in Iowa and perhaps higher in New Hampshire.

In terms of strategy, Pete believed that if he was totally committed to Reagan—which he was, naturally—and if he was the innovative idea guy, that would provide him with visibility and recognition nationally. He hoped this would provide the firepower to get him recognized, and if he was recognized then he would be a very viable candidate—the alternative to whoever beat Bush in Iowa and New Hampshire. We actually thought that Kemp would beat Bush in Iowa and New Hampshire. Obviously that didn't turn out to be very prescient on our part.

In terms of issues, we wanted issues that were very broad, had a broad impact, and hopefully had a direct impact on people. Three of our five issues did: first, the voucher system in education; second, our social security proposal which would give people an opportunity to opt out of the social security system and manage their retirement money themselves; and third our program for random testing of high school students for drugs.

One of the other two issues, the welfare proposal (if you don't work, you don't get paid), also had a broad impact emotionally. And then we offered the proposal to eliminate $25 billion in farm subsidies—an issue which, although it certainly didn't affect most of the people, had a broad appeal politically.

Our goal was to get 15 percent in Iowa and come in third, and we hoped Bush would not get more than 25 percent and that he would come in second. We hoped that would give us a lift and that our position would improve in New Hampshire, not necessarily to second but to above 20 percent. Bush would again come in second, and whoever came in first would not do significantly better— ideally a little worse—than he did in Iowa. The result would be that we would become the alternative to whoever had beaten Bush in Iowa and New Hampshire.

In terms of what happened, we thought it went very well until the end of the summer of 1987. The Robertson victory at the Iowa State Fair was a big setback for us. The Wall Street crash was a big setback for us because that created a lot of uncertainty on the part of the American people and moved them toward wanting the status quo, toward staying with Reagan and Reagan's vice president. And to be perfectly honest, the first debate hurt us. The "Pierre" comment people obviously remember.

But I think what hurt us most is how well George Bush did. He didn't make any mistakes—or any significant mistakes—and consequently he didn't lose in either Iowa or New Hampshire. We also didn't come in third in both Iowa and New Hampshire, so it was all over for us.

Martin Nolan: For Richard Gephardt's campaign, Bill Carrick.

William Carrick: Having gone into the movie business, I thought, "What's a clever title for the campaign?" Since all campaigns ought to be B movies, I thought maybe we were, "The Campaign That Was Eaten by Iowa."

Dick announced on February 24th. He brought some resources to the campaign even though he was a relatively unknown member of Congress. One, he had the support of 80 of his colleagues, which turned out to be valuable. He also had been identified with some powerful ideas: tax reform, tough trade policies, and the Harkin-Gephardt agriculture policy. He also spent a good deal of time in Iowa doing all sorts of legwork, meeting with people.

By the time he announced we had an impressive group of veteran Iowa organizer activists behind the Gephardt candidacy. We also had made less impressive, but significant, efforts in New Hampshire. Theoretically, we were positioned to finish a decent second in Iowa to then prohibitive-favorite Gary Hart. Then the events of May unfolded and Gary Hart fell out of the sky. The next thing we knew was that *The Des Moines Register* poll had Dick Gephardt a two-to-one favorite in Iowa over the next closest contender, which I think at that time was Bruce Babbitt.

Suddenly the Gephardt campaign was dramatically changed. Instead of being an impressive challenger hustling away at the frontrunner, we were suddenly the front-runner. But we were a premature front-runner who was not exactly a prohibitive favorite. From that day on, there were no subtleties. There was no "spin." The media and politicians had one view: "Gephardt's got to win in Iowa. The Gephardt campaign is over if he doesn't win Iowa."

From that point on every resource and the entire focus of the campaign was weighed against our "must" victory in Iowa. As we went through that summer, Paul Simon's candidacy emerged and started to build, Biden started a resurgence, Dukakis started to catch on—all of which we saw in our private polling and which started to show up in public polling.

We were still living, however, with this straightjacket of "Gephardt's gotta win Iowa." There was no financial viability without an Iowa win. There was no realistic chance of getting the nomination without an Iowa win. We continued to organize very successfully in Iowa. We also made progress in New Hampshire and in the South, with the support of a lot of southern members of Congress. We had developed skeletal organizations for Super Tuesday.

The withdrawal of Joe Biden, however, had a significant impact on our candidacy. We spent 10 days as the unindicted co-conspirator on the Biden tapes. In that period we fell from first to second and continued to slide. Then we were down to single digits and everyone had written us off in Iowa and everywhere else. I remember one of the network correspondents called up to say, "Well, kid, you're out of it. We're pulling our crew off. You're finished. It's nice to see you." Bam. He's gone. We lost a network crew, which underscored where we were politically.

At this point, Simon had started to move very strongly, and then there was another major change in the Iowa political landscape. The same Gary Hart who had caused all the problems for us back in May reentered the scene and reshuffled the cards. Simon had spent money early on media. Despite pressure to go on television, we had waited on our media buy in Iowa. We ended up timed perfectly for the reentry of Gary Hart. Hart's emergence gave us a smokescreen. In the public polling, everybody was behind Hart, but nobody believed it. The media and political community always assumed that it was a mirage.

The day after Christmas, Gephardt started a resurgence, first with Dick's own personal performance. As the campaign hit bottom, Dick was never better in terms of how he performed on the stump and how he developed the message personally. Day to day as things got worse, he got better. Gephardt reached down into his gut and told people what he believed in, in an emotional presentation.

The media campaign was crafted. It amplified his issue positions. We started a comeback that resulted finally—after another brief run at us by Simon—in our Iowa victory. The reward for that was absolutely the toughest scrutiny I think anyone got in the campaign, with the exception of the aberrational events that happened to Hart and Biden.

The news media unloaded on Gephardt from Iowa to Super Tuesday. After finishing second in Iowa, Simon defined his future survival as dependent on a second-place finish in New Hampshire. We got a dose of negative advertising in New Hampshire from Simon and Dukakis. Instead of being in the classic position of the Iowa winner against the New Hampshire favorite, a Dukakis-Gephardt confrontation, we ended up having a donnybrook with Paul Simon for second place. Dukakis was sort of our elder statesman, above the fray.

I remember that the night after the Iowa caucuses, the polling numbers for New Hampshire were Dukakis, 37; Gephardt, 18; Simon, 12. The final result was Dukakis, 37; Gephardt, 20; Simon, 18. So nothing moved in New Hampshire other than this struggle for second between Simon and Gephardt. There was no momentum or flow. First it was a round of Simon attacks on Gephardt followed by our counterattacks. Governor Dukakis got a substantial win without being challenged. The Dukakis victory was not impressive by historical terms, but the opposition was split.

We moved on to South Dakota. Everyone asks, "What were the

high points of the campaign?" The high point for us was South Dakota, where we conducted a week-long campaign, spending $65,000 to buy 2,000 rating points. We started with our two-minute bio and ran our entire media campaign, outlining all our issues, finishing with the Belgian endive spot, which broke on the weekend before the election. In was a perfectly constructed campaign. We went from 11 points down to win by 12 points and did that in the course of seven or eight days. That was the high point.

From then on we got caught in a crossfire between Gore and Dukakis on Super Tuesday. They spent substantial advertising dollars attacking Gephardt in the South and destroyed our Super Tuesday prospects. We were low on money and could not counterattack. After a failed attempt to revive the Gephardt campaign in Michigan, Dick withdrew from the race.

Martin Nolan: Next is Frederick DuVal for the Bruce Babbitt campaign.

Frederick DuVal: The way we saw it was that, at the end of the Mondale campaign, the party was clearly going through a tremendous search for new ideas and a new generation of candidates. Although Hart was a front-runner, he was not a dominant front-runner. It was going to be a very flat race, with a tremendous opening for an ideological war inside the party. It was in that context that governors got extremely hot in the late 1970s and early 1980s.

Democrats were noticing the tremendous paradox between their failure to win the presidency and losing regions, the West and the South in particular, across the board, while carrying statehouses with tremendous majorities in the Rocky Mountains and in the South. We saw this as a tremendous opening for a governor. Added to that, there was an interesting situation. You had Republican governors in all of the major states except New York: Jim Thompson in Illinois, Bill Clements in Texas, and George Deukmejian in California. We didn't have any governors naturally positioned for the race based on their coming from a large state.

And you had a number of the most prominent governors blocked behind senators who were positioned to run for President. Bill Clinton was backed up behind Dale Bumpers; Dick Lamm was backed up behind Hart. For a while Dukakis was backed up behind Ted Kennedy. We saw there was an opening for a governor making the case of why it was that the Democratic party was doing well at the statehouses. We wanted to take that message to the national stage. That strategy worked—but for someone else!

The party was thirsting for new ideas. The niche we attempted to fit into was that of a successful governor in a state—a Republican state—with a message of economic and budgetary success and, most importantly, one with a whole set of new ideas and approaches. We put that message strategy together with a very, very novel and unique field strategy of putting all of our eggs in one basket—Iowa. It's not exactly the first time that's been tried.

Our advantages were that we had a full-time candidate and we had an extremely loyal group of organizers who for the final six months worked for virtually nothing.

Our weaknesses were enormous—not a tremendous amount of stature, not a tremendous amount of money, no base to speak of. But the one really positive thing we did have was a candidate with an unusual degree of guts and courage and fortitude and personality and character. That became the essence of the campaign. We attempted to turn those strengths and those weaknesses into a campaign strategy. Even the fact that Babbitt was initially very poor on television we attempted to turn into part of the strategy.

We tried to present Babbitt as the uncandidate, the antipolitician, the truth-teller; not slick on TV; not racked up with a lot of endorsements; but a man pushing unpopular ideas which we felt most of the public instinctively knew were right and correct and were the ideas that were coming but did not yet have common currency in public opinion. We attempted to challenge the voters, and what happened was—well, we got blown out. I think somewhere in the Bible it says, "The truth shall set you free," and in our case it did that very quickly.

Our failure in Iowa was based on a couple of things. First, the Dukakis campaign eclipsed a great part of our positioning. Second, I think that we never were able to establish a long-term calendar credibility—not enough money, not enough base. Even if he were to survive the early tests, where would he go? Every other candidate had some advantage in the election calendar. Virtually everybody else came from a state with a neighboring primary state early in the calendar. Sophisticated Iowa caucus attendees wondered where Babbitt would break through later in the calendar. That hurt us.

Third, I think the 15 percent threshold in Iowa served to plummet us down rather than up, and I think the threshold has that effect in both directions. And funny, and most important, I think ideas are kind of like aging wine. They get better with age. They take a little time to breathe. We pursued a set of ideas that, while advancing them very successfully, we were not successful in making them credible enough or popular enough to establish a base around them and turn that into a viable campaign.

In closing, from our point of view, our secondary objective to winning was to advance a specific set of ideas about the deficit, about Mexico, about children, and about a few other things. I think Governor Babbitt has a long-lasting legacy in advancing those issues.

If there's a moral to our story, it is that the first goal you have in setting out on this course is to win, but the second is if you're going to lose, lose early.

Martin Nolan: From one extreme to the other: For the campaign of Michael Dukakis, Susan Estrich.

Susan Estrich: We lost late. The truth also set us free, but it took a little longer. I'd like to start by congratulating the Bush campaign. I think no one knows better than the person who's trying to figure out a way around your strategy when someone's got a good strategy, a strong strategy. It may have been a different one than certain folks in our campaign were comfortable with, and we can debate that all day and all weekend, but you had a clear strategy. You executed it well. It was very tough running against you, and I guess it's the first time I've seen Lee [Atwater] and Roger [Ailes] since, so I just want to take a minute before I begin on our strategy to congratulate you for yours.

Lee Atwater: Thank you.

Susan Estrich: It's a lot more fun for me to talk about the primaries, so I think I'll start there. Going into the primaries, our initial assumption—I think, like everyone's—was that Gary Hart was going to be a formidable factor and that the question was who could emerge as the alternative to Gary Hart. We thought for a number of reasons that Michael Dukakis could. First, in message terms, we had a case to make that Mike Dukakis was the candidate who not only stood for new ideas but had actually made them work. Second, we had New Hampshire. I think somebody mentioned already the regional advantage. Jack Corrigan's best line, I think, was that winning New Hampshire was always a good idea for us, and it proved that way. And third, we had a financial base both here in Massachusetts as a sitting governor who had demonstrated strong fund-raising ability as a gubernatorial candidate with the Greek community nationally.

Those were our initial assumptions. Without Hart, it changed. Remember the Seven Dwarfs? We were in a field that didn't have an obvious front-runner, and it kept shifting on us.

Our imperative was to survive Iowa credibly enough to hold that lead in New Hampshire. Our great concern obviously was that if we lost badly in Iowa, we wouldn't go into New Hampshire as a credible candidate. New Hampshire, as many of us know, has a

way of turning on its friends and neighbors. We were able to succeed in part because of a very strong organization on the ground in
both states.

I think we turned out about 98 percent of our "ones," our strongest supporters, in Iowa for that astounding third-place finish, which
we turned into something of a moral victory. I also think we benefitted a bit from the confusion on the Republican side. The bounce
that Dick Gephardt might have gotten going into New Hampshire
was reduced and as Bill remembers, we won New Hampshire.

We went into Super Tuesday with a four-corner strategy. I think
some of the reforms that the party put into effect clearly did not
have their intended effect. We were able to win the delegates on
Super Tuesday and turn it into a victory by winning in Texas and
Florida, where we'd gone in and organized early; by winning in the
West; by winning in Maryland; and by winning in the Northeast.

I could talk endlessly about the fun of Michigan, the joys of
Wisconsin, and the pleasures of New York, but to make a long story
short, we ended up in a two-man race. After Jackson won Michigan, somebody called me and said, "You know, this may be the
best thing that's ever happened to you." Believe me, it did not feel
like it then. But it did narrow the race. We ended up in a two-man
race, which at the time obviously helped us.

Looking back, we came out of the primary superficially much
stronger than we really were. We were the beneficiaries of being the
winner every week against Jackson. And, we looked moderate as a
result, but we lacked a foundation. I suppose you could view the next
six months as our unsuccessful effort to build that foundation.

Our strategy for the general election had three basic points. The
first was that Michael Dukakis cares about people like you. We
highlighted this by trips in the summer to mid-sized communities,
focusing on jobs and drugs and housing. We had a series of specific
policy proposals on each of these areas.

Second was a convention that focused on Michael Dukakis, the
man of American roots and a product of the American dream. And
finally, it was the emotional closing argument that Michael Dukakis
is on your side. I think we did our best at this prong of our strategy,
which obviously built on the traditional strengths of a Democrat,
but that's not enough to win the general election.

It is on the other two points of our strategy that we did not do so
well. The second point of our strategy had to be to make the case
for change. We knew we couldn't win without it; we had to turn the
election into an election about the next four years, not the last
eight, about America's place in the world economically, about the

future, not the past. We did not succeed in that argument, I think, quite plainly. In part, I'm sure it's because we didn't make it with enough edge or power, and we made mistakes along the way in making that argument. Even more, I think, we were undermined by external economic conditions, which if there ever was a broad constituency for change in this country, undermined it. We didn't have a strategy that succeeded in turning that around.

The final element of our strategy, and maybe the one that I still think about the most, was the whole issue of leadership and character and how that was to play out. We began by thinking that that would be an important element of our fall strategy, that we would emphasize not only competence, not ideology from the convention speech, but the value of integrity. You saw this at the convention and throughout the campaign—that Mike Dukakis stood for high standards. That's the kind of campaign he would run, the kind of governor he had been, the kind of President he would be. On these issues we ended up on the defensive. Character played a lesser and a different role in the election than we thought.

I think the governor was hurt by the attacks on him—the mental health rumors, the attacks on patriotism, the harbor and furlough issues—and perhaps most of all by the perception that he had failed to fight back, which went to his character.

I think there were many who thought that those Bush attacks would go to Bush's character. In the last few weeks of the campaign he may have paid some price for running a negative campaign, but he paid a much smaller price than Michael Dukakis did.

Our campaign paid for the perception, and I say perception not in an attempt to escape responsibility, of not fighting back. We did fight back on occasion. The problem is we didn't fight back effectively, and we didn't sustain it. We created a perception that we weren't fighting back, and I think that hurt us much more than the tone of the attacks hurt Bush.

Finally, George Bush's character and leadership qualities—far from being a liability for him in the general election as they were in the summer—were, with some help from the press on Quayle and some wise work by some folks here, an advantage.

So character played a different role than we thought it would play. Bush was not hurt by the attacks in the way we thought he would be. The kinds of issues he chose, far from seeming less important in some way than our mainstream middle-class agendas, defined the election and defined them to Dukakis's disadvantage.

We're all a lot wiser and smarter now. We made a lot of mistakes along the way. I look forward to talking about them, I guess.

Martin Nolan: Next candidate to announce was Al Haig. Dan Mariaschin.

Daniel Mariaschin: There was indeed a strategy for the Haig campaign. There was an assumption that there were certain constituencies out there which would support a Haig candidacy: retired military, of course, blue-collar, ethnics. There was a sense in his travels through 1986, speaking around the country, that there was some support. But we were clearly handicapped from the beginning by several things.

We started late. We were late in organizing; a late start in organizing meant a late start in fund-raising. The fact that Haig was a non-traditional politician, that he had not held elective office, that he had not been around the track before—these were things that ultimately caught up to us.

The strategy was very simple. Notwithstanding some high negatives, particularly based on the day the President was shot and General Haig's military background, we still had, next to the vice president, the highest name ID in all of the polls. So we thought we would use the high ID in order to get a hearing to demonstrate that we had a candidate who was conversant with issues beyond the foreign policy and defense sphere. And so in mid-summer of 1987 there was a series of speeches on the economy, on education, and on long-term health care.

Starting late, we knew we had to front-load and that meant doing well in Iowa and New Hampshire. Super Tuesday looked good to us because we felt that we could do well in the South if we were able to move beyond New Hampshire.

Second, while we had this strategy, we knew we'd have to look to events beyond our control for something special, something different, to cause voters to consider the Haig dark-horse candidacy seriously, and which anticipated an atmosphere in which voters would say, "We aren't satisfied with the status quo and business as usual. We have to turn away from the front-runners to a Haig (or to another candidate)."

We had the crises to cause this critical change in thinking, but the crises were really slow-moving. For example, there was the reflagging in the Gulf, which could have led to some major foreign policy upheaval, but it was slow motion and the collateral damage that grew out of it was contained. Then there was Black Monday and the economic collateral damage that would cause voters to move away from the status quo. But that was not there because the problems were limited largely to the market. So those incidents which might have caused voters to look to an Al Haig simply didn't do so.

Third, because we were a small low-budget operation, we needed someone else's troops on the ground. We needed one of the other candidates—but probably not one of the two front-runners—to bow out of the race relatively early so we could siphon off some of that support to help us in building a staff and an organization. As it happened, when the Laxalt campaign ended we did pick up some staffers, but it was far too late to really help us.

As a consequence, if you will forgive the military analogy, we had to operate a command post exercise—firing away basically in scatter gun fashion from Washington, with a sense that there would be a payoff if we spoke out on many issues and hit some target. In bottom line language, we simply were operating out of Washington and out of New Hampshire a couple of days a week and going to Iowa. We had no troops in the field, a small staff—the smallest staff of any of the campaigns. I think we had 40 on staff at the highest point.

We simply were overworking the candidate and didn't have the backup. We discovered early on that this was going to be a race of personalities. It wasn't going to be a race of issues. Increasingly the press cast the race as a two-man race, and everyone else, including the farthest back of the dark horses, Al Haig, simply wasn't getting the kind of serious play that was needed to generate a candidacy with wide support.

In the campaign, we were stressing executive experience with a candidate who had not held elective office and who did not have a voting record, but who had a record of four decades of public service. We were talking about the presidency as the chief executive position in the country, and we talked about Haig having been secretary of state, chief of staff in the White House, NATO commander, and a corporate executive.

But the lead in the battle of the résumés—and often Haig's was compared by the press with the vice president's—unfortunately didn't add up to points for us. The fact that General Haig had not held elective office and had not had the opportunity to build a political organization certainly affected his prospects.

We decided in October to jettison Iowa and to concentrate on New Hampshire. Our objective was, to use the general's words, to finish a respectable third or fourth there. We thought we would move on to Super Tuesday in a good position if that happened. It didn't. We simply didn't have the staff on the ground in New Hampshire to effectuate that kind of outcome.

The debates interestingly gave us the exposure and the equal footing that we needed to score some points, most noticeably on the INF issue, which served to remind voters of Haig's extensive foreign policy experience and executive ability. What we were left with, because personalities rather than issues were what voters and the press seemed to be interested in, was the option of leveling criticism at the front-runners to cause voters to make a comparison between our candidates and them.

There was an ad in the New Hampshire papers and in the Boston papers, for example, comparing Haig to Kemp, and other "comparison" approaches. In the process, we were given a lot of credit for feistiness and a lot of credit for expertise and for our foreign policy issues. We were also given a lot of credit for our candidate being able to speak his mind and the courage of his convictions, but that simply didn't translate into any success in the polls or more serious play in the press.

And so there we were on February 12, with the snow coming down, deciding that the way it looked there might be 3,000 or so votes for Al Haig in New Hampshire. Bob Dole at that time we understood was up by 8 points. We thought that perhaps 3,000 Haig votes might, in fact, put him over the top. Of course, it didn't happen. We bowed out actually four days before the primary.

Martin Nolan: Next candidate to announce was Jack Kemp, and speaking for the Kemp campaign is Ed Rollins.

Edward Rollins: First of all, there were a couple of assumptions that all of us Republicans, tacticians or whatever, had at the beginning of this campaign, and certainly, they were all false. All strategy was built on that.

First and foremost, we underestimated George Bush—just as in 1978 when he first announced for President, he was totally underestimated by the Republican establishment. He went out then and beat such candidates as Howard Baker, Bob Dole, John Anderson, Phil Crane, and others. He did much better than expected and obviously ran a much better campaign than anyone anticipated. The 1980 Nashua debate convinced a lot of Republicans and conservatives and a lot of Reagan people that this guy could not stand up to the hard scrutiny.

Adding to that was the 1984 campaign in which George Bush was put in the very untenable situation of going out on a daily basis to defend the Reagan administration against Walter Mondale, Geraldine Ferraro and everybody else. Ronald Reagan, in turn, did not appear before the national media. Bush had a miserable campaign in 1984. He was very disturbed by it afterward, and, I think, a lot of people said, "This guy, we can take a real shot at him." He was not as strong as he could be, but I'm just saying to you that no one could have stood up to that scrutiny in 1984.

Then I think you compound that with the bigger foreign policy disaster, Iran-Contra, and Ronald Reagan's numbers going down in 1985 and 1986. Obviously, George Bush had a close association with the President, and a lot of people, including myself, said, "This guy can't win."

George Bush himself put together the very best team in America. His first choice was Lee Atwater—my very close friend and deputy for four years—who he brought in right off the bat, two weeks after the campaign in 1984. By bringing in Bob Teeter and people like Roger Ailes, Bush showed that he understood politics. He understood the necessity of putting together a strong team. Lee Atwater lives and dies politics, and, I think, George Bush himself lives and dies politics 24 hours a day. They put together a first-rate team across this country. There weren't any weaknesses in the team and there weren't any weaknesses in organization. They put together probably the most effective fund-raising apparatus that anybody ever had. Ronald Reagan in 1984, without any problem whatsoever, had 5 thousand $1,000 donors. George Bush in 1984 had 17 thousand $1,000 donors.

Saying all that, all of us ran around saying, "This guy is vulnerable. We could knock him out, knock him down early. Once we get him down, he's a bleeder. It's over. If Bob Dole's the alternative, obviously a Kemp-Dole campaign across the country will be a very significant campaign."

Kemp couldn't knock Bush down in Iowa, but we thought Dole could. We thought we could take Bush out of New Hampshire. We thought if we could raise somewhere in the neighborhood of $16, $17 million, stay viable, get beyond Super Tuesday, take one or two states, and go west where we were the alternative to Bush, facing a weakened Bush or a weakened Dole, we could be the candidate.

Obviously, what happened was that Jack Kemp was an inside the Washington Beltway candidate. He had 100 percent name ID among conservatives. His name ID among people across the country after a lot of effort was probably 77 percent, and those who knew him thought of him as a former football player and not necessarily as a presidential candidate.

A member of the House obviously has great difficulty moving up, but, I think, Jack was a much better candidate than his campaign was. I think anybody who's never been through this process and goes through a year's campaign and doesn't make a serious blunder is a pretty significant candidate. But the problem, I think, is that Jack had spent 18 years in the House, had never run statewide, and really was a novice when it came to actual politics.

Jack is the ultimate optimist, and day in, day out he had crowds out there who were telling him he was wonderful. Members of the House were telling him that. He had been the idea guy behind a lot of the Reagan programs, but his message was an old, stale one. There wasn't any difference between him and Bob Dole and, obviously, George Bush.

What we all do in this room is try to rerun the last campaign. The truth of the matter is we need to sit down and look at each campaign differently. Every cycle since 1972 has changed dramatically. Iowa was important, so therefore we put all the focus on Iowa. The truth of the matter is you could probably skip Iowa and still be a viable candidate.

The difference in this go-around was Super Tuesday. Lee obviously understood the South better than anybody in this room and, by moving the South Carolina primary forward, he set a strategy that was almost impossible to beat. So what we had to do was raise sufficient money and hold that money back so that we could be viable and stay beyond Super Tuesday. We raised a tremendous amount of money—$17 million. But we were always behind the eight ball relative to Bush and Dole, who had much more stature, much more name ID. At the same time we were being nickled and dimed to death by conservatives who were saying, "My God, Bush is weak. Why aren't you moving? You're sitting there at 7 percent." We kept trying to explain that you don't move till there's battle and there wouldn't be a battle until we reached Iowa or New Hampshire.

Then there were people like Laxalt, obviously being pushed by Pat Robertson and Du Pont, and Jean Kirkpatrick talking about getting in. The conservatives themselves kept saying "He's [Kemp] not the candidate."

But the more fundamental point that everybody in our side underestimated was the moment Ronald Reagan put his arm around George Bush and said, "This is my guy," to the conservatives across this country. That was it, Bush was okay.

When the early Iowa polls showed that more than 50 percent of the voters there didn't want Bush, our assumption was that it was a great big wide open market and we could make inroads. But what we found when we tested even more closely was that the people who approved of Ronald Reagan, which a majority of Republicans actually did, were split between George Bush and Jack Kemp, with George Bush getting about 80 percent of them and Kemp getting about 20 percent.

Those Republicans who did not like Ronald Reagan, did not like his policies, were all for Bob Dole. So we were in the very awkward position of trying to make inroads into the Reagan base, the Reagan approval base, against someone who obviously had at least the implied support of Ronald Reagan. Saying all that, the bottom line is that it just wasn't there.

There were lots of mistakes that we made in the campaign. Once we didn't do well early on, our campaign ran out of money just like every other campaign, and obviously got out of the ballgame quickly.

Martin Nolan: For Senator Paul Simon's campaign, Terry Michael.

Terry Michael: I don't think I'd be refuted by many here if I said that, when Paul Simon made his decision to run for President, he was probably the least calculating candidate in approaching that decision. In fact, most of you probably gave him the Democrats' Al Haig chair for long-odds prospects when he finally did jump in. If I had to choose a movie title for the Simon campaign, it would be, *They Laughed When He Sat Down to Play the Piano*.

The Simon campaign began back in August or September of 1986 when about a dozen of his colleagues joined in what, I guess, was a spontaneous letter which said, "You've got to get in to fill the void that exists in this campaign." I remember meeting with him in October of 1986, and he was laying out a rationale of how he could have a chance of winning if he couldn't persuade somebody else to fill the void—and that somebody else was Dale Bumpers.

He wanted Dale Bumpers to run. And, as a matter of fact, by about February he was convinced that Bumpers had told him he was going to run. Convinced of that in early March, Paul announced that he was not going to run for President. Then, about three or four weeks later, after Dale Bumpers suddenly announced to the world that he was not going to enter, Paul made a decision to run. He got in in early April.

His rationale was partly based on geographic proximity to Iowa, obviously. But also it was a cultural proximity to Iowans and to the people of New Hampshire—offering the small-town guy, nice guy, respected guy, the standup guy image. He felt he could sell himself to people in those small states the same way he had sold himself in Illinois politics for 35 years. I think to understand that, you have to understand the sense of self this man has, which is his great strength. And like other men with great senses of themselves, he could defy conventional wisdom because he just thought he could do it.

In addition to both that geographic and cultural proximity, he also said, "Well, I've done well with labor over the years, and labor is a major factor in Iowa." He also believed "I'm an old-fashioned activist kind of Democrat, and I think that's what this year's going to be all about. It's not going to be a generational thing. We're coming to the end of the antigovernment era, and I stand for what the Democratic party's always stood for, an activist use of the tools of government, and that's going to sell this year."

So he basically got into it because he really thought he could sell himself to people in those two key states. He began the campaign by using the Democratic heroes. He particularly used Truman and tried to create the view among voters that he was a candidate in the Harry Truman mold.

The downside of that obviously was that with an excessive use of that positioning he could appear to be the candidate of the past, and to some he already looked like the candidate of the past with that bow tie and those horn-rimmed glasses. So it was kind of a dangerous proposition to be positioning himself as a Harry Truman kind of candidate when many were saying this was a baby boom generation election.

When we started to move in Iowa, I think people misinterpreted the Simon appeal. Some saw it as an ideological appeal in "liberal" Iowa, when indeed it was an appeal based on biography. Unfortunately, that's about as far as we ever got in Iowa. After his promise to balance the budget in three years, part of our selling proposition— Paul Simon's credibility—was attacked by Bruce Babbitt and Dick Gephardt.

We started losing some of that bonding we had been creating on the basis of biography with a lot of voters in Iowa. And then, Gary Hart reentered and things got jumbled up. Just at that point in time, Gephardt came in with the Hyundai ad. We were left in the position of having been a front-runner and having to fight back to be a front-runner once again. We almost did it, coming within a few points in Iowa.

The second phase of our strategy then was to stay in the race by using a base we thought we had developed in New Hampshire. We were at about 19 points in New Hampshire, second only to Dukakis. We always felt that if we won Iowa, we had enough of a base in New Hampshire to challenge Dukakis there. Losing by only several points in Iowa, we thought we still had an opportunity in New Hampshire and another shot at the nomination if we could make New Hampshire a contest for second place and come in ahead of Gephardt.

We lost by three points again. The next phase of our strategy came the next morning when Paul said that if he didn't win South Dakota or Minnesota, he was going to be out of the race. That lasted about 24 hours until we got back to Illinois and talked to the state chairman and others. They didn't seem to think it was a real good idea to leave hanging our Illinois delegate candidates—the Democratic elected officials and others whose names would appear on the Illinois ballot in March as candidates committed to Simon. It's a direct election of delegates primary.

So we dropped our "either South Dakota or Minnesota" strategy and indicated to the waiting world that yes indeed, the nominating process was going to be starting over again in Illinois after Super Tuesday, because there was going to be gridlock from the Super Tuesday results. And we refined that as we went along. Many of you believed to some degree that there was going to be some gridlock, and there was still potential for somebody to break out.

We won in Illinois, to the surprise of some. And with this victory we got another shot at reviving our campaign—the same kind of "one last shot" that Gephardt got in Michigan and Gore got in New York. We felt if we could turn the Illinois victory into something in Wisconsin—the state where Paul Simon's roots were, where his father was born, and the home of progressivism—we might be able to then take advantage of the gridlock theory.

And so we got our last shot. And boy did we get shot in Wisconsin, where we ran out of scenarios.

Martin Nolan: From the lonely slopes of the Rockies and the Continental Divide, for the Gary Hart campaign, Sue Casey.

Susan Casey: As Simon was supposedly the candidate of the past, I think most people felt that in 1984 Gary had really helped the Democratic party make the change from a party of the past, and it turned to future leaders. In 1988 he felt strongly that that decision was already made to move forward, and it was just a question of who.

He had this notion that what was important about running for President was the ability to govern, and he thought that if he could tie the ability to govern with the ability to win—and he did not have total confidence that it could necessarily be done—that would be the sort of process that one ought to have when you're talking about running for the presidency. So when you looked at the race, it's obvious why issues became so important. They were important to him and to the way we thought we could win the general election as well as the primary election. As all of us Democrats know and learn over and over again, it's not enough to win the primary.

All along it was important to be able to not only win primaries but to attract independents to compete at the general election level. And the way to do that was to put forth the idea that being prepared to govern was important.

His message in the campaign really was, despite how naive it sounds, based on issues, on developing a framework in foreign policy and domestic policy and on laying a foundation for governing that would be successful in a general election.

Now, we had a great deal of confidence that if the election came to that, if the Democratic primary election came down to who best could govern, then Gary would be successful. If the general election came to that, he would be successful because he was indeed prepared to govern.

But we knew it would be very difficult to move the election in that direction because practical politics always interferes. It would certainly be, we thought, a year-long process to move the debate in that direction.

We didn't know we were going to have such a short time. We always looked at the primary process as a full cycle, not that he would be the front-runner going into Iowa and New Hampshire and win the election very easily. We saw that Gephardt was doing very well in Iowa. We knew Dukakis, being so near New Hampshire, had great support there. In those early states, we knew we had to do well—first, second, or third—well enough to stay in it.

We had a good financial base. We were prepared to see it through Super Tuesday. We thought the real race would start after Super Tuesday.

It was clear to us that Jesse would come out of Super Tuesday, we would come out of Super Tuesday, Al Gore would come out of Super Tuesday, and maybe one or two others.

The field would narrow after Super Tuesday, we guessed, to four or five people, and then the real race would begin. Our strategy was to try to maneuver the message throughout that year, to try to make the ability to govern the cutting issue and in the end to win because that would be the criteria by which the Democratic candidate was chosen.

Our strategy was to be strong financially, husband our resources, and come out strong after Super Tuesday. Then we thought it would be a battle all the way to California. There was never a sense in those early days, despite the polls, that it was his race, that he was indeed the front-runner, because he wasn't in a lot of ways. He didn't have the institutional support as we all know.

That sums up what we wanted to do. And then along about May we sort of stopped (laughter), and then he really seriously got back into the race with the same notion. If nothing else, he wanted to try once again to move the Democratic candidates into focusing on the issues so that we would have a candidate come out of that process who could compete in the general election and could win.

Gary Hart felt strongly that with the changes in the world we needed new foreign policy, we needed to deal domestically with the economy, and unless the Democratic candidate could lay out that kind of framework and could show the public that a candidate could govern, we would not have a chance.

Martin Nolan: In the campaign calendar we've only reached the spring of 1987. People were trying valiantly to overcome their bashfulness to announce they were going to run. There was a brief moment in which Paul Laxalt of Nevada was a candidate, an official candidate. I'll ask Ed Rollins to say a word or two. Ed, I think you have to represent two camgaigns.

Edward Rollins: Well, as Matt Reese and Roger Ailes and I are the three old gray beards in the political side at least, there are four words that we always hate to hear from a candidate, "Money? It's no problem."

No one had more affection from the Reagan supporters than Paul Laxalt, and obviously if the American public wanted four more years of Ronald Reagan, Paul Laxalt would have fit that mold very, very well. They are very similar men. They're very close friends.

About a year and a half before the election when Paul was first approached by a lot of people saying, "You've got to carry on the Reagan mantle," we sat down. I said, "Paul, there are two things you have to do. First and foremost, you have to raise $10 million to be a viable candidate. And the period that you have to do it is between the Super Bowl of 1987 and the Super Bowl of 1988." That means $200,000 a week, which is a very, very significant sum of money as anybody who's been in this business knows. He said, "Money? It's no problem. I'll just get a bunch of my friends to go raise $100,000." I said, "Paul, you may have 100 friends and you may have 100,000 friends, but you don't have 100 friends who can raise $100,000." He said, "All right. I'll get 1,000 of my friends to raise $10,000."

Well, to make a long story short, Paul waited very late in the game. He did not announce until very late, and most of the people who would have supported him had already gone to Bush and other candidates. He went out in the course of two months and tried to raise money. He raised less than $2 million; basically, he got out of the race very wisely and didn't leave any debt.

Martin Nolan: For Joe Biden's campaign, Tim Ridley.

Timothy Ridley: After Senator Biden's departure from the race I was asked what it was like to manage his campaign. I likened it to being the General Secretariat of the U.N.—without the benefit of a peacekeeping force. (Laughter) What was the strategy and message of the Biden campaign? Not a simple question. You see, we were not so much a campaign as a confederation of nonaligned states. (Laughter). So we each had our own strategy and own notion of message. I once suggested that we bring in the rival campaigns and auction off some of our surplus strategies. (Laughter)

In a sense, we were very long on making the decision to run. And the decision, once made, resulted in a very short campaign. I describe the Biden campaign as the three-week presidential campaign. Senator Biden formally announced on June 9. Three weeks later Supreme Court Justice Lewis Powell announced his retirement. After the Powell decision, the campaign was highly distracted, without a full-time candidate and plagued by a dual mission.

Senator Biden first faced the decision to run for President five years ago. In December 1983, Pat Caddell came to him with an analysis of how Biden might make a late entry into the 1984 presidential campaign. It was a plausible analysis that later provided the strategic foundation for the Hart insurgency. Joe opted against a late entry in 1984, and in making that decision, his 1988 campaign was probably set in motion. When somebody has to face the decision of whether to run for President as opposed to *could* he run; he's 50 percent of the way to being an announced candidate. Subsequently, Senator Biden did all the things one does in preparing to run for President: campaigned across the country for Democratic candidates, organized a PAC, and so on. He also did something that struck some observers as peculiar. He went out and recruited every sociopath in the Democratic Party, including myself, to be part of his political brain trust. (Laughter)

The basic strategic assumption of the Biden campaign was this: In 1988 Democrats would be hungry for a nominee who could move the country forward with a compassionate message delivered with great passion. There was only one other candidate who could rival Joe Biden on this score—Reverend Jackson. Joe was very taken by some of the nongovernmental elements of what it meant to be President. A President isn't just the leader of a government. He's a leader of a society. Senator Biden thought the President had to be able to move and motivate the American people. There are many things to be said about Joe Biden. I think few would dispute that he was and is a man who can move people.

A second assumption: We felt Senator Hart was very weak in Iowa and very vulnerable to a Biden candidacy. At the time Joe left the race there were polling data that verified Iowa was very receptive to the senator's candidacy. Our tracking polls had Joe Biden solidly in second in Iowa on the eve of the Bork hearings. Finally, we assumed we could raise the money. In fact, I had the very odd experience of mananging a presidential campaign that ended with $500,000 in the bank.

The ultimate decision to enter the 1988 race was complicated and delayed by several unforeseen developments. First, we Democrats won back the Senate. Second, Senator Kennedy decided to forego chairing the Judiciary Committee. The job of reorganizing the Judiciary Committee fell to Chairman Biden. Two years ago at this time we were debating what these developments might mean to Joe's candidacy. What happens if Lewis Powell resigns, or Thurgood Marshall dies, or whatever. What does that do to your presidential campaign? We thought through those unpleasant scenarios. Our worst case hypothesis was Lewis Powell retiring in December [1987]. As it turned out, our hypothetical scenario occurred. Powell resigned in June [1987]; and events unfolded from there, of which we're all aware.

Martin Nolan: For Al Gore's campaign, Fred Martin.

Frederick Martin: I'm reminded, Tim, what happens to the other campaigns when a candidate withdraws. While it's a tragedy for the candidate withdrawing, his withdrawal puts tremendous pressure on those who remain, because what happens is that everybody turns to you and says, "Well, are you going to get their people? Are you going to get their money? Are you going to get their support?" And of course we never did. It dawned on me after Senator Hart withdrew the second time that everyone could withdraw and it still wouldn't get any better!

I resist the temptation to begin with the outcome, the conclusion, and then interpret all the facts that happened in the light of that outcome. Instead, I want to try to give you very quickly what our thoughts were about strategy as those thoughts were developing, what assumptions they were based on, what problems we thought we had, and how we tried to address them.

The strategy was to try to use the new calendar and take advantage of 20 states casting their votes on the same day, on the 8th of March—two-thirds of them in the South—to win a bunch of those states. We thought we had a good chance to do so with the candidate from the South. We also believed that if we were successful, we would then be present for a side-by-side comparison and close scrutiny alongside the one or two others who remained. We thought there would be only two or three remaining on the 9th of March as strong and viable candidacies. And I should add, I strongly believed that with Al Gore's personal qualities and strengths as a candidate we had a good chance to win that close comparison.

The assumptions that we were operating on were: One, a late-starting campaign cannot compete in time and in money, the two most precious things in a campaign. We were unable to put campaigns in place everywhere without those two essential assets. As to time for instance, I would remind you that the first trip that Al Gore took to Iowa was during the week that Senator Hart withdrew from the race. We were that late in getting going.

Assumption number two: We believed that the other campaigns which followed a conventional strategy would very likely be drained of their resources by doing so. And we thought, as a consequence of that, that a series of them would have to withdraw during the four to six weeks after Iowa.

We had as a final assumption that we too would not have enough money in the bank after competing on Super Tuesday to spend in the states that came up after that. The only way we would get money sufficient to compete after that date was if we got a large enough bounce coming out of Super Tuesday to generate more fund-raising.

As to weaknesses: One, we saw all along that there was the intense danger of being becalmed in the month of February when we had voluntarily excluded ourselves from the intense press scrutiny surrounding Iowa and New Hampshire. Two, we knew that it would be hard to demonstrate progress for our campaign—to the press and to the voters—particularly if we were not competing in that month, but also all through the campaign. And we knew that it was important for us to demonstrate progress because we had a young candidate who started late and who came from Tennessee.

Weakness number three: We believed that we would not have time or money to invest in states that were going to vote after Super Tuesday until Super Tuesday came and went, which meant that we would not have a foundation laid in those states, all of them in the North. This was a problem that we saw early on. And then finally, we believed that it was not axiomatic that Al Gore would be the southern candidate—that is, not certain that Al Gore would automatically receive a great deal of southern political support before March 8.

We took steps to address these problems and also to implement our strategy: One, save our money during 1987. We spent under $3 million in that calendar year. That was about a third of what our competitors spent on average.

In fact, our goal was to save so we could spend the money in February in the states that were casting their votes on March 8. And we did that. We spent close to $3 million during the four weeks, most of that on media in states casting their votes on the 8th of March.

Two, to become the southern favorite, we needed to prove that we could get support in the South. So we went about getting political endorsements and support during 1987. Three, we attempted to demonstrate progress with debates. Debates for us were a blessing. They were a way for a candidate without a great deal of money and without a great deal of time to try to do by personal performance what others were able to do with their field operation and with more time.

I resist the temptation to undergo a self-autopsy. I think you can do it for me and do it better.

Martin Nolan: For Jesse Jackson's campaign, a manager who's been elected to office a couple of times himself: Former mayor of Gary, Indiana, Richard Hatcher.

Richard Hatcher: Well, I'll begin by suggesting that Reverend Jackson's campaign probably began about 20 years ago. There was a fairly quiet revolution taking place in urban areas of the country, and blacks were running for and being elected to the mayor's office and other local offices with a certain degree of regularity.

Basically that created a foundation for the Jackson campaign of 1988. Many of those cities, which were of some considerable size, represented the key to winning certain states. The mix of blacks, Hispanics, and others was such that it was a natural constituency and became a very natural base for the Jackson campaign in 1988.

Jesse Jackson had run for President in 1984 and had run what was basically a symbolic campaign. However, we learned a great deal from that effort in 1984. For one thing, there was very little knowledge of how to run a national campaign among people who were close to and who were inclined to support Jesse Jackson in 1984. The experience of 1984, in fact, created a cadre of people who had some understanding of what a national campaign was all about, so it was very helpful.

Second, Jesse Jackson himself was an extraordinary candidate. We were convinced that of those persons who had announced for the nominations in both the Republican and Democratic party in 1988, he was far and away the best candidate in the sense that he had the ability to communicate and to motivate people better than anyone else out there.

He ran a coalition compaign. While there had been a substantial increase in voter registration among minorities, in the South especially, there were other fairly large voting blocs in the country that were experiencing substantial troubles. The farmers were having tremendous difficulty. The steel workers and organized labor in general were in serious trouble. These represented natural places where Jesse Jackson could go with a message and receive a reasonably good response.

Running for President for Reverend Jackson was a case of continuing to do what he had been doing for the last 20 years. He had been going around the country making speeches.

He also had an extraordinary capacity to get on the evening news without paying for it. For some reason the news media liked him—enjoyed quoting him—and so he was able to get an awful lot of free exposure and free attention.

Our largest job in the campaign, to be very frank with you, was to have enough money to keep the plane that Jesse was on in the air. That was a major challenge of the campaign. We learned very quickly that people who did not like Jesse Jackson were probably not inclined to vote for him under almost any circumstance. We found that people like that underwent a change if they saw him or heard him in person. In fact, in some instances, they would even become workers in the campaign. We knew it was really important to us that he be exposed to as many people as possible.

We went into the year with a commitment that we would run in every state. We did not intend to avoid a single state regardless of the composition of the citizenry of that state. We also made a commitment that we would remain in the campaign to the end. We were not going to drop out under any circumstances.

The Iowa primary was an interesting one for us—really Iowa and New Hampshire because they were both essentially no-lose propositions. No one expected Jesse Jackson to do anything in Iowa. No one expected him to do anything in New Hampshire. We did not disappoint anyone either in that regard; but it didn't matter because no matter what he did, if he did anything, that would be more than people had expected.

So we saw Iowa and New Hampshire as simply legitimizing primaries, that is, as simply showing that we were serious and major players in the campaign. We did not do very well in Iowa and New Hampshire, and yet it was clear that we were viable.

Then very interesting things began to happen. I believe we came in second in Vermont, which was a bit of a surprise to people, and we did very well in Minnesota. It was our strategy to get to Super Tuesday. Obviously Super Tuesday had been planned as the Waterloo for a candidate like Jesse Jackson. The whole idea was to produce a moderate nominee for the Democratic party.

However, those who devised that strategy obviously were thinking of the Old South and not the New South. The South had really changed dramatically, just as in many ways the country had changed. There had been a tremendous amount of voter registration activity in the South, and we saw Super Tuesday as really being made to order for Jesse Jackson. It was a situation where we felt he was going to do extremely well. As it turned out, he did. He won more states on Super Tuesday than any other candidate and for the first time, our campaign began to be competitive in terms of delegates. Then the campaign turned north, to Illinois, and we felt at that point we were beginning to develop momentum.

We ran into a problem in Illinois in Paul Simon. I think he had announced that he was out of the race, that he was not running anymore. This campaign produced something that I think was unprecedented in national campaigns. In the past if a candidate dropped out of the race, he actually dropped out of the race.

Something new was developing in this campaign, however. It was called, "I'm suspending my campaign," and that's what Paul Simon did. He had suspended his campaign so that instead of it being dead, it came back to life in Illinois. Illinois is where Jesse Jackson had spent his last 20 years, and we were convinced that he would win that state. However, when we went into Illinois and lost—that is, we came in second and Paul Simon won the state even though we knew that his campaign was over—we stumbled. That really slowed our momentum.

However, we went to Michigan and we won Michigan. I believe that we won Michigan simply because Michigan had same-day, on-site voter registration. College students came out, registered, and voted for Jesse Jackson in large numbers.

We lost the nomination in Wisconsin. We could have won Wisconsin, but I think we made some really serious tactical and strategic errors there. As a consequence, we lost Wisconsin and sort of limped into New York.

New York was the first place where the campaign became racially polarized. Up to that point it had not been. The race factor really had not been significant, or at least it had not manifested itself publicly. When Mayor Koch launched his blitz, it really polarized not only the state but the rest of the country. The other thing it did which hurt us very badly was to knock Al Gore out of the race. We needed at least two people surviving at that point aside from Jesse Jackson.

The rest of it, of course, was all downhill. I would conclude by saying I think the campaign did change the way people think in the country. I think that it moved us a step closer to the day when perhaps the most segregated office in the country—the office of the President—will become integrated.

Martin Nolan: From one reverend to another. For the Pat Robertson campaign, Marc Nuttle.

Marc Nuttle: If the Tax Reform Acts of 1986 and 1987 were a lobbyist's work bill, then Pat Robertson was probably the working press's Material Support Act of 1988. The supporting cast of Jim and Tammy Bakker, of course, was out there in the headlines for quite a while. The highest-rated "Nightline" telecast was an interview with Jim and Tammy Bakker. I didn't mind that. It was just that the high level of coverage lasted for 18 months. Good grief.

Our campaign assumptions were basically these: First, George Bush would control the party nationally. He had a lock on the local party in about 25 states, and we had no chance of taking over those 25 state parties in the primary from within.

Second, the trip theory in politics does not work. That is, the candidate who trips early and falls will never get up. It didn't happen to Walter Mondale and it didn't happen to Gerald Ford. I didn't think it would happen to George Bush. Third, the press, the public, and the Republican party would never believe that Pat was going to win until he actually did. Therefore, we'd have to win and keep winning to maintain credibility. We also thought that the trip theory might work against Pat, and it ultimately did.

I'll highlight the primaries for you in a minute, but it might surprise you to remember that Pat Robertson either won or came in second in the first seven Republican primaries. Now, those were geopolitical and organizational assumptions. The candidate assumptions were basically these: We had high negatives, and we were less acceptable than George Bush to party officials, elected and appointed, across the country in every sector and always would be. We had a credibility threshold that we had to build, a foundation of acceptance.

In addition, we expected to be criticized for lack of experience, for never having run for public office before, for not having published policy papers, and there would be questions on how he would govern. There was very little tangible evidence or track record. And, of course, there was his ministerial background. This generates a built-in fundamental suspicion among the American electorate, both Republican and Democrat.

At the national and state level our strengths were our organizational bases everywhere except the Northeast corridor. This potential base was pretty constant all over the country, with a little bit of increased strength in the South.

We had a financial base that we were very familiar with. We had that one nailed. We knew how to approach it, how to raise money from it, and we knew how to match funds from it. We ultimately raised about $24 million. With matching funds, we had a little over $30 million. Actually, we thought we could do $35 million. Most of the money raised was in hand by the end of February. The financial trend lines were set and on projection.

The campaign, I believe, now holds the record for matching funds and therefore small contributions. The average contribution was less than $100. There were upwards of 200,000 contributors in total. This entire contributor list was developed in six to nine months—not bad for starting from ground zero.

These assumptions dictated a few axioms of tactical necessity. One was that we must compete everywhere if we were to maintain credibility—every state, every primary. We had to organize completely from outside the party. Pat primarily didn't seek party endorsements or endorsements from senators or congressmen.

We had a couple of state chairmen who were sympathetic and a few committeemen who came aboard. But the difference between this campaign and the Reagan effort was that when Reagan emerged, he moved on the party at the grassroots. The Reagan organization also achieved some vertical takeover; that is, some chairmen, some governors, some senators, some congressmen endorsed him. We had none of that. The Robertson campaign was a grassroots, precinct campaign.

Further, we determined that we must maximize spending. This wasn't something that we just hoped for; it was a basic tenet of the strategy. You must raise it and spend it judiciously according to the plan. We had to have it on time, and we had to have it early.

Lastly, it was imperative that we win a few small states that were open ballot primaries, and we had to win one big state. You can look at the spending reports and determine which large state we targeted. It was Texas. We thought we could organize Texas. There were 10 congressional districts in which we could identify our following. These were nontraditional Republican districts. We thought we could make a difference in those districts.

From this strategy and those dictated tactics, there were three organizational strategies: compete in all the caucus states, which represented about 24 percent of the delegates to the Republican National Convention; compete in certain congressioinal districts for the three-per-district winner-take-all delegates, another 24 percent of the total delegates; and win three small state primaries and one big state.

We targeted 125 congressional districts mainly in nontraditional Republican areas where a very few votes captured the district and the three district delegates. Alabama, Georgia, and Mississippi were the small states we targeted to win and Texas was the large state. Following Super Tuesday, it was anticipated that our support would accelerate as other candidates dropped out.

If Jack Kemp or anybody else had withdrawn earlier, we might have picked up some of that support. About 4 percent of Jack Kemp's supporters were listing Pat as their second choice. In certain states in the South this additional 3 or 4 percent would have brought the campaign over the 20–25 percent threshold formula of required votes to get a portion of the at-large delegates.

Our theme and message was basically the same as those of many other campaigns. It was classic Reagan—less government, strong national defense, discipline in education, local and state control of curriculum of education, and economics.

Pat does have a good academic background in economics. He spoke on this subject very well, particularly with regard to banking and Third World debt. On a balanced budget, Pat proposed where the cuts would come from. He addressed entitlement programs, family values, abortion, marriage, prayer in school. Pat's real expertise is in international trade, international banking, and international exchange rates. CBN operates in several foreign countries. He has been published on these issues. These topics may have been a little esoteric or kind of highbrow for some audiences, but they still were credible speeches in Washington, D.C.

The underlining image to be developed was that of a statesman with a religious background rather than a religious man with a statesman background. He had the political background, his father having been a senator. The basic Robertson voter was an evangelical, born-again Christian. The breakout coalition beyond the basic base was new right conservatives, economic conservatives, particularly those who sought a balanced budget constitutional amendment and line-item veto. Such conservatives could care less what your background is as long as you're right economically.

And believe it or not, we were getting around 5 percent of the Republican party traditional vote. Pat's speeches were classic vintage Reagan, right across the board. The speeches were not on ideological social issues only. We embraced the 1984 Republican party platform. Pat was very comfortable with it: His speeches came across well, and he delivered them well. Putting those little pieces together, we were inching up into the 20 to 25 percent category of all voters in certain key states.

Now, for the general election, I want to say one thing. We did have a plan for all the way through the general election. We anticipated that if we ever did win the Republican nomination, there would be fallout from the Republicans. A good 8 percent would abandon the party because of who they thought Pat was. But, believe it or not, our highest approval rating was among black voter groups and Hispanics—60 percent approval. It's our belief that we could have gotten 25 percent of the black vote in the general election, which is double the normal Republican percentage. We also planned to target Catholics and blue-collar voters in the upper Midwest. These groups did not seem to have any problem with Pat as the Republican nominee. He just wasn't their first choice in the primary. He was a high second choice.

Since the campaign strategy and tactics required extensive precinct organization, a decision was made to make organization part of the exploratory test. To measure the viability of a national precinct plan, we initiated the exploratory presidential committee by broadcasting live by satellite to 218 locations nationwide simultaneously from Constitution Hall in Washington, D.C. The effort captured an audience of between 200,000 and 300,000, with 50,000 new contributors generated in one night. The event was self-liquidating.

Of all the things in the campaign I did, I wouldn't change a thing, except now I know a few ways to do that type of broadcast a little bit cheaper. It can be done a little more efficiently. We replicated the event at the state level a few times, in Michigan and in Texas, for example. We broadcast from Dallas to 20 remote sites and from Detroit to 16 sites. This is a very cost-effective way to communicate to volunteers. The next technical stage will be two-way communication. That will be cost-effective soon.

The criteria established for the exploratory "testing the waters" committee to determine a viable presidential candidacy was 3 million signatures on a petition circulated nationwide urging Pat to run. It takes 6 million votes to win the Republican nomination. If 3 million names could be obtained of persons indicating they are dedicated to Pat Robertson and if they were situated in strategically located areas, then we could conclude that we had a good chance to win or at least to make a real difference.

What happened is this. In Michigan we gave it a good fight and the campaign won some credibility. Next was Hawaii. They tried to move the election date a couple of months when local opposition forces decided that Pat was going to sweep the caucuses. It wasn't the Bush campaign; it was somebody from the party at the local level. We had the organization and numbers of people to completely dominate the election. We took 100 percent of those delegates. Then was Nevada. Alaska fell in there, which we also dominated. Iowa is where we got the big bump, probably the high point of the campaign. We came in a strong second in Minnesota and South Dakota.

That made seven primaries, and one of those was an open primary. At this point things were kind of nice. Our negatives were down to 32 percent among all voters, 25 to 26 percent among Republicans. It was still too high, but it was manageable, particularly in low turnout states.

It is important to remember one thing. Only 60 percent of the eligible population in the country is registered to vote, and of the registered voters only 50 percent participate in the general election. Therefore, in a general election only 30 percent of the eligible universe participates. In close elections, 15 percent to 16 percent of the eligible population is electing men or women for President and senator. In the primaries, this voter apathy produces only about 15 percent total participation. If you know your base and can identify it, you can achieve great election percents with 10 to 15 percent of the voter population. We were on that track. That's how you can compete even with high negatives if you can control certain things.

So what happened? Two things. One was a series of statements that the press called "funny facts." It is debatable as to how the statements came about, but not to belabor that now, there was a series of unfortunate statements that cost us credibility, not only with the public but with our own base.

The other main reason that Pat Robertson lost was the Bush campaign. I have to give them credit. It was a well-managed, disciplined, organized campaign. I was with a publisher yesterday who asked if I believed that Bush was out of the race after Iowa. I said absolutely not, for two reasons. One, I knew the Bush campaign was organized down to the precinct level in over 20 states. Their voters were identified. Two, Bush was dominating in several Super Tuesday states.

I didn't have as good information in New Hampshire as I had in the South, but I could tell it was close in New Hampshire. I had the highest regard for Governor Sununu as a technician. But, even if Bush lost in New Hampshire, a firewall had been built in the South, beginning with South Carolina.

In the general election, the Bush campaign embraced not only Pat Robertson's issues but also his staff. Bush brought us into the campaign and gave us every access. I have a poll with me which indicates that 82 percent of the Robertson supporters not only voted for but worked for and tried to contribute to George Bush. That base represents somewhere around 8 to 10 percent of the total vote. When viewed in terms of general election impact, it represents a 6 to 8 percent difference for Mr. Bush on election day.

Thank you very much.

Martin Nolan: Last week, the secretary of state-designate and Bush campaign chairman Jim Baker spoke at a dinner honoring David Broder. And Jim Baker was saying that David Broder represents a kinder and gentler nation. David Broder is so kind, so gentle, he makes Mister Rogers look like Lee Atwater.

Lee Atwater: I thank you. Due to time I'll probably just concentrate on the primary. I did first of all dispense of two key strategy decisions very quickly that were both general election and primary strategies.

Decision number one was media, which is all important; early strategy decision: hire Ailes. Number two was the debates, which we knew were going to be all important in the primaries; strategy decision: hire Ailes.

We made about seven assessments at the outset of this campaign. The first three I'll go over very quickly. Number one was that George Bush was a durable candidate, a very durable candidate, and much more durable than the pundits and the media and his political opponents would ever give him credit for being.

I was on the other side of him in a brutal fight in the South in 1980 when I was running the Reagan operations down there. I thought we had pounded him into the dirt, but he was able to come back after that and not only compete but actually win states, important states like Pennsylvania and Michigan. I watched the guy, and I've been working with him on and off since 1973, and I knew that he was much more durable than he would ever be given credit for.

Second, and probably I think one of his biggest advantages, was that he would be severely underestimated throughout the entire process. He'd be severely underestimated by the pundits, by the media, and by his opponents to such a degree that it would always end up being to his advantage. I remember one time telling him that I felt he'd be so severely underestimated that he could prove himself on something; and within 24 hours he'd be equally underestimated, and that that would help him all the way.

Third, his experience as a national candidate would be probably the most solid single advantage he had. If somebody came down from Mars and asked, "How'd you get elected President? How did you get the nomination?" I'd say, "It's this crazy damn thing, this political stuff, but the one rule that stands out to me is whoever goes around the track the most usually wins the primary and general election."

If you look at Ronald Reagan, if you look at Richard Nixon, if you look at Mondale and so forth, whoever goes round the track most has the best advantage for a bunch of reasons: Experience, understanding the national media, understanding the ebb and flow, understanding how things are played out. There were many times I sat in that campaign and remembered back to times when my mentor Ed [Rollins] and I sat through crises and thought they were the end of the world. You understand how something plays out over time.

So those were three things. Another was something that our excellent strategist Bob Teeter brought to my attention at the very outset of the campaign: what he called the invisible circle theory. That is, basically there's an invisible circle that you really need to get in. It's a circle, I guess, of acceptability to be considered by the American people as a candidate for President, a real candidate for President. And at the outset of this race there was only one guy in that circle and that was George Bush.

Now, you don't automatically get to be President if you're in that circle. I think Humphrey was in that circle; Rockefeller got in the circle. In other words, that circle basically means this: If people woke up the next day and heard he was President, they would say, "He's all right. He could do that," whether they're for him or against him.

There were a couple of people hovering around the circle at the time. Gary Hart was hovering around the circle in the other party, and Bob Dole was hovering around the circle in my party. I always felt as though whoever got the Democratic nomination would get into the circle, or at least get right up to it.

It's like you're out there in limbo; you see all the fins coming at you. The whole strategy is to get one oar in there, when you see a fin, get up to the post and start beating the hell out of him. If you want to talk macrostrategy, one strategy is to sit in the damn boat and keep beating every fin you see coming at you.

The other assessment was that George Bush in many respects was Ronald Reagan, Jr. It was his own personal strategy of sticking with Reagan right on through. I think it paid off. It would definitely pay off big in the primary. Even in the midst of the Iranian thing, I knew that Ronald Reagan was a deity in our party. I was also convinced that at worst he would never be a liability in the general election and would probably end up being at least a geopolitical asset. That was another assessment we made.

Another almost tactical assessment we made was to always announce our tactical and strategic decisions way out front because people would figure we were spinning them. The only way you could turn people off and keep them from following a strategy was to announce it first.

The other critical assessment in the primary season was identifying the nature of the party. As a guy who'd spent all his life inside the party my feeling was that everyone plays on the basis of the last election. The last primary election for our party was in 1980, and in that case the right wing of the party was the nominating wing of party. If you go back to our party, the moderate or eastern wing dominated up till 1964, when the Goldwater crowd took over and in effect nominated candidates thereafter. In 1980 when Reagan got that nomination, in effect he was the nominee of the party.

Well, my sense was that the axis had changed dramatically and people didn't realize it. What we had in 1988 was a party that Ronald Reagan had brought more to the right, and in effect there was no longer a classic moderate wing of the party. But by the same token, the party brought Ronald Reagan more to the center. The new nominating wing of the party would be what I termed, for lack of a better word, the mainstream conservative wing of the party, which would be about 70 percent of the vote.

Now, a rule I learned from one of my first mentors, John Sears, was that an early front-runner can always lead the race. So we made an early incursion over to the right with two or three things in mind. One was that if we went right, everybody would be totally enveloped in this conventional last-campaign wisdom and go running publicly over to the right. If you all remember that early campaign, it was very publicly criticized.

We went over to the right and everybody followed us there. We got two things out of that. Number one, because the right wing had shrunk, we had what I call the mainstream-conservative wing, and also the far right, new right wing, which was only about 25 percent. When something shrinks like that, all of a sudden, the structure really counts. We thought we could co-opt 25 to 30 percent of that structure. I never underestimated what Pat [Robertson] was going to do. I knew he would co-opt another 15 or 20 percent of that structure.

Number two, any time a political movement shrinks dramatically, very quickly it becomes almost impossible to unify. And so my assessment was that if we got over there and moved quietly on out very quickly after co-opting what we could get, we would leave everybody else over there playing in that ballpark. And no one could ever unite it because of the nature of the rapidly shrinking universe. But if they did unite it, they'd still be sitting on only 25 percent of the vote. So that was not only a major strategy assessment but also a series of major tactics that we did very, very early.

Now, on the other strategy/tactical decisions we made, I felt strongly there were only two things that George Bush needed to do other than stick with Reagan that would preempt anybody from ever being able to get him on the right. One was to be hard-core on taxes, which as you all know he was. Number two was to be hard-core on the anti-communist cluster of issues. If he did those two things, no one could ever move out on him on the right and he would have all the freedom in the world to start getting giant chunks of the 70 percent mainstream group.

Calendar strategy obviously played a big part in this. That began 10 months out; when I spent three or four days in Iowa doing all the things I do when I go into a state. I made the assessment that I didn't see how we could win Iowa. We decided that we should never say that publicly and that we should fight hard in Iowa but we had to be prepared to lose Iowa.

That forced us to look at the thing very carefully and make another critical decision: that this year more than ever before voters would be indifferent.

There is an indifference to politics. Voters are frankly somewhat jaundiced about all institutions this year. It's been a trend I've seen developing in the last ten years. We thought there would be a very short attention span not only in the primaries but in the general election. In 72 hours, regardless of what happened in Iowa, if we ran a good campaign on the ground, we could prevail in New Hampshire. If we could get South Carolina 72 hours before the rest of Super Tuesday, we could get 8 or 10 points just off a good victory in South Carolina.

After we made the Iowa decision, I made a personal decision that I never announced to anyone: I was going to New Hampshire to meet with John Sununu. And we also made a decision, by the way, that I think was a proper primary decision—to really concentrate on these governors. There were three governors that I felt had strong enough organizations in their states—if we could get them lined up early—to bring about a win no matter what else happened. They were John Sununu in New Hampshire, Carroll Campbell in South Carolina, Jim Thompson in Illinois.

I've always placed a great deal of importance on Illinois. Regardless of what happens by the time you get around the circle, if you can win Illinois you're probably going to go ahead and win the primary.

So I went and saw Sununu. I went to dinner at his house at 6 o'clock and I said to myself, "I ain't leaving here 'till this guy commits." About 11 o'clock, when he hadn't committed, I said,

"John, I ain't leaving until we get this thing worked out. Here it is 11 o'clock, so let's get it done or I'll be here till the 15th."

So the elements of winning New Hampshire were getting Sununu lined up and, of course, the magnificent campaign and Roger's work and what Sununu did. I totally agree with Ed [Rollins]. We were 3- or 4-point guys max in any given situation. More important than anything else our candidate showed every strength he had in New Hampshire.

Then, of course, we had South Carolina and then Super Tuesday. The one miscalculation we made in the primary season was, frankly, that we felt we could, in effect, end our primary for all practical purposes on Super Tuesday, but that at least one viable candidate would be left and it would be Dole. I figured we would not end up with a two-man race with us versus a right wing–oriented campaign. It would be us and another guy inside of the 70 percent group. Dole was the main one, but I thought that Dole would be badly crippled. The calendar was good enough for him— Wisconsin and so forth—to go on, and we could get the free publicity and so forth. Susan indicated really what happened.

Briefly, on the general election, what we were worried about was going into the Democratic Convention in a situation like Gerry Ford got into when he got 16 or 17 points behind. If we let that happen, we would end up giving him 10 more points. Then we'd be 27 points behind at the end of their convention, and at 27 points behind, you could run a damn good campaign and still just may not be able to make it.

And there is the old axiom, there's nothing like an impending hanging to focus the mind. Roger and Bob and I and a couple of others started having some serious focus groups. We went to Paramus, New Jersey. We found out three things from those groups: Number one, neither candidate had any kind of image around this country. Number two, it was an issueless election, which let us know that we had distant help, that peace and prosperity would jump back into consciousness after people started focusing on the election after Labor Day and that that would be helpful.

Third, we had a macrodisadvantage which had been hurting us badly: We were on the wrong side of an historical cycle, which I do believe in. But if we could get to the post-Labor Day period, our macroadvantage, which was the electoral base and the organization we had, would come into play. The fourth finding, of course, was the famous six or seven issues that we discussed. The people in the focus groups were conservative Democrats who all voted for Reagan in 1984 but were for Dukakis in 1988.

We found a few little issues that we decided to go with. Our strategy was to cut their lead in half before the convention. We figured that if we could get it down to 7 or 8 points before the convention, they'd get their 10 out of the convention which would put them at 16 or 17. That's doable.

In a nutshell, the strategy was that if we could make it to game time and get in the game, and if the game wasn't going to start till late, we could win. But the ticket of admission to game time was being about 8 or 9 or less points behind going into our convention, then using our convention as a leveling mechanism. We thought we could win with our candidate's experience with some good issues that we felt would be underestimated by the pundits and by the other campaign; by hammering like hell on them; and then by having the advantage of this electoral base. I guess that's it in a nutshell.

Martin Nolan: The last candidate to enter this race was Bob Dole. Bill Lacy.

William Lacy: Lee described the invisible circle. I think that Bob Dole, who really is a brilliant tactician, brought himself into that invisible circle in the last months of 1986, during the Iran-Contra episode.

Very early in the campaign we really thought we had a two-man race between the vice president and Bob Dole. We essentially thought at that particular point that there were two avenues that we should follow in terms of trying to defeat George Bush. The first was message: that is, to articulate a reason why Republican voters should switch from George Bush to Robert Dole. The second way that we thought we might be able to beat George Bush was to beat him politically: to defeat him early, decisively, often, and, in effect, really shake his coalition, shake his support, shake his organization. Of course, neither of those ultimately worked.

In terms of message, one of Bob Dole's greatest strengths was his ability to argue the leadership issue. All our polling throughout the country fairly consistently showed that Republican voters were willing to accept the notion that Bob Dole was a very strong leader. But the big thing the vice president always had going for him in all of our research was experience—that was a killer for us—and specifically, foreign policy experience.

Those of us who know Dole well—and most of you have watched him for a long time—know that he really is a very tough guy. We always thought that one of our best arguments would be to ask Republican voters, "Who would you like to see sitting across the table from Gorbachev?" Well, when we tested that in our first poll we found Republican voters wanted to see George Bush sitting across the table from Gorbachev. So the foreign policy area was a very, very difficult area for us.

The second thing that was really interesting was people's response to this statement, "George Bush deserves to be the nominee in 1988." About two-thirds of the Republicans agreed. So we knew we had a real tough road in terms of selling a message.

Politically, we had a big advantage, and that advantage was Iowa. We always knew that we would be strong there. I listened to Bill Carrick's comments about how you could be so absolutely consumed by Iowa. We didn't do that. We, in fact, had looked at some past elections and realized, if we had Iowa, what we would have to do to step beyond that. What several people—Ed Rollins, I think was the first—mentioned specifically was that the Bush firewall in the South was really our immense stumbling block.

When we started getting back survey data from the South at the end of 1987, we saw the kind of leads and strengths and all of the attributes and characteristics that the vice president had. We knew immediately that we no longer could simply win early and win often and, say, finish strongly in New Hampshire but not win it. We knew at that point we had to win New Hampshire.

With that kind of a situation I thought we should begin with Michigan. Instead, we took a walk. We were hoping that Robertson would defeat Bush there. That didn't happen.

But we still had a very strong showing in Iowa, thanks to a good organization, the right message, and a very bad political environment for the President which rubbed off on the vice president.

We went from there to New Hampshire. We spent a lot of time trying to plan what we would do after we won Iowa. We sort of assumed we would win Iowa and tried to plan out what to do to maximize the impact. One of the problems that we had in New Hampshire, among many, was that a lot more voters there really believed that George Bush was the conservative candidate in the race. And as you know, Republican voters in New Hampshire are conservative. They believed by a two-to-one margin that Bush was more conservative than Dole and even by about 15 percent that he was more conservative than Kemp. We were never really able to overcome that.

We tried a maneuver that week on foreign policy to go to Bush's right, and it really succeeded up until about the weekend. That weekend Lee and Roger put the taxes and the straddle ad on TV. We knew it was coming. We had written memos on it. We knew what they were going to hit us on, and they still caught us unprepared. We violated really what has become a fundamental rule, I think, of strategy: You always must react in some way, not necessarily respond, but react to any kind of an attack. And we didn't do that.

We lost New Hampshire and in effect that was the end of the campaign. We did very well following that, in South Dakota and Minnesota. The vice president just took a walk on both those states, and we therefore didn't really get any stature out of those wins.

Then we went into South Carolina and, as Lee described it, that was really impossible for us all along. Perhaps in retrospect we should have tried to take a walk on South Carolina to see if we couldn't downplay what was inevitably going to be a Bush win there. Whether that would have worked I don't know. Then came Super Tuesday, which was really a total disaster for us and a great victory for the vice president and for Lee.

I still believe Bob Dole could have been elected President. I think we lost for three reasons. Number one, we really never came up with a way to articulate a reason why voters should be against George Bush and for Bob Dole. They liked Bob Dole. They liked what he stood for, but they started out with a preconceived idea that they wanted George Bush to be their nominee. We could never beat that.

Second, our failure to react—and this is a very specific situation—to the ad in New Hampshire sort of sealed our fate. Finally, and perhaps most important, was the Bush campaign, the vice president's performance, which was superb. The fact that he had a linkage to Ronald Reagan was probably a good thing for him in every state except for Iowa, Minnesota, and South Dakota. Further, a fine team was put together by the Bush campaign side. I think those are the primary reasons why the Bob Dole campaign never really made it.

Chapter 2

CHARACTER COPS AT WORK

Introduction by Paul Taylor

One of the most wry commentaries on the 1988 presidential campaign was a letter to the editor printed in the newspaper I work for, *The Washington Post*. It was elegantly brief. "A prediction regarding next year's presidential election," wrote a reader by the name of Jeff Balch. "No Democrats will be left in the race by the time we reach primary and caucus season. George Bush will run unopposed in November, and lose."

Balch offered his weary prognostication in October 1987 after Gary Hart and Joe Biden had slipped out of the presidential race, each on his own banana peel. We were in the midst of what one wag called the "Year of Living Childishly." Presidential candidates were being grounded at a ferocious clip—less by scandal, it seemed, than pratfall.

One had an unauthorized sleepover and was out of the race just six days later. Another copied someone else's words. Poof! Gone in two weeks. Then the campaign manager who got the copier in trouble had to resign for being a tattletale.

Then things really started to unravel. A Supreme Court nominee was forced to remove himself from consideration after he confirmed a National Public Radio exposé: Yes, he'd once (okay, maybe two or three times) smoked marijuana. That tumble in an adjacent branch of government triggered a small avalanche of confessions back out on the campaign trail. Candidates for offices large and small suddenly began holding press conferences to recount the circumstances of their youthful experiments with controlled substances. A race was on: Could the politicians come clean before the reporters hunted down their college roommates?

Something fundamental seemed to have changed in the way reporters were scrutinizing presidential candidates, and the guess here is that Balch's letter was poking fun as much at the way reporters were watching as at what they were seeing. That was the campaign when journalists became character cops.

To our critics, we were behaving more like bulls in a china shop, rampaging through dark alleys of the psyche, peeking beneath bedsheets, trampling over privacy rights, trivializing the quest for the presidency. They said we were creating the sensational stories we were reporting.

Gary Hart was obviously not blameless for the circumstances that led to his downfall, the critics said, but did his behavior give reporters the right to snoop outside his townhouse after-hours, or to ask the "Big A"—adultery—question at a press conference? If they hadn't done these things—never before done in a presidential campaign—would there have been a story? A downfall?

Our defenders said we were performing a valuable public service. Gaudy as the process sometimes was, we were the first line of defense against another "flawed presidency."

The voters seemed to want to find all they could about the character and judgment and veracity of their next leader. The candidates understood this. The core material of presidential campaigns in our personality-soaked political culture had come to be more and more about autobiography, authenticity, and character. It only stood to reason that press scrutiny into these areas would grow closer, deeper, harsher, deadlier.

Besides, someone had to prune the field, to "get rid of the funny ones," as one 1988 campaign manager put it. It simply wasn't practical for voters to make choices among 12 to 15 contenders for the throne. There was too much information to wade through; the national circuits would overload.

In the old days, this gatekeeping function had been performed by party leaders. But they no longer had much role or credibility in presidential politics. So there was a vacuum—into which rushed the unofficial, unelected screening committee of the modern political era, the character cops of the Fourth Estate.

By all means these journalists should scrutinize, shot back the critics, but they should choose their yardsticks and microscopes more wisely. "There's got to be something more to this than working your way through the Ten Commandments—adultery, false witness, etc," Duke professor James David Barber, a presidential scholar who had long advocated that the press don the uniform of the character cop, said in 1987. Barber was worried that Greshams law of character coverage seemed to have taken root, in which the sensational drove out the substantial.

Whichever side was right—there was surely some truth to both perspectives—the scrutiny did turn the campaign into a kind of demolition derby. The year 1987, in particular, was part carnage, part carnival. Two Democrats went down as a result of trial by media ordeal—and in both instances, the verdicts were rendered months before any voters had any chance to ratify or overrule the unsparing portraits of them drawn by newspapers and television. The time was out of sync—as if, in a football game, a period of sudden death was being played before the opening kickoff.

The Republicans were pretty much on the sidelines that year, observing the Napoleonic dictum of not interferring with the enemy when he is in the process of destroying himself. But all was not well in their kindgom, either. The year 1987 found GOP front-runner George Bush derided in the political press as a "wimp." The charge seemed to have enough bite with the voters that his strategists came to view 1988 as a kind of manhood rite; once the serious campaigning started, Bush, above all, would have to show he was tough enough to be President.

Thus in the summer and fall of 1988, the nation was introduced to George the Ripper, that snarling, liberal-bashing "read my-lips" concoction that had never been seen before—or since. This may be the crowning irony of the year of character copping. A system of scrutiny designed to take the bark off the candidates winds up rewarding the one who did the most creative job of putting some bark on.

All sorts of questions were raised by this aggressive reporting.

Are the old rules about coverage of a candidate's private life—that it should remain private unless it affects his or her public performance—passé?

Or, where the episodes of 1987 and 1988 exceptions to a still-functioning standard?

If that's no longer the standard, are there any new ones?

Is there an "invisible hand" in the marketplace of public opinion and mores, as Bush campaign manager Lee Atwater posited, that reins in press excesses?

Is there a statute of limitations in these matters, or are youthful transgressions of the Ten Commandments just as reportable as current ones?

And is there any way for the press to report the fact that false rumors are being spread without spreading them itself?

We spent the first morning of the campaign decision-makers weekend conference batting around all of these questions and, predictably, coming to consensus about almost nothing. We did lay down what I think is a rich account of what it's like to have to plot strategy and tactics in an era when the rules seemed to be changing.

For example, the question arose whether it is better for the target of a rumor to get it out in public and try to shift the focus of the press's curiosity onto the evil soul spreading the rumors. Atwater said his campaign did that to great effect when rumors circulated in 1987 about Bush's private life. But Sue Casey, a top Hart campaign aide, said that Hart had tried to do the same thing a few weeks before his fateful encounter with Donna Rice. Instead of making the womanizing rumors go away, she said, it invited more stories.

The easy explanation for the difference, of course, was that one rumor proved to have substance, while the other was never substantiated. But not so fast. Dukakis campaign manager Susan Estrich noted that even though virtually all of the reporting on the unsubstantiated rumor that Dukakis had once received psychiatric care was focused on who was responsible for spreading it, her candidate still suffered a precipitous decline in tracking polls for the two days the story was in the national news. "It was 'Dukakis Not Crazy—Details at 11'," she lamented.

Character copping proved to be an unsettling exercise all around—for reporters, politicians, and voters. Whether it was an aberration of the last campaign or a permanent feature of all future ones—the verdict awaits 1992 and beyond.

Meantime, if anyone has any bright ideas of how to run for the presidency in the midst of all of these shifting tides, FAX them immediately to the campaign manager Class of '92, now assembling in Washington, D.C., and other suspicious locales. They're going to need all the help they can get.

The Discussion

Paul Taylor: I thought that scheduling the press session first was like treating you all to your dessert before we made you eat your collard greens. This is an opportunity for you to comment on how we in the media did our jobs. I recently came across a passage I think you'll enjoy: "Generally, the press performance was fairly typical for a presidential campaign: ubiquitous and voracious; oriented to polls and horse races, glitz and gossip, warts and gaffes; largely unsuccessful in their efforts to avoid being manipulated; demonstrating meager interest in issue substance and candidate competence actually relevant to governing; and informative, resourceful, and professional." That was the introduction to the 1984 campaign managers' panel on the press. So the more things change, perhaps the more they stay the same.

Bob [Beckel] and I want to work roughly chronologically, focusing on episodes where press scrutiny became a central part of the campaign. We can all have fascinating philosophical conversations about what role the media ought to play in a free society, and there are a lot of wise men and women around the table, but our sense is that the first thing we want to do is lay down a record of what actually happened.

So our questions to you are going to be: How did you react to the press scrutiny? Did you think that because of this press scrutiny the rules were changing, that the game had changed somehow? We will generally start by asking the principals in the episode involved, then try to expand it out and have other campaign managers react to the circumstances they saw unfolding.

Robert Beckel: There are some obvious episodes concerning the press and how you all reacted to it. All campaigns are not going to be involved because some of you are better at ducking controversy than others. If you want to jump in and ask questions, go ahead. We want to get down to specifics as to how you reacted to certain events. We are also going to be short on time, so we're going to try to move it along.

Paul Taylor: Let's start with April 1987. Gary Hart is announcing for the presidency; he's the front-runner in the Democratic field, and there are a series of articles written around the time of his announcement that raise the so-called "womanizing" issue. Probably the most memorable one was a quote in a *Newsweek* profile which ran just before he announced: A friend and political ally of Hart, John McEvoy, was quoted as saying that Gary will be all right, he will win the nomination as long as he can keep his pants on. I believe there was something similar in a *Washington Post* Style Section piece. I recall a lot of the straight news articles right at the time of the announcement, and many of them had a paragraph that contained some variation of the phrase "plagued by rumors of womanizing."

Sue Casey, what was the mind-set of the Hart campaign as he announced and was reading these things in the press? Did you think that the rules were changing on you? Did you think you had a problem on your hands?

Susan Casey: Well, it was very clear to us, thanks to all of the members of the press, exactly the way they were going to address our campaign. It's an irony in a way. There was general consensus that Gary was very prepared to run a good campaign and that he was very prepared to govern on the issues. They [the press] couldn't really find much fault in many many areas, so they had to find something else they could examine. And the press very clearly laid out to us directly, to one another in conversations, and to all of you in the other campaigns as well that they were going to focus on "character." That would be the area they would have to delve into to satisfy whatever curiosities there were because there were no other vulnerabilities. Right up to the first of the year every conversation with members of the press began with, "So what is it about you?" The subject captured every article that was written—not just a paragraph, but entire articles.

In fact, I think that entire *Newsweek* article was on how are we going to have this man reveal himself, what are these hidden things? That was the whole focus of the press.

We took the long view. It's a year-long campaign, this is what they're going to do, it's the only thing they can do, we will have to tolerate it. And, as Lee said yesterday, if you have been around the track, you know this is going to happen and you've got a year. And Gary was, as anyone who ever interviewed him during that period knows, pulling his hair out that he would have to sit through these long interviews with the total subject being "what's inside him, what is this secret, why are there all these things we cannot quite understand?" Well, how do you answer?

If any one of us had to sit through those interviews, we'd be thinking, "Here I am, I have laid out a record, but this is what they want to talk about." We knew it was there, and so we went through the process. Gary agreed he would go through this profile kind of process with the press, if they needed it, up until the time of the announcement. We decided we would get it done, if that's what we had to do. If they wanted to ask all these questions, we would do it, and then we'd stop after we gave them their fill.

We did not have a strategy to deal with the character issue. We felt Gary's character could be laid out over the course of a year based on a whole lot of history of character, including independence and courage in a lot of different areas. We felt this examination stage would pass.

The stories in and right around the announcement were very, very frustrating, but again, there was a sense within the campaign that this is what they were going to do and they were going to have to go through the process and we would have to go through it with them. We didn't sit around asking how we were going to deal with this, how we were going to get past this. It was part of the process and it would pass.

Robert Beckel: Let me ask a follow-up question. You said that the press was going to ask the character questions, that this was going to be the year of the character. Out of curiosity, was this a Hart phenomenon, or did anybody else get those kinds of questions about character about your candidate?

Edward Rollins: Kemp had a lot of scrutiny early on, in two ways. We didn't know whether our strategy would be to line up 15 airline stewardesses to deny one side or 25 football players to deny the other side.

Susan Casey: Can I just speak to that? I went back this week and reread a lot what was written in the press to look at that very issue. Had the times changed or was it Hart? I think it was Hart. I mean, it was Kemp, too, a little bit because of past rumors, but it was primarily Hart. Everyone seemed comfortable, I guess, in every other area, but there was the one area they weren't comfortable with, and therefore for Hart this was his thing. I think for each candidate the press looked to the one or two things that were the vulnerabilities, and I think it was clearly a Hart phenomenon very early on.

Paul Taylor: Sue, you got the phone call on that Saturday night from Hart saying he had these *Miami Herald* reporters outside his townhouse. Events unfolded very rapidly over the next week. Tell us your reaction to the scrutiny that occurred. What was your strategy? What was your reaction? Did you think the fire was going to be as big and engulfing as it was?

Susan Casey: Well, it wasn't something we thought would just go away real fast. When I think about this whole issue of character, it's not so much whether the press should have covered it, it's not whether the press needed to reveal these things or whether the story should have been covered or written: it's the intensity, it's the color, it's the depth. I think what happened in a 24- to 48-hour period was not that there was a story that *Miami Herald* reporters had spotted a woman at a townhouse. But there were nine or ten very colorful stories—in *The New York Times,* for instance—the very next day and four or five minutes on the evening news on every channel.

Robert Beckel: I was going to ask you about that. In that 24-hour period, from the campaign standpoint, did you all decide who was going to speak to the press and who wasn't? Was there a specific meeting where you said, "Now we've got a fire storm on our hands, who's going to take the point on this?"

Susan Casey: During the night Bill Dixon decided he would fly to D.C. to find out what was going on because we didn't really know. Gary called and said that some reporters were around who said they were going to do a story the next day. We weren't sure just what. Okay, so there's going to be a story tomorrow. We didn't really know what happened until the morning when we got a copy of the story. Dixon was in D.C., Bill Shore and Paul Tully and Emerson, all of us, were back in Denver, and we got on the phone together and tried to clarify who was saying what to whom. Dixon apparently was talking with the press in D.C. I guess he went over to our D.C. office. And he would be the person who would be speaking to the press mainly.

Robert Beckel: Did he make a point to the people out in Denver that nobody was to say anything in the press in Denver, that he would handle it in Washington?

Susan Casey: I guess that is sort of the way it came out, but essentially we had no response. You know, we did not know what happened. When people called us, we said we'd wait until the next day to see what happened. Before we had a chance to see what was really going on, it was well beyond a manageable kind of entity.

Paul Taylor: Let me ask you this question and then invite any of the other campaign managers to speak. In retrospect, thinking about managing that crisis over that six-day period, is there anything you think the campaign could have done differently to get out in front of it, to get above it, to make it go away? Or did you think once you had the first story, Hart's candidacy was going to be gone in a big hurry?

Susan Casey: I think that once the story was in *The Miami Herald* it was gone. It doesn't mean we couldn't have done things differently, but I think it was gone once it was out there. I think if Gary had called the night before and said, "Look, guys, something has happened; it's very serious. This is the kind of story it's going to be tomorrow morning. By the time it hits the stands, we've got to be prepared." Instead we had a vague notion of what had happened—last night something happened; he ran into a reporter; there's going to be some story. That was sort of the sense we had until we saw the story. And then by noon, the reaction to the story—it was far gone.

Robert Beckel: One last question. At any time before the whole *Miami Herald* thing, knowing you had a lot of Hart stories from 1984, did anybody sit down with Hart and ask him specifically what to expect for stories for the year? Do you know if that took place, that Hart said, "Here may be my vulnerabilities," and everyone decided how to handle them?

Susan Casey: I've read quotes in the press from different people saying, "Well, we sat down and we explained it to him." But Gary's personal life was Gary's personal life. It was not a campaign item.

Paul Taylor: This was the opening episode of this long marathon campaign. It obviously sent huge ripples across the political landscape. Those of you who were preparing campaigns or already had campaigns underway, what was the message from this episode? Was the message that the rules had changed, that areas previously thought to be out of bounds were now in bounds? Did you all have strategy sessions? Did you ask embarrassing, tough questions to your candidates about what the press might find? Anybody jump in? All right. We will nominate somebody. Let's nominate Lee.

Lee, as you remember, shortly after that there was an effort by some folks to move a "George Bush-has-a-mistress" rumor into the public domain. It got serious enough that the decision was made in the campaign to have George, Jr., address it. When he did, that was the one moment when it surfaced in the press.

Lee Atwater: I'm trying to think who he addressed it to.

Paul Taylor: But you must have had a lot of conversations around that time, and that rumor came back, as we know, a year later. But talk about that. Talk about your own assessment of what the landscape was.

Lee Atwater: Backing up for a minute, I remember very well the day before I knew about the Gary Hart/*Miami Herald* situation. My partner and friend Charlie Black and I were driving to Roanoke to Ed Rollins's wedding, and before I left Washington, I picked up *The New York Times*. They give you half of the Sunday paper on Saturday, and so I was reading *The New York Times Magazine* article about Gary Hart. I finished reading the thing and said to Charlie, "You know, this guy is a terrific front-runner on paper, but he's not going to make it—just no way—because we have 10 months left in this contest and he can't have a story written about him that doesn't (a) talk about him changing his name, (b) talk about him changing his age, and (c) talk about being a womanizer. Every time the guy has a fund-raiser, federal marshals show up. There are character arrows that are going to be shot through his heart for the next 10 months, and he's going to be bleeding to death by a thousand cuts." That was my assessment, not knowing anything at all about what was going to happen.

I also told Charlie that what would be interesting was that the

"Seven Dwarfs" thing that was popular at the time would be shattered because Gary Hart was a pretty big man. So with Gary Hart in there, the dwarf beating the big man was better than dwarf beating dwarf. So somebody was going to be a big man because Gary was going to be taken out because of these things.

I agree with Sue; there was no question in my mind that for the most part it was a Gary Hart phenomenon.

I have always had great faith in what I call the invisible hand. When things get out of hand, either on our side in the political community or in the media, it gets back fairly quickly. So what I figured would happen would be a temporary hysteria, but that very quickly some other candidate would get in the soup á la Gary Hart, but that the candidate would be innocent. Unfortunately, that candidate would get wrecked, but that incident would bring everything back in line. But it never quite happened that way. But I've got enough confidence in the way things work that I never thought this was going to be a long-term problem plaguing us throughout the campaign.

Robert Beckel: Let me ask you specific questions about the adultery story on Bush. Bush's kid came out and said publicly to the press "There is no big 'A' story." Was that a conscious decision to send him out there or did he want do do that himself?

Lee Atwater: It was a conscious decision for this reason: Tuesday of the week prior to that I received in one day some phone calls from the press about this thing. It was hysteria. I've never seen anything like it. The second day, the rumor hit the Hill, and from 12 to 5 o'clock we literally got probably 40 or 50 calls from the Hill. The third day, it started melting down into the states, and we were getting calls in from the states. At that point what I figured would happen, after observing the Gary Hart episode, is that a favorite game would be played. It's the old game we saw a hundred times; *Time* calling up and saying, "Well, *Newsweek* is going with it. We heard *Newsweek* is going with it," or "*The Washington Post* is going with this. CBS is going with this thing." Everybody was manipulating the media.

It became clear to me that no responsible organization was going to go with it. But it was a lead pipe cinch that some mid-level or off-the-wall paper was going to go with it by the next week.

Just think about this, fellow campaign managers. You have had over 500 calls from virtually every important person in the media. You know it's going to get out. So you're dealing with this situation. Does it get out with some mid-level newspaper and then everybody says, "Oh, well, we hate to do this. We didn't want to touch this story. But now it's out, and so we've got to put it on the front page." You're dealing then in a totally rear guard defensive posture because what you have got to do is explain. So when you see a Mack truck coming down the road at you, you ought to try to deal with it on your own terms.

What crossed my mind was that we needed to get it out on our own terms and in mid-air to shift the nature of the story from the rumor to who was the dirty trickster putting out the rumor.

By the way, when the story came out, within 24 hours it was flat dead. Why? Because the whole story shifted to whoever was putting this out was a dirty trickster and this was vile et cetera and no one would put it out.

Susan Casey: Why didn't that happen for Hart the same way?

Lee Atwater: You didn't play it quite the same way we did.

Susan Casey: Before May 3 the same thing was kind of happening. Then in that plane, right around announcement, when there were more press questions about this womanizing thing, he said, "You're the one telling me it's coming from other campaigns." Why didn't you do that story?

Lee Atwater: The instant he did that he stepped in flypaper. That Style story—I looked at that and said this fellow has gone about three notches further than he needed to go.

Let me make one last point now. There was no conspiracy to get that out at the time. It was total coincidence that while all this was going on I had lunch with a couple of reporters from *Newsweek*. We talked about a great many things. At the end of the conversation we got into it, and as a result George, Jr., did end up talking.

Robert Beckel: Did you then call George, Jr., and say, "George, we need a member of the family out there to do this?"

Lee Atwater: No. It didn't happen like that.

Roger Ailes: George went out on his own, didn't he?

Lee Atwater: No. We were sitting around in my office on Saturday, and I was also talking to the reporters. George was in there. When I hung up, George said, "Well, I want to say something." George was very determined about it.

Robert Beckel: So you said, "Let's do this. This would be a good way to deal with this."

Lee Atwater: Yes.

Howard Fineman: Let me ask, since I was on the receiving end of that,—

Lee Atwater: I don't want to give out my source.

Howard Fineman: Whether you discussed this with anybody else in the campaign. It was a pretty big decision to make.

Lee Atwater: That is confidential information.

Howard Fineman: That sounds like a yes.

Lee Atwater: I really didn't.

William Carrick: One thing on the Hart situation was fundamentally clear, and Lee alluded to it. There was an overwhelming consensus in the national press corps that they were going to get at this question of Gary Hart's personal life, his life-style, and it was going to get maximum exposure. It was a relentless pursuit. The question of whether other campaigns fueled it or not, I guess we could get into that, but its probably irrelevant.

Susan Casey: You could just mention it.

William Carrick: It was not really something that was produced by the opposition campaigns. It was a dynamic that was in the national press corps. It was going to be relentlessly pursued by the news media pretty quickly in the campaign. I think others would probably corroborate that because that is what we got back from the press on a daily basis: "What do you know about Hart?"

Paul Taylor: Was it your view and the view of the other campaigns that were up and running at that point that this was a special circumstance because of who Gary Hart was or that were we playing in a whole new arena, with the press much more intrusive, much more aggressive, much more into the kind of character scrutiny that some have called psycho babble?

Roger Ailes: Search and destroy.

Paul Taylor: Search and destroy. What was your mind-set at the time?

William Carrick: For my part, I think the answer to your question is yes to both things. It was a special circumstance with Gary Hart and it was a new era. There's no question it got sillier as it manifested itself beyond the Beltway journalists. I can remember that when the Hart thing hit Gephardt was out in San Jose. The next time he got on the phone, he said, "You're not going to believe this. Some local reporter just asked me if I have ever committed adultery."

Robert Beckel: Let's get back to one other point. There were campaigns, Democratic campaigns, that strategically figured Hart was vulnerable on this side and did everything they could not to discourage the Hart discussions. Are any of the Democratic campaigns willing to own up to the fact that they talked to the press?

Did it become part of your thinking that Hart was vulnerable way before *The Miami Herald* thing? That you knew you had a front-runner who was flawed?

William Carrick: I don't think anybody had to do anything. It had nothing do with the other campaigns. It was moving on its own momentum and was driven by the national press corps.

Edward Rollins: Well, if he had not sinned again, past sins probably wouldn't have mattered. How this game changed, I think, was that present affairs or future affairs were on the board. You could deal with them. As for past affairs, I don't think anybody in the press really dug beyond the initial stage. The big difference with Hart is that he had gone on and made such a big deal out of "I don't do it, go ahead, follow me." And people went out to prove he was a liar. I think that the integrity issue sunk him more than anything else, more than the adultery issue.

Paul Taylor: Do the rest of the people around this table agree with that statute of limitations?

Roger Ailes: I would be interested in hearing the press comment on that. Is there a statute of limitations or isn't there?

Paul Taylor: Well, the answer is that we don't know.

Roger Ailes: It depends on whether you need a story that day.

Paul Taylor: No. The answer is that we are very uncomfortable laying down strict rules because we tend to want to be able to judge everything in its own context. Every story has a different context. But this question of past behavior takes us to the Biden episode, which came next on the calendar.

Roger Ailes: I don't know when this happened, and I don't know whether the media drove it or what drove it, but there was a tendency to make this a soap opera and make it the year of the person. We had Mr. Mean, Bob Dole. We had Romeo. We had the Ice Man. We had the Wimp. We had Crazy Al.

Edward Rollins: Half those words are yours. (Laughter)

Roger Ailes: They're all mine, but the point is this: Each of these candidates then had to prove he wasn't what the characterization of him was. And that was set up, I think, in every story by the media. Well, he's known as a wimp; can he get over it? He's known as a mean guy: can he get over it? I don't know where that fits, but I did see that throughout the campaign.

Paul Taylor: In the presentations last night about what the initial thinking was, I didn't hear a whole lot of discussion about new ideas or where we want to change the country. The discussion tended to be (a) tactical calendar considerations and (b) he's a nice guy.

Roger Ailes: That's suicide with the press.

Paul Taylor: But my point is that a lot of the campaigns were based on presentation of self and on biography. Isn't it natural then that the press scrutiny will be about biography?

Roger Ailes: I think you can defend who you are better than you can defend your ideas. If we come out with a sweeping view of how to change things, there are going to be some flaws in it. And the next 30 days of stories are going to be about the flaws. Therefore, you have made a terrible mistake in trying to present an idea which may be helpful.

Robert Beckel: I think you made a good point. There were certain characterizations developed around the candidates.

Roger Ailes: Cartoons.

Robert Beckel: That's right. Cartoon is a good word. How do you take advantage of it? We will talk about it as we move down into your case and yours, Susan.

Susan Casey: I want to follow up on something Roger said. Some candidates had some things that they had to beat, that they had to get past. That was set up by the press.

Ed, you said Gary Hart made such a big deal of it that that's why the press went after him. Gary Hart didn't make a big deal of it. He didn't say, "Hey, this is what we're going to talk about," or every chance I get I'm going to say, "I didn't do it, follow me around." The entire record of April was "there's something here, there's something there." What else can a candidate say except, "no, there isn't; no, there isn't; no, there isn't."

Did Hart set himself up for this because he kept going around making it the issue? He didn't make the issue. The press made the issue.

Edward Rollins: I had a candidate who also had similar accusations out there. We just had a strategy, even before Donna Rice came on the national scene, to take steps in the course of the campaign with our candidate. We never let Jack be alone with his deputy press secretary, who is a woman. Joanne [Mrs. Kemp] always traveled with him. We were very careful on a whole variety of situations because we were aware of what was coming. I think the bottom line with Gary is that he wasn't as careful as he probably should have been.

Susan Casey: No question. No question. No question. (Laughter)

Allan B. Hubbard: Could I ask one question that has perplexed me since it happened? Why did George, Jr.'s comment to *Newsweek* kill the story? Kill the rumor? Kill the press's interest in it?

Lee Atwater: It shifted the nature of the story to who the dirty tricksters were—that the rumor was unfounded and whoever put it out was dirty and malicious. Then guess what? No one would promote the story anymore. So the story died on the vine because everyone immediately became too scared, intimidated, to spread the story around. So (a) there was no one to spread the story around, and (b) there was no story because the rumors were unfounded, and then it died.

Allan B. Hubbard: So the lesson is that you should deal with it head on?

Lee Atwater: On these kinds of things the lesson is to sit down and look at the situation and act at the time of the situation. If you generalize on these little sticky situations, you're going to get burned.

Paul Taylor: This is out of sequence. You had the whole thing bubble up again on you in the fall of this year. You had the stock market fall 40 points in one hour on the rumor that *The Post* was going to print a story that Bush had a mistress. That event required everybody to make some mention of it. You had the *LA Weekly* publishing a story on the rumor. What was the Bush campaign strategy at that point?

Lee Atwater: There was no strategy because we knew it wouldn't go anywhere.

Paul Taylor: You had to talk about it.

Roger Ailes: We had complete confidence. If anybody had this story, it would have been a front page story in *The Washington Post*.

Lee Atwater: My only observation is that the other campaign was trying to make an issue that we were running a negative campaign or we were running a cheap-shot campaign. When their field director was on record they made a wise decision on how to handle it. But, nevertheless, it was during that very point in their campaign when they were trying to make those kinds of things the issue against us that the whole thing bubbled up—the stock market thing. Frankly, I thought it played fine for us under the circumstances, and I knew it wouldn't go anywhere. Roger did, too, because we had been through it.

Roger Ailes: When they [the press] have it, we're going to be doing damage control. We're not going to be doing anything but damage control.

Lee Atwater: Let me ask Susan. I figured at the time that you all hated it as much as we did.

Susan Estrich: We couldn't touch it.

Lee Atwater: You couldn't touch it, and you knew we would be smart enough to blame it on you.

Susan Estrich: We couldn't touch it with a ten-foot pole. We had heard from umpteen news organizations that had tried to get this story, and no one had. I think Lee is right. What was working for us best at that time was that we had finally been able to make George Bush begin to pay the price of what we called his negative lies campaign. The last thing we needed was a backlash of sympathy for George Bush—him being the target of the same kind of rumors—so that everyone would say they couldn't stand the election. Personally, I remember these *L.A. Weekly* people coming up to me.

Lee Atwater: The night of the debates?

Susan Estrich: Yes.

Frank Fahrenkopf: There was also a reporter from the *Village Voice* who was running around.

Susan Estrich: And I hadn't even read the damn thing, so I could say, "Keep away, I'm not pushing it, I didn't read it." I think by that time it had become perfectly clear, if not through the Hart case then through your handling of the story the first time around and through the Biden people's initial handling of the tape story, that the best thing to do when you get hit with a rumor like that is to spin it back to the people who are pushing this kind of nasty rumor. The last thing we could afford was to look like we were trying to spread rumors about George Bush's personal life. In fact we had one staff person who spoke out of turn about George Bush's personal life in a comment in New York, and she was gone that night. We could not have that inside our campaign.

Robert Beckel: Can we take a step back to the primaries, because there are some campaigns here right now that were impacted directly by the Biden incident. Ridley is not here right now. Let me pose questions to the Biden campaign, the Gephardt campaign, the Dukakis campaign, and then the Babbitt and Gore campaigns.

Let me ask this question, Bill Carrick. During the initial flurry about who leaked the press story, somebody in the Biden campaign told me they were absolutely convinced it was the Gephardt campaign that leaked that story. I said, "How do you know?" He said, "We were told by the Dukakis campaign." My sources were very good.

Let me ask you this. How did you react to that information, and how much energy did you have to take out of your campaign to deal with the fact that for at least five or six days you guys were fingered as the leak?

William Carrick: It was 10 days. It was an incredible experience because we knew it wasn't anything we planted. We had plenty of people who were likely suspects. We had a lot of animosity between the Biden psychopaths, as Tim Ridley called them last night, and our psychopaths. And it was an attitude of "if we're going to go down, we're going to take them with us" in some quarters in the Biden camp. Later it all unraveled, and it was obviously the Dukakis campaign's problem.

But during that period CBS went out twice on the nightly news with stories stating unequivocally that Gephardt did it. We were in the situation, particularly in Iowa, where Dave Yepsen of *The Des Moines Register* had been part of this story. The paper was refusing to write anything about the story in terms of analysis, interpretation, or even follow-up stories. *The Register* was staying totally away from it, and Iowa is a one-paper state. That was a hell of a problem because all the Iowa voters were getting was the CBS wild story and the political rumor mill. Meanwhile there was nothing in *The Register*. So the assumption was Gephardt had done it.

We were actually in the field doing focus groups. Democrats were saying, "I'm not voting for Gephardt," and that he was behind it. We were guilty until the Dukakis-Sasso confession.

Robert Beckel: So your real problem was CBS and the way CBS picked it up with, I presume, no evidence to go with it. It got into the body politic when CBS made certain allegations.

William Carrick: Paul Taylor called me seven times a day asking well, what if CBS had a real live news story that had aired. It was beyond speculation. It was beyond the personal animosity between the political campaigns. This was on the air. It contributed to Gephardt's going from number one in the polls in Iowa into a tailspin down to third or fourth.

Robert Beckel: So you think it seriously affected the polls?

William Carrick: I think there was a Gephardt momentum that had been building over the summer, and I think the Biden incident stopped our momentum and put the Gephardt campaign in a slide.

Martin Plissner: Bill, let's get one thing straight about CBS. I think you know how that happened. Are you saying your staff did not pass out materials on Biden?

William Carrick: No, I'm not saying the CBS story was malicious. But it had substantial political impact.

Martin Plissner: You don't really want to go into all the details.

Paul Taylor: There were a lot of spinoffs. Ed, you made the point that you thought the operating assumption was that past behavior was generally off limits; current behavior would get you in trouble. Here was the Biden episode. It began with the use of Kinnock's prose without attribution. Then you had the series of small cuts. You had the "plagiarism" incident in law school, you had videotape from earlier that year where he blew up at someone and overstated his academic record. You had use of an RFK quote without attribution. Again within the space of two weeks a candidate was dropped from the field. The voters were still six months away from getting involved in the process. Did the press create a caricature of Joe Biden? They strung together these four or five episodes. Did you campaign managers around the table feel this was out of hand?

Edward Rollins: First of all, I think plagiarism—there was a recent incident here at Harvard—lasts forever. Adultery only counts in the present term. The truth is, don't falsify when you're writing about it. I think the bottom line comes down to this: There were certain candidates in this campaign whom the American media viewed as not up to the job, and I think Joe Biden was one. I think they felt he was projecting an image different from what he really was. I think they felt Gary Hart had been a fraud in 1984. I think they felt some of the other candidates were not quite up to what they perceived as being presidential.

So I think there was a real effort to dig and find and examine these candidates under greater scrutiny than the front-runners—with the exception of Hart, who obviously was a front-runner for a time—or candidates who had a proven track record. I think in Biden's case people didn't think Biden was quite what Biden appeared to be, and they were going to look hard on it. And the moment they found some falsification, they were more than willing to jump and pounce.

Robert Beckel: Let's get specific. In this campaign atmosphere, you have Biden down—two people now down. In the midst of the Biden thing, did you make any campaign management decisions? This thing was out of hand; you could either make some moves to protect your candidate or take advantage of the opening.

Terry Michael: We saw it as an opening, with both Hart and Biden down, because we were positioning our candidate as the credible candidate—the guy you could trust, the guy you could believe in.

Paul Taylor: Were there conversations that others had of a different nature, along the lines of: Listen, gang, we better get out in front; better go scrub your closet one more time because you can see a train wreck coming?

Lee Atwater: I can say that.

Paul Taylor: Ron, you were not around with Jesse at that period, but I remember Jackie Jackson, I think right after the Hart episode, coming right out very aggressively and basically saying what goes on in our private life is off limits. I sometimes wonder whether she was the best shield that anybody had in this campaign.

Ronald Brown: Well, I guess my own assessment is that it was probably her decision. I don't think it was a campaign decision. I think an attack on her husband at that point was an attack on her. She was defending herself as well as him. Jesse was, in my judgment, not really in this kind of mix. It was in his interest to have a bunch of candidates in there. He didn't want to see them drop so soon, didn't want to see it down to a two-person field so early. A two-person field, at that point, was contrary to his strategy. His campaign was not really affected as much by these kinds of incidents. I would not put Jackie's response in the category of some profound strategic decision. My belief is that it was a visceral response.

Robert Beckel: It was Jackie reacting hearing it?

Ronald Brown: Yes.

Robert Beckel: There were two other campaigns that were affected after Biden. Then you had the nominees to the Supreme Court, one who blew dope.

Two campaigns made a decision, the Babbitt campaign and the Gore campaign, to talk about marijuana.

Frederick Martin: I assumed, having been on the Ferraro plane in the fall of 1984 for three months, that not only was everything in your personal life going to be discussed, but even things in your parents' personal life and even rumors about your parents could be discussed. After that campaign, anyone getting involved in a campaign the next time had to be prepared for anything being asked. You had to discuss everything that could possibly come out long in advance and decide how you would handle it long in advance, before anyone ever asked a question—without going into any detail, that's what we did. We were prepared for the possibility of a question being asked.

Robert Beckel: Did you make that decision in light of the [Supreme Court nominee Douglas] Ginsberg stories or did you make the decision before that?

Frederick Martin: We had made the decision to deal with the question forthrightly and honestly and quickly, if the occasion arose. It arose.

Robert Beckel: Fred, how about the Babbitt campaign?

Frederick DuVal: In our case, our reaction to the Hart story was to talk about the potential issues and how we would deal with them. The only one we thought we would have was marijuana. We reacted the same way. We weren't going to bring it out, but if it came out, we were going to respond to it very quickly and honestly.

In our case I think there was a difference. In our case, in addition to it being past behavior, which makes a difference, Babbitt volunteered it. He actually brought it up on an airplane flight. He asked Marilee Schwartz, "Aren't you going to ask me if I ever smoked marijuana?" He also dealt with it totally unequivocably. He didn't moralize. He didn't say, "At the time it seemed acceptable, but now I regret doing it." He said, "Yeah, I did it. It was acceptable at the time, I was curious." That didn't give it any more psychological sort of fuel to make it a second-day story.

In contrast, I think, Fred, you guys in your first-day reaction equivocated a little bit and then dealt with it in a way that turned it into a two- or three-day story. For us it was over in 24 hours.

Frederick Martin: The question was asked of Senator Gore at 3:00 in the afternoon, and at 8:00 the next morning he had a press conference. We thought that was about as fast as we could act.

Robert Beckel: Can we go back one minute? One final point on this. Lee made the point that he thinks there is an invisible hand that, if things ever get too far out of hand, the media draws back and checks its behavior. This episode, the marijuana thing, seemed to me to be fairly short. It went away. Did this send another signal of normalcy and restraint?

Lee Atwater: I think that after Biden, followed by the marijuana, the invisible hand started taking effect and guiding down. As a matter of fact, what I was worried about was that after you had Biden, you had two Democrats, you hadn't had a Republican in the soup. We were getting ready to man our battle stations. The next one would be not on scandalous type stuff, but on issues and so on. The press view would be to go after a Republican and go after him on some main stuff. Then the marijuana thing came up and the invisible hand took place. We got through that whole little era.

Robert Beckel: These stories did change the climate for you?

Lee Atwater: Absolutely. I would like somebody here to jump up and disagree with me, but it was the eeriest thing. Regardless of how you felt, it was going to play out at the end. It had a very eery period.

Rober Ailes: We thought we were a target.

Paul Taylor: In addition to losing two candidates in this time period we lost one campaign manager by way of a three-cushion shot of who said what to whom.

Anyone who wishes to take this up in the Dukakis campaign? In retrospect, could you have handled that situation differently once the Biden story broke? Could you have handled it in a way that would have resulted in John Sasso's staying on in the campaign? Were there tactical blunders you made in that period?

Robert Beckel: Can I add to that? During that period, although CBS got some hits here by going with that story, there is no question that there were some people in the Dukakis field operation who were targeting one particular person in the Gephardt campaign. It was Trippi who was getting a lot of allegations coming from some of your field people. Was that a situation you all knew was going on?

John Corrigan: I can't speak for everybody. I can speak for myself. There were other people who were speculating on what was happening. You know, frankly, some people like Joe, some people don't. The Gephardt campaign did participate with the follow-up story about the speech that resembled a Humphrey or Bobby Kennedy speech.

William Carrick: That was written by Phil Traustein of *The San Jose Mercury-News,* and he sat on it for six months. It was in his files. And when the story broke, he brought it out. It was old news that got recycled.

John Corrigan: I don't know the whole truth about the story. I know what I did. I know what John did. I have some sense of what Paul did. I have a couple of points about the Biden incident. First, the only thing we were aware of was the similarity between the Biden speech at the Iowa State Fair debate and the Kinnock speech. We were not aware of any rumors of plagiarism in law

school, which apparently the White House was spreading in antici-
pation of the Bork hearing. We were not aware of the resemblances
to the Bobby Kennedy speech. In participating in spreading the
truth about Joe Biden, we were thrown into a much larger pattern
of behavior that we essentially were not fully briefed on.

Second, there's a big difference and, I think, a much larger issue
here. Lee talked about the invisible hand, how the invisible hand
corrects something. It does not necessarily work in the way that the
standards are the same for every campaign or every candidate.
What the Dukakis campaign did was tell the truth about Joe Biden.
Then there was a cover-up of the source. And only once was there
an on-the-record false statement. That was Paul's statement in
Time magazine.

Later on in the campaign, when I think there were differences in
the dynamics and differences in the race, there were outright lies
told about Michael Dukakis for which there was no political price
paid and for which there was no subsequent witch-hunt for the
person who spread this story.

Immediately after the Democratic Convention a rumor was
spread that Michael Dukakis had seen a psychiatrist. That shifted
us 8 points that week. That's the margin between defeat and victory. Other things happened in the course of the campaign which
attributed to our defeat, but the most fundamental thing in this
business—I think in politics, in government, in journalism—is facts
and lies. That's a very fundamental distinction. There were lies told
about Michael Dukakis. There were lies that he was seeing a
shrink. There were lies being spread about his wife burning the
flag. We paid an enormous political price for telling the truth.

Roger Ailes: All candidates are subject to rumors, as George
Bush was. Part of the trick to this game is who is resilient. That has
to do with their electability.

Robert Beckel: First of all, I have got a few questions on
Dukakis. Why was it that the press was consumed with who was
leaking a story on the Biden incident? Did you all have the feeling
there was an unfair kind of emphasis by the press on the issue?

William Carrick: There are a lot of points that Jack Corrigan
raised that I think ought to be discussed. But I do think the Biden
incident was an important one. One question obviously has to do
with the net consequence of this: Should Joe Biden have withdrawn from the race based upon these series of incidents? They
made a judgment to get out, but I don't know that that was the
right judgment. I think he might have been able to survive this.

Second, I think the whole question of why Dukakis paid a big price had to do with the 10 days where somebody else—the Gephardt campaign—was being blamed for the Biden-Kinnock tape incident. I think it is likely that our campaign and the other campaigns, once all this started, had people putting gasoline on the fire. But none of us committed the original crime. The Dukakis campaign did. Jack made a good point. Maybe there wasn't a crime, and the tapes were distributed as standard hardball politics. The Gephardt campaign didn't commit the crime of planting the tapes. The price Dukakis paid was created by an internal decision to wait 10 days to deal with their guilt and to stop trying to blame others for something they did.

Paul Taylor: In retrospect, Jack said the problem was the cover-up. From the Dukakis point of view, you told the truth about Joe Biden. Had you said the day after the Joe Biden story came out, "Yes, we're responsible for the tapes," would your end of that story been over and done with? Or did you think that was too risky a course? Did you have those kinds of conversations?

Susan Estrich: I didn't, which is why I sit here now.

John Corrigan: I don't recall discussing coming forward. But there were certain news organizations which protected their sources: NBC; *The New York Times,* with the exception of Craig Whitney, who started a process of elimination; and *The Des Moines Register. The Des Moines Register* essentially narrowed the list of suspects.

Paul Taylor: Your take on that was, "We told the truth." If that was your take that week, why not come out and say, "Yeah, we did it, we told the truth." I think there was a lot of comment back then that went to the question, "What was the sin here?"

William Carrick: There was another dynamic. This was in the context of Joe Biden being the chairman of the Senate Judiciary Committee. We were dealing with a Supreme Court nomination. And that dynamic had a very powerful political edge to it, particularly in a place like Iowa, which is dominated by activists who are very interested in the civil rights issue and the complexion of the court.

Paul Taylor: Was that on your mind?

John Corrigan: No. That's a fair point. We were thinking about Iowa.

Paul Taylor: Was it on your mind that if you came clean that you were the source, you would pay a price in Iowa because the activists would say you cut the knees off this guy just as the Bork hearings were starting?

John Corrigan: Frankly, I don't remember that. We weren't interested in helping out any of our Democratic opponents. We weren't interested in helping out the Gephardt campaign. We had just gone through a debate. Some of them were characterized as attacks on Gephardt. Mark Johnson—Is that his name?

William Carrick: Mark Johnson. Marty [Plissner] and I can spend an hour on this. It's not worth getting into. CBS said on the air that the Gephardt campaign was pushing negative information on Biden on Capitol Hill. Somebody in our campaign gave material—a news clipping—to one of their correspondents. And I confessed already that we were guilty of putting gas on the fire once it started. But the Dukakis campaign was the perpetrator and instigator of the entire episode.

Paul Taylor: Let's move on and let's pick up on a comment that Roger Ailes made, that the press seems to set up character tests by drawing cartoons or caricatures of the candidates. In the fall of 1987 George Bush was about to announce for the presidency, and *Newsweek* came out with a story, "The Wimp Factor." Howard Fineman has agreed to fall on the sword and tell us about the use of that word on the magazine's cover.

Howard Fineman: I don't think there is a sword to fall on, because it was an important subject and dealt with straight forwardly. This was one of the key issues of the campaign, George Bush's character. But the key question is the use of the four-letter word "wimp." Maybe I'll just give you a little insight on what I know about that. I think that putting a cover line on a magazine is the last and highest—or lowest, depending upon your point of view—job of the editors of the magazine. We weren't going to do a political cover with George Bush on it without trying to state as succinctly as we could what the issue was. And the fact is that in the political community, among people who followed this business, the question in shorthand was, "Is this man a wimp or isn't he a wimp?" That word was common currency.

One of the things we tried to do during the whole campaign season at *Newsweek* was to get behind and inside the thinking of professional politicians. That's what the "conventional wisdom" chart was all about. That's what a lot of our stories were all about. We weren't going to hide from public view what the professionals were talking about. So we made the decision to go straight at the subject, and we did. The story itself was written by Margaret Garrard Warner, who ended up being a panelist on the presidential debates. We all know how those people were picked. If you felt the story itself was so out of bounds, Margaret never would have ended up on that panel. I think by having her on the panel, you indirectly said the story itself was valid.

Now the word "wimp" got some people angry, one person in particular—which you guys might want to talk about. But to my way of thinking, it was a childish reaction on his part.

Edward Rollins: I totally disagree. I think it's absurd to say inside the Beltway or in this room that people talk about George Bush being a wimp and it therefore ought to be a cover of a national magazine. A news magazine has a higher responsibility than *The National Enquirer* or what have you. Margaret did write a very in-depth, lengthy story, but the bottom line is that the six million people who see "wimp" couldn't tell you what was inside the story. That became a very big factor. And by your running it on the cover you basically put it out there in the public arena. To be perfectly honest with you, I thought it was the most irresponsible thing that your magazine did during the entire course of the campaign.

Lee Atwater: What I thought it was, and what I do think it was, is the biggest example in the whole campaign of a media organ participating in the process. The First Amendment very clearly does not prohibit that. So it's legal. But the first campaign school I went to—a little campaign seminar, when I was growing up—said there's only one day that you're going to have good press in a campaign. That's the day you announce. Well, here's a guy announcing for President of the United States, and a national news magazine creates a prop. I walked in that night and there was Tom Brokaw interviewing and using that as a prop. For the next 10 days that magazine cover was used as a prop. It was a conscious decision to participate in the process. Again, the Constitution clearly allows that.

I agree with you, Howard. It was not the story but, guess what, not enough people read *Newsweek* every week to make any difference in terms of national consciousness. But guess what else? I went jogging this morning and I saw *Newsweek* on four newstands. Guess what I saw? The cover.

I think it was an example of something that happened this year more than I've ever seen in my twenty years of involvement. It was as if the media became a participant in the process. So you had our campaign, the other campaigns, the candidates, so forth.

Paul Taylor: How did you guys deal with the "wimp" issue? What opening did that give you?

Lee Atwater: There are three points I want to make. Number one, George Bush was not perceived as a wimp in our party or in this country. The fact of the matter is that that was an echo chamber perception, meaning the people in this room multiplied by however many other people like us run around following this stuff all the time. The net effect was that for the next 10 days—and we were having news conferences every day in those days, 209 news conferences—all we got were people waving *Newsweek* magazine and so forth.

But what was interesting was, 10 days later, the first debate in Houston. In effect, the *Newsweek* story played out well for the vice president because for the first time the public's consciousness was raised on this so-called wimp question, and the vice president got up 10 days later and knocked that one right out of the ballpark. I was out for the 10 days after the debate in Houston and the question was never raised. It really was never seriously raised again in the campaign.

Second, I felt at the time that because of that the vice president would be in an unprecedented situation in the event he needed to do some comparative campaigning later on. He would be inoculated from having that comparative campaigning backfiring on him.

Roger Ailes: A couple of things. First, I guess you referred to me as overreacting to the *Newsweek* cover. We got repeated requests for a shot of George Bush. They wanted to do a nice story on him for his announcement. They let everybody in the campaign, including the press people, know this was going to be an announcement story. But they said they would like a shot of George playing tennis. I think somebody smelled a rat on that and eventually sent one with him in a speed boat. Could you imagine him leaping through the air in a tennis outfit? That's what they wanted to do. So there was a little bit going on there.

Plus, it was very clear to us that one of the editors simply didn't like George Bush. It was clear to us that the original story filed by Margaret was not exactly the story. The wimp thing got blown up dramatically by the editors. And it's always been my contention that if you're going to do that based on the rumor he was a wimp, there were certainly rumors that Dukakis had no heart, had no emotion. What about a cover on "Computer Heart" Dukakis? The Dukakis camp didn't feel they were getting fair coverage on that thing.

Second, I had breakfast with Vernon Jordan. He said that women and men view the word "wimp" in different ways. He said that a lot of men see it to mean a homosexual. I happen to disagree with that, but that was Vernon's assessment of that word. It's a cloudy word.

The other thing we felt was that it was an unfair shot on his announcement day because of the magnification given by every morning news show that he was scheduled to go on the next morning. He had no ability to get ready for it. It broke that night; he was going on the next morning. He had to face every piece of news regarding his announcement as a magnification of something that *Newsweek* wanted to pin on him.

Robert Beckel: Let me jump over to the Dole campaign for a second. You wanted to say something about how you guys reacted and saw that as an opening or not an opening. I couldn't imagine you couldn't see it as an opening.

William Lacy: I've got to say that nobody from the Dole campaign ran out that day and disavowed the article and said it was totally wrong. We were doing a lot of research and we were finding that if you really press people—Republicans we're talking about— about doubts they had about the vice president, the doubt usually expressed was, "Well, we don't know if he's strong enough and tough enough." At the same time our guy was clearly very tough, a skilled negotiator. We always thought that if you compare him to Bush versus Gorbachev, everybody is always going to take Bob Dole. But then we saw numbers that showed voters, Republican voters, really preferred Bush over Dole in dealing with Gorbachev. And that gave us cause to ask if strength is really a big issue. I think that indicated what was going to happen in the general election in terms of this issue. It wasn't really there.

Robert Beckel: One last question to Howard. Did the "wimp" word cause internal controversy at *Newsweek* after it was done?

Howard Fineman: Let me say a couple of things. First of all, George Bush was vice president for a long time—a very well-known figure. The old practice about valentine announcement days stories is, I think, passé, especially in the case of a sitting vice president as well known as he was. And there were some questions about his toughness. What it really comes down to is the use of the word "wimp."

The cover line itself said "Fighting the 'Wimp Factor,' " with the words "Wimp Factor" in quotes. Now I have to say, if there were any of our editors who thought that putting quotation marks around the "wimp factor" was going to negate the use of the word wimp on the cover, they were kidding themselves, obviously. Yeah, there was some debate about it. I really don't want to go into it any further than that.

But, as I say, we were writing a headline for a story. The way we write headlines involves the use of a picture and the use of a few short words designed to grab the attention of dedicated joggers like

Atwater. That's our forum. I think it was a strong word, a controversial word to use, but I think it was justified.

Edward Rollins: I just want to go back to the point. It's great to say that in the story you were saying nice things but you didn't have anything to do with the headline. I think you have to take responsibility for the whole thing. We all did a lot of polling, and nowhere in an open-ended poll did I ever find the word "wimp" used with George Bush.

Howard Fineman: If we had written a headline "Is He Tough Enough?" and had run that picture, I don't think we would be having this discussion at all.

Edward Rollins: You wouldn't.

Marc Nuttle: One thing to remember that permeates through all this discussion about the press is that if you poll the American electorate, about 80 percent will tell you they received most of their information from the print or broadcast media. Of those responding about 75 percent say that they initially do not believe it. Therefore, they're deriving negatives one way or another. Imagine a campaign that was under constant character review. I did a lot of research on that. When the press constantly implies to the public that a certain candidate is deficient in some way or can't win, it helps the expectation game. Two candidates benefitted from that, George Bush and Pat Robertson, particularly in the debates. Neither was expected to do well in the debates for different suppositions: Pat because he was weird, George because he was weak.

And when they both showed it wasn't true, the electorate would look at that and say, "Gosh, somebody misled me." It would have a backlash effect, and the candidate would get a lot more credit than he deserved. But the fact remains that the negatives were so high in this campaign and so unprecedented for several candidates. I think the press is partly responsible for this occurrence.

Paul Taylor: We have talked an awful lot about the episodes of the press's very aggressive scrutiny of the candidates' characters. Does that create a tactical opportunity for the candidate under scrutiny to appeal to the good judgment of the American people by, in effect, press-bashing? Bush had a celebrated confrontation with Dan Rather, and Bush went after Jim Gannon in a debate in Iowa. Then there was some press-bashing in the whole Quayle episode toward the end. There was a response to the tough press scrutiny. Roger, what is your view of the openings created for aggressive press scrutiny?

Roger Ailes: The openings are there only if you can take advantage of them. One of the things that the "wimp" cover did was to play to our strength. The hidden secret of this campaign was that George Bush was always a better candidate than anybody ever gave him credit for, and everybody was trying to make him a joke. But George always gets up for the fight, and he's the kind of guy who is able to create a tactical advantage.

With regard to the Rather thing, I got a call at home Sunday night from Peter [Teeley]. He said, "I think this CBS News thing is going to be worse than we thought. You had better get down to Washington." I started checking around. I had a source inside CBS News who went outside to a pay phone and called me and said, "I'm sorry to have to tell you this, but they're running around the CBS newsroom saying they're going to take George Bush out of the race tonight. They have hired a Democratic consultant to work with Rather over the weekend to debate. They have created a five-minute show which is going to indict him by putting him on the screen with some sorry characters who have some problems. Then they're going to hand him a blindfold and Rather is going to execute him. So you guys better get ready."

When you're in that kind of a situation the question is, Do you use a blindfold or don't you? And do you fight back or don't you? I caught up with the vice president at Andrews Air Force Base—got in the back of the car. He didn't believe that it was going to be a political execution or an attempt at a political execution. I said, "Why don't we plan for it just in case?" Basically, we decided we weren't going to take it lying down. That's how that episode happened.*

Paul Taylor: Did you, in fact, feed him the lines he used that night?

Roger Ailes: He doesn't talk about what he tells the President, and I don't discuss exactly what lines I give him, but I certainly wasn't adverse to him using the line, "Would you like us to judge your whole career by the time you walked off the air?" We had another one which is even tougher, and he never had to do it.

Robert Beckel: You did use the press as an issue at various times during this campaign, correct?

Editors Note: Tom Bettag, executive producer of the "CBS Evening News with Dan Rather," has submitted a lengthy rebuttal which states in part: "The Ailes account does not correspond with my experience. The interview was set up through a series of phone calls between Pete Teeley, who was then the press secretary of the Bush campaign, and myself on the preceding Thursday. I went out of my way to stress that the interview would follow a long and very pointed story and that the interview would be tough and sharply focused on the content of the story. It was clear that the overall subject was Iran-Contra."

Lee Atwater: Let me make a point. This was Roger's strategy. The strategy that we had across the board in debates, in these confrontational situations, was this: That George Bush is a counterpuncher. The nature of the man is such that he does not go out and start a fight, he doesn't start controversy or confrontation, but if he gets hit, he hits back. So there was not an instance you can point to in which he started the fight.

Roger Ailes: In fact, he was prepared that night not to fight.

Lee Atwater: Dan Rather threw the first punch. Pete du Pont threw the first punch in the "Pierre" incident. And in every incident, unless the other guy started mixing it up, there was no fight.

Paul Taylor: Well, a counterpunch is a strategy.

Lee Atwater: Sure. But it was based on the fact if the other guy acts unfairly, dish it back to him.

Roger Ailes: Including the press. So if you think the press hits and you think it's unfair, hit it back.

Lee Atwater: And that's my point. It was a conscious strategy. All you have to do is examine the four-year campaign, and you can see that happened.

Robert Beckel: There were some serious suggestions during the campaign concerning the two preachers, Robertson and Jackson. We know that there were a number of news organizations that aggressively pursued Jackson stories, from adultery to money in his campaign, things that came up in 1984. We know about the Robertson stories, about Korea. There have been some suggestions around that those stories on Jackson did not break because these news organizations were afraid to take him on because he was black. And in Robertson's case they were willing to take him on because he, obviously, was not. Ron, did you have any sense that they were holding back?

Ronald Brown: I didn't. I said before that I thought that Jackson was never really in the mix as far as having to react to what was happening to other candidates. There were two principal reasons for that. One was that he had been through it in 1984. There have been 10, 12, 15 books written about him. I think the general feeling was there wasn't much more that could be done to hurt him.

But, more importantly, there was an overriding issue with Jackson. There was an overriding impediment with Jackson which, in fact, superseded any of these other things, and that was the issue of race. So if the question is, Was race a factor? of course, it was a factor. I don't think it was a factor which protected him. I think it was a factor which was out there above and beyond everything else. So you never got to the other issues with Jackson. It wasn't necessary. You knew there was this one major impediment that would in all likelihood keep it from happening in 1988.

Marc Nuttle: I believe it was a major factor and therefore called for a major strategy in our campaign. I made the assumption that we would be attacked and attacked unmercifully, which I think we were. The difference with the Robertson campaign was we had a base that was loyal. Pat's followers didn't believe what the press said. I could use that to my advantage in a couple of ways. The reason we picked Bedford-Stuyvesant as the place to announce was to draw as much lightning as we could. I mean, the only thing I underestimated was the intensity of the demonstration in the streets of New York and the Bronx. But to our base it was wonderful. The announcement, the militant homosexual demonstration, and the resulting coverage really boosted our organization and intensified our support in the South.

As for the statute of limitations on past behavior, the Korean War allegations were within the reasonable time check because Pete McCloskey had made it an issue. We should have answered it, and we did. We proved McCloskey's claim to be without merit. That should have been adequate.

We checked Pat's background thoroughly and planned for anything that might come out. The only thing I didn't know about was his marriage date 32 years before. I think that was beyond the statute of limitations. It was irrelevant, had no bearing on his current character, and required no response. I guess there was no statute of limitations on character checks, period.

But the point is still that to our base it was not important. We didn't have to break out of our core coalition until after Super Tuesday. So again, the assumption we made was correct, planned for, and used to our advantage.

*   *   *

David Runkel: When we were talking about the press yesterday, we did not get a full discussion of the events which led to the withdrawal of Senator Biden from the campaign. Let us return to Paul Taylor.

Paul Taylor: The subject of discussion was press scrutiny and the press as character cops. Tim, I think that the best way to start is for you to walk us through. It's the middle of September 1987. And one morning you wake up; there's a front-page story in *The New*

York Times and a page-two story in *The Des Moines Register*. Both say essentially the same thing, that Joe Biden has lifted passages of a speech he had given two or three weeks before from Neil Kinnock without attribution. About 12 or 13 days later he was no longer a candidate. Walk us through what it was like.

Timothy Ridley: The interesting question is: What the hell was a candidate for President of the United States doing building a major campaign theme around a quote from a failed British politician? With Lewis Powell's resignation, the campaign went into suspended animation. We intentionally decided to forestall efforts to refine the campaign's message through the summer and focus almost completely on the Bork hearings. Those hearings were Senator Biden's Iowa caucus. By mid-August we were totally, almost exclusively, focused on Bork.

I personally viewed the "Kinnock theme" as, at best, a stop-gap message. Joe first saw the Kinnock tape in July [1987]. He was obviously taken with it. The senator saw certain parallels between what Kinnock had to say and what he [Biden] believed. There were also certain biographical parallels between Biden and Kinnock. So Senator Biden started using Neil Kinnock—with attribution. His campaign knew he was using Kinnock—with attribution. His rivals for the nomination knew he was using Kinnock—with attribution.

In August *The New York Times'* Robin Toner reported that the senator was in New Hampshire, that he was using Neil Kinnock with attribution. Two days later *The Boston Globe* had a similar story of Biden in New Hampshire using Kinnock. Later, the senator went to the Iowa State Fair. In his closing remarks—the senator had two minutes—he hastily used Kinnock without attribution.

Some ask what we could have done to at least tourniquet the damage caused by this simple mistake. One of the things that we could have done was to issue a simple press release, in a timely manner, acknowledging that Senator Biden had made a mistake. Period. We would have taken a hit but that would have been the extent of it. There were others [inside the campaign] who argued, "Look, the senator has been out using Kinnock and people know that he has been using Kinnock and the senator's been saying that it's Kinnock—this is no big deal."

Paul Taylor: But you did have that conversation the very afternoon of the Iowa State Fair?

Timothy Ridley: Yes. But typical of the Biden campaign, we never came to a resolution on what to do, so in this instance, as in many others, we did nothing.

The week prior to the beginning of the Bork nomination, Maureen Dowd [*The New York Times*] had received the "attack video." She was working the story. Our view was that we were in the middle of the biggest constitutional fight in 50 years and didn't want to be bothered with whether or not Joe Biden's great-grandfather was a coal miner or a mine inspector. Besides, her paper already acknowledged Biden's attributed use of Kinnock.

On the Friday before the Bork hearings, Maureen informed us, "It's coming tomorrow," meaning her story would run the Saturday before the beginning of the Bork hearing. I remember getting up at 6:30 a.m. and going to Union Station to buy a copy of *The New York Times*. I paged through *The Times* but couldn't find the story. I couldn't find the story because it ran on the last page I expected to find it—the front page!

If we want to turn at some point in this conversation to press ethics, I would argue vehemently with the editorial judgment that put that story on the front page of *The New York Times*. I'd take particular issue with the editorial judgment that ran the story without acknowledging that *The Times* had previously reported Senator Biden was using Kinnock with attribution.

In any case, the story was very damaging. Did it occur to me that this was the beginning of the end, that Senator Biden would have to get out of the race [because of the Dowd story]? Absolutely not.

Later that day I saw the CNN coverage, in effect, of the Maureen Dowd story. It was devastating. It was devastating because it was quintessentially a TV story. When you took those two video clips [original Kinnock, Biden in Iowa] and put them side-by-side, it communicated something that hurt the senator beyond all proportions to his simple mistake. That night Ken Bode did a piece on NBC.

On Monday, the day before the beginning of the Bork hearings, we got a call from *The San Jose Mercury* about a speech Senator Biden had made at the Democratic convention in Sacramento, California, in January 1987. It seems there were two passages of the speech that used Bobby Kennedy quotes without attribution. We were initially at a loss as to whether or not this was the case. But, in fact, there was Bobby Kennedy language in that speech, and Senator Biden delivered it without knowing it was Bobby Kennedy language.

Robert Beckel: Did Caddell write the California speech?

Timothy Ridley: Yes. Tuesday we went into the Bork hearings. *The San Jose Mercury* story had broken. Neither of the other two networks [ABC or CBS] had yet followed up on the Saturday Maureen Dowd story.

Here is the situation: All three networks interrupted their day-time programming for Bork's opening statement, and for Chairman Biden's opening statement and his opening round of questioning. They continued coverage through Senator Kennedy's opening round of questioning.

There were those of us in the campaign who believed that the Bork nomination was over after that first round of questioning by Senator Biden, given what Bork conceded on the privacy issue. Bork made devastating admissions about his views on privacy, which the rest of the world may not have understood yet. But as the hearings and floor fight played out, we knew those opening admissions would undo the Bork nomination.

That night all three networks devoted their opening coverage to the first day of the Bork hearing. All three networks then moved immediately to Senator Biden, rehashing the Maureen Dowd story and *The San Jose Mercury* story. These stories included the video juxtaposition of Senator Biden and Kinnock, and of Senator Biden and Bobby Kennedy footage 20 years prior. At that point it was clear to us this simply was not going to pass.

On Wednesday we received a call from Leslie Stahl of CBS, who said, "Listen, I'm just checking this out—this is probably too weird—could this possibly be true—but I've got to check it out." We also got a call from *The Wall Street Journal*, "Did Senator Biden plagiarize in law school?"

The campaign was aware that there had been an episode in law school. We never viewed it as plagiarism. Joe described it to me at one point when I was playing confessor to the candidate earlier—much earlier in the year.

On the basis of the Stahl inquiry, we went to the senator. Now, here you had the Chairman of the Judiciary Committee leading these hearings over the fate of the Supreme Court, and we had to ask him, "Senator, did you plagiarize in law school?"

That afternoon we dispatched a law classmate of the senator's, a partner in Sullivan and Cromwell, to Syracuse to retrieve the senator's law school record. By 7:00 p.m. the file was in Washington. Syracuse [Law School] had not viewed the incident as plagiarism. If they had, the chairman of the Senate Judiciary Committee would never have graduated from Syracuse Law School. Subsequent to Senator Biden's withdrawal from the race, the Delaware State Supreme Court concurred. Senator Biden had made a mistake in a "legal methods" paper he wrote during his first six weeks in law school.

That night after the conclusion of the day's hearings, we convened and made the decision to call a press conference the next morning and release the senator's law school record—in its entirety. We held the press conference—put out the record. The law school record was not flattering. The press conference was brutal. Joe's performance was uneven. He walked directly from the press session to begin chairing the third day of the Bork hearings.

At this point there were people in the campaign who thought the campaign was over. More importantly, people were very much concerned with the senator's ability to continue chairing those hearings, to lead them fairly. We were concerned that the presidential campaign was jeopardizing Joe's ability to do these things—that the troubles plaguing the campaign might inadvertently assure Robert Bork's going to the Supreme Court. So at this juncture, the campaign was divided on whether or not the Biden candidacy was over. Nevertheless, everyone knew we were wounded. Everyone knew the wound could be fatal.

We made a decision—this is now Thursday—to wait out the coming weekend to see if Senator Biden got any credit for his steady stewardship at the Bork hearings. He didn't. Instead, the weekend talk shows and Sunday papers rehashed, in gruesome detail, the troubling events of the week—Kinnock, law school, et cetera. This confirmed for me that the campaign had run its course.

Sunday afternoon we received a call from *Newsweek*. They had a C-SPAN tape of Senator Biden in New Hampshire, at a house party where somebody asked him about how well he had done in law school. The senator, in this exchange, was rather agitated and made certain claims about his academic record—some of which were true, some of which are arguably true, and some of which were not true. That then became the news story for Monday—which was the beginning of the second week of the Bork hearings.

We were polling all through this period. The bottom fell out from under us in Iowa and in New Hampshire on Monday night [on the basis of the network coverage of the *Newsweek* story]. Going into the Bork hearings we had ourselves solidly in second place in Iowa and New Hampshire. Monday night the bottom fell out.

There was wide speculation on Tuesday that Joe was going to get out. A decision was made on Wednesday, at the conclusion of the Bork hearings, that he would get out, and on Thursday he did.

That's the chronology of events.

Paul Taylor: Let me ask one question: Had the initial two stories occurred at some time in the campaign when you didn't have the Bork hearings right on the plate, do you think events would have unfolded differently? Do you think that (a) the press wouldn't have given it the scrutiny that it did, and (b) would you have had more freedom to respond differently, to stay in the race?

Timothy Ridley: I don't know. If all these stories had unfolded simultaneously, as they did, outside of the context of the Bork hearings, I suspect that Senator Biden would still have made the decision to leave the race.

Again, I would say that any one of these events, in isolation, could have been managed, could have been contained. The fact that they came in a serial fashion was, I think, devastating to Joe's candidacy. Remember, we had this paramount consideration. What was the effect of all this on Senator Biden's ability to lead the fight against Robert Bork.

Robert Beckel: You had some serious disagreement on the campaign about getting out, though; wasn't that the case?

Timothy Ridley: No.

Robert Beckel: Or at least one figure had a significant problem with your getting out?

Timothy Ridley: Yes. Pat Caddell felt that the senator should stay in the race. The senator obviously felt differently. His family felt differently. His other key advisers felt differently. I felt differently. Pat argued that we should put "the press on trial." I believed that would be a hard case to prosecute.

Robert Beckel: Did you get a sense that the press had now gotten their next Hart case?

Timothy Ridley: No. I sensed ambivalence. I sensed, among the press, a feeling that the "counts of indictment" against Biden were shaky. And even if they were solid, they didn't add up to the verdict that resulted.

Again, remember, this was not a print story. This was an extraordinary TV story. An exceptional TV story. And the video indictment, the various video clips set side by side, were an exceptionally powerful indictment. You could genuinely argue the large, small, and fine points of what mistakes Joe Biden had made in his life, but reduced to these video juxtapositions, the average American news-viewer's verdict could only be brutal.

So I sensed ambivalence among the press. Among select journalists, I sensed disgust. You know, the "stop-me-before-I-kill-again" self-examination. Why this ambivalence on the part of the press? Why the discordance—the discordance between those criticisms that could be fairly and accurately made about Joe Biden—and the picture that emerged of Joe Biden during the days leading up to his withdrawal?

Is it fair to say Joe Biden was capable of exaggeration, casual disposition toward "detail," sometimes lacking discipline? Yes. These things could arguably be said about Joe Biden. Is it true Joe Biden is a pathological liar, fundamentally lacking integrity and moral bearing? Absolutely not. The press knew that.

So I sensed ambivalence. Out of this ambivalence came a new freneticism. The witch hunt—the "who shot Joe" story. Who delivered Dowd the "Attack Video"? In this sense, Joe Biden and John Sasso were victims of a similar press pathology.

Paul Taylor: You have had a year to think about this. What's your judgment about the role of the press in this episode? There are two diametrically opposite views of this. One is that the system worked. The system, like it or not, is for the press to function as the gate-keepers and the screening committee in the early stages of the campaign. And, they moved in very swiftly and easily and, as it turned out got a candidate out of the race. There were no voters involved in the process at all. The other view is that it was a feeding frenzy by the press. These things really didn't happen in sequence; the only people who arranged it in sequence were the people in the newspaper and the TV business, three or four in a row. What's your conclusion?

Timothy Ridley: I don't have a general conclusion. There are specific stories I can look at and say that it was very fair—tough, unpleasant to read or watch—but fair. What still bothers me is that there was only one attempt, that I am aware of, on the part of the press itself to look at what the press was doing in this instance to Biden.

Eleanor Randolph of *The Washington Post* wrote a story on the Monday before the Bork hearings and took *The Times* a bit to task for having run the front-page story, if my recollection reads correctly. It also raised the spectre of orchestration—was this just coincidence that this was all happening on the eve of the Bork hearings? The stakes were very high here. In some sense the stakes were higher than Senator Biden's presidential campaign. The stakes had to do with the balance on the Supreme Court. There were all sorts of possible villains. My thinking went to the White House.

E. J. Dionne: I wanted to make a small point and ask a question. The small point is that, in fact, the original story did say that Biden had used the Kinnock quote with attribution before. It wasn't placed in the story where the Biden campaign would have put it, which is somewhere near the lead, but it was right there and said it clearly.

I got the impression immediately after Maureen's story appeared that your strategy was to savage the press and, in particular, savage my colleague. You really went after that story very aggressively in two ways. One, you went after the story itself, and two, you tried to divert the press, with significant success, to the issue of who leaked this stuff. Was that a conscious strategy on your part? Eleanor Randolph's follow-up was not a follow-up on our story in the traditional sense. It raised questions about our story. You succeeded there and in other cases to kind of encourage that movement.

And I'm asking you: Was that a conscious, thought-through strategy, because at this end it sure felt like that.

Timothy Ridley: Right. We felt like we were being attacked because, as later events revealed, we were being attacked. There was a strategy, on our part, to attack the editorial judgment that put the Kinnock story on the front page of your paper [*The New York Times*]. Your paper had already reported Senator Biden was using the Kinnock theme—with attribution. The one instance in Iowa where he didn't use attribution, is that a front-page story?

There was a strategy to focus on the story itself. Frankly, there was an exchange, a very unfortunate exchange between Pat Caddell and Maureen [Dowd]. In that exchange, Pat [Caddell] was vulgar—profane. Please do not interpret that exchange as representative of what the Biden campaign's strategy was for dealing with Maureen's [Dowd] story.

E. J. Dionne: But my sense was that the strategy for at least 24 hours was to try to ride it out by really trashing that story and then also, secondarily, by moving the focus of the story away from what Joe Biden had done and toward the source of the story. You were helped by the little line in Dave Yepsen's story that referred to the attack video. Putting aside whatever language he used, was that a strategy?

Timothy Ridley: Within the 24-hour window, that was the strategy. By 48 hours we were dealing with a different problem; we were dealing with *The San Jose Mercury* inquiry. I sensed an escalating crisis that was overtaking Maureen's story.

Paul Taylor: There was a secondary story which was "Who struck John?" Who planted the thing? We got into that a little bit yesterday. Let me go back one time, Jack, because you talked about that some.

It always struck me that the "guilty party" wasn't particularly guilty of anything. And you made that very point yesterday. Was there a strategy consideration given to coming clean at the beginning.

John Corrigan: There are a couple points I made yesterday that I would like to make again. One is that we were aware of only one incident, which was the closing statement at the Iowa State Fair and its resemblance to the Kinnock piece. We were not aware of the law school incident and had paid no attention to the New Hampshire incident. We were not aware of the San Jose speech. So we were, when we put together the two pieces of tape, interjecting ourselves into a much larger controversy than we ever anticipated.

Paul Taylor: This is the "I didn't mean to kill the guy" defense.

Timothy Ridley: The way I describe it myself is that John [Sasso] meant the "attack video" as a brush-back pitch, not a beanball. As a matter of fact, the Biden campaign didn't even know these other things were sitting out there waiting to blow up, so nobody could have known, least of all John Sasso.

John Corrigan: That's an important point. And the second point is that what Sasso did was tell the truth. What others in the campaign, myself included, did was to essentially spread the truth. And it's a very different standard in terms of political price. And a different standard was applied by the press with respect to that conduct as was applied to the general election. And I think that's an important point, rather than who did it or what.

To answer your specific question, I don't remember participating in any discussion where we thought about coming forward. But, frankly, it was a fairly intense period of time.

Paul Taylor: Do you think John Sasso left the campaign at that point because he distributed this "attack video" or because he covered it up for a couple of weeks and let his candidate go out one Monday morning and deny that anyone in his campaign was involved.

John Corrigan: I think that he can be legitimately criticized, and he said this in the past, for letting Dukakis say nobody in his campaign did it. But I don't think that's as big a question as some of the other things that we could debate.

Paul Taylor: I'm interested in the psychology here.

John Corrigan: The other thing I wanted to make sure was in the record was that other stories were being spread at this time, and I think that might have had a lot more to do with the Bork hearings. We weren't thinking about the Bork hearings. We were thinking about Iowa, New Hampshire. The White House, I was told by people in the networks, was spreading the law school plagiarism story for the specific purpose of undercutting his credibility as a questioner of Robert Bork.

Edward Rollins: I pooh-poohed the White House's involvement before, but as you told the story today, Tim, it did trigger an event that obviously was part of the Maureen Dowd story.

A young fellow worked with me in the White House political office, and I was not in the White House political office at this time nor was Lee Atwater, so the normal trickster techniques that you would blame on us don't apply. This was a nice, young, innocent guy, Jeff Lord, who used to work for John Heinz; he was a Robert Kennedy Democrat. He was watching the California convention on C-SPAN—this wonderful thing that now brings politics into our daily lives—and he was watching Biden give this speech, rattling off these words. And he memorized them. He knows them all. He got an RFK record and he played it again. He then called Maureen Dowd and said, you know, you're digging into this thing, and here is another example of plagiarism.

He freaked that night and called me up—with my great experience into getting into trouble with the press, he knew what an expert I would be. I said that he'd better get over to James Baker and Ken Duberstein and tell them what was happening.

That was the Maureen Dowd lead coming out of the White House. Now, obviously, the White House may have done other things, but I sort of dismissed it yesterday, and that was a factual bit.

Robert Beckel: But you also had the situation of the California newspaper, which had been sitting on that story for a while.

Edward Rollins: Right.

William Carrick: Bob, just let me just say this. I think it's important with this thing. One thing that Tim didn't mention is that *The San Jose Mercury News* is a Knight-Ridder paper. *The Des Moines Register* subscribes to the Knight-Ridder service. And the Phil Traustein story appeared on the front page in all of this.

Robert Beckel: You, or some people inside your campaign, did make a decision to make the who-dunit a strategy. You guys were convinced, or at least that was the impression that was given, that the Gephardt campaign had been responsible for the leak in this story.

Timothy Ridley: That's probably a good example of the rambunctiousness of the Biden campaign. We had a lot of free agents. They were very adroit at free-lancing.

Dave Doak is a dear friend of mine. We started in politics together. Very early in this process, when the "blame Gephardt" frenzy was at its height, Dave came up and said, "We didn't do it, and I'm giving you my word as your friend, we didn't do it." And I went to Senator Biden and said I really believed the Gephardt campaign wasn't the culprit.

At this point we were already to Tuesday and, as you know, this thing had incredible velocity to it. No kind of micro-gambit like "Who Shot Joe" was going to salvage the situation.

Again, Pat Caddell believed vehemently that it was Dave Doak and Bob Shrum, his former partner, who had pulled the trigger.

Robert Beckel: After you had that conversation with Doak, there were still people in your campaign who were absolutely out there pushing the fact that it was a Gephardt campaign leak.

Timothy Ridley: There were some very long-standing vendettas being attended to with no regard to the "truth" or Joe Biden's best interest. Caddell was a big, uncontrollable problem with respect to this. It was unfortunate.

Nevertheless, I sensed that the press was going to make someone pay a price for the "undoing" of Joe Biden. Still, it was not the position of the Biden campaign to go out and try to point a finger at a likely villain, simply because there was no consensus within the campaign on who to blame. I suspected the White House. Caddell suspected Gephardt. With great prescience, John Martilla suspected the Dukakis campaign.

What preoccupies my recollection of these events is the sense that the press was intent on making someone pay a price if Joe Biden left the race—someone, anyone, anyone but the press itself. I was struck by the press's unacknowledged intention to exact a price for what was about to happen to Joe Biden. Someone had to pay. A witch hunt must be organized. In hindsight, I believe, the witches organized the witch hunt.

E. J. Dionne: But what I was curious about was to what extent would this story never have taken the turn it did afterward—not in reference to you, but in reference to everybody else—if for that 24-hour period you had not successfully pushed the story in the direction you did. I had the impression that you guys, more than anything, were responsible for creating this search for the villain.

William Carrick: E.J., one thing that really amplifies what Tim said, the thing that was really driving the witch hunt, was this wonderful little phrase of Dave Yepsen's in *The Des Moines Register*—"attack video." Then everybody was looking for the villain because they knew from Dave Yepsen that somebody had done it from an opposition campaign. That was on the table and a matter of public record. So it wasn't like somebody was speculating whether it was the White House.

Obviously, we had the Jeff Lord thing, and maybe, we can conjecture there were other incidents. But the bottom line was that it was clear, based on the Yepsen story, that a Democratic opponent of Senator Biden's had done something to generate the original story by giving them the simultaneous Kinnock-Biden video.

One other point is that Tim Ridley and Dave Doak talked during this period, and Tom Donilon and I were talking. Basically we confessed what we did: Mark Johnson had given a set of clippings to Phil Jones at CBS, including the Phil Traustein story in *The San Jose Mercury News*. That became a story on CBS, that the Gephardt campaign was spreading negative information about Senator Biden on the Hill.

We confessed that it happened after Mark Johnson told me what he did. You know, he was totally shattered that something he considered very innocent had become a big nightly news story.

Timothy Ridley: E.J., I would just like to make the point that as this was going on, I didn't feel that we were being very successful in deflecting much of anything. We didn't deflect the Kinnock story. We didn't deflect the plagiarism story. There was an incredible velocity to the events undoing Senator Biden's campaign. It's extraordinary to contend we spawned and successfully advanced the "Who shot Joe?" story in light of the momentum of events and these failures.

E. J. Dionne: The point that I was making is not that you succeeded in doing what you intended to do but that you did half of what you intended to do—from your point of view, the less important half.

William Carrick: E.J., what we recognize is that you people in the press are much more thin-skinned about these things than we are.

E. J. Dionne: I am honor-bound to defend my colleague.

Chapter 3

CAMPAIGN ORGANIZATION

Introduction by Howard Fineman

"Campaign organization" is not the dry, mechanical subject it seems at first glance. In presidential elections it is the very stuff of victory—or defeat. Winning requires the quick construction of a vast yet nimble enterprise, able to handpick a coffee klatch for an Iowa livingroom or buy a million dollars worth of television ads overnight. It must win a game whose rules are ever-changing on a playing field of mammoth size and daunting complexity. More important, it must be the crucible of hard decisions—some profound, others merely tactical—that often are made in a vacuum and at break-neck speed. Campaigns must decide what works and what is ethical. Like any other institution, campaigns are the lengthened shadow of the leaders who create them. If you know his organization, you are likely to know the candidate, his leadership style, his view of politics.

In 1988, campaign organizations were doubly important and newly controversial. There was no war, recession, or other political storm to fill the sails of national campaigns. More than most, this contest was what the candidates and their aides chose to make of it. And so it was that Willie Horton became famous. A black murderer who raped a white woman while on furlough from a Massachusetts prison, Horton became a household word almost solely because George Bush's campaign chose to make him one. That decision, in turn, made Bush's own "handlers" an issue, though not a particularly effective one. In commercials for Governor Michael Dukakis, they were portrayed as slick, cynical characters, all jowls, suspenders and blow-dried hair, devising fiendish ways to smear The

Duke. In 1988 the world of campaign management looked inward and met the enemy—itself.

The Harvard conference highlighted the differences in attitude, structure, and operating style of the two general election campaigns. It seemed clear that the focused, disciplined Bush campaign never wavered from its basic strategy: make the other guy—whoever that turned out to be—the issue in the contest. When Dukakis became the likely nominee in May, the Bush organization was primed for transformation into a heat-seeking missile. The Dukakis campaign was not ready to respond. In winning the Democratic nomination, Dukakis's campaign had performed ably, piling up cash, picking up delegates, and making no bold proposals. But in the fall his organization never jelled and neither, therefore, did his message nor strategy. Money was abundant, as were cadres of dedicated workers in the field. But the will was missing, perhaps because Dukakis's own view of politics was in the way. Whatever the reason, his campaign organization could not decide on a consistent or effective strategy to repel Bush's attacks or to advance a positive message.

Of course, after the fact every winning campaign looks brilliant, every losing one inept. But it did seem from the testimony of the conferees in Cambridge that Bush's team had more continuity, a more comprehensive game plan, and a greater ability to follow through. Roger Ailes, master of no-holds-barred media, was signed up for the Bush team at the start in 1987. He demanded, and was given, firm control over the delivery of Bush's "message"—all speeches, interviews, and advertising. Campaign manager Lee Atwater created a vast "opposition research" department, reporting directly to him, that developed reams of "negative" material on Dukakis the moment it became clear he was the likely Democratic nominee. Bush himself, at least as portrayed in the conversation of his aides at the conference, stayed out of the way, and for the most part was little more than a willing (and noninterfering) payload atop a powerful rocket.

It seemed equally clear at Harvard that the Dukakis campaign never was as tightly assembled or as urgently and forcefully directed. In 1987 it had lost its initial leader. John Sasso had quit after admitting he had secretly distributed videotapes that undermined a rival Democrat. Sasso's deputy, Susan Estrich, brilliantly steered Dukakis to the nomination. But while the Bush team began its "fall" campaign in late May, the Dukakis organization remained publicly consumed by its dealings with Jesse Jackson through July—first by questions about his possible selection as Dukakis's running mate, then over his role and prerogatives at the convention. As it turned out, Jackson was as much the star in Atlanta as Dukakis himself, perhaps to Dukakis's detriment in the fall. In our conference session, Jackson's Atlanta negotiator, Ronald H. Brown, argued that the Dukakis team had had no choice but to focus as intently as it did on the delicate diplomacy of dealing with Jackson. The convention, Brown said, may well have been disrupted by Jackson's delegates and supporters outside the hall had the Dukakis campaign been seen as less than solicitous.

Perhaps the Jackson challenge drew organizational energy away from other tasks. Perhaps the peripheral presence of Sasso—a worshipped figure whose eventual return, like the Messiah, was always being awaited—made forging unity at headquarters in Boston difficult. Whatever the reason, the Dukakis campaign had organizational problems. Unlike the Bush campaign, it never was able to harness the best and the brightest of its party's trained campaign professionals in Washington and elsewhere. Instead of a single "media guru" with strong authority, there was a succession of advisers, none with the requisite clout. Instead of a few simple themes ("read my lips," "the L-word people," "a kinder, gentler nation"), there was a changing lineup of muddled ones. Instead of an organization chart that bespoke a clear strategy, there were ill-defined responsibilities. And instead of a candidate who let his "handlers" handle, there was a headstrong governor who, understandably, insisted on following his own ideas and instincts about what would work and what was proper.

Listening between the lines, one could hear in Cambridge the sound of campaign aides complaining about—but also praising—Dukakis. They indicated that he opposed waging the kind of scorched-earth campaign he thought Bush was running. The only consistent strategy his campaign *did* agree on was to tell voters that they should have been offended by the odor of Bush's campaign. So it was not surprising that Dukakis's inner circle was determined to make the same argument at Harvard. For scheduling reasons, our session was the only one at which the Bush high command (Atwater and Ailes) was confronted by the top ranks of Dukakis's leadership (Estrich, campaign chairman Paul Brountas, and political director Jack Corrigan).

As a result, our conference session on "campaign organization" evolved—exploded—into a debate on the role of ethics in campaigns. It became a clash between the Dukakis campaign's righteous indignation, bordering on the holier-than-thou, and the smug Realpolitik, laced with cynicism, of the Bush campaign. It seemed, as the election contest itself had seemed, like a clash of cultures. The session distilled itself into a series of confrontations over facts, intent, and ethical rules.

Was the Bush Campaign's "Revolving Door" Spot Unfair and Misleading?

Brountas questioned the accuracy and intent of the Bush campaign's famous "revolving door" spot. In the ad, long lines of convicts pass through a prison turnstile gate. Willie Horton's name is never mentioned. Instead, the announcer says that Massachusetts had allowed "convicted murderers" out on weekend furloughs. A graphic shows the number 268 (the number of all types of convicts furloughed). The announcer says "many" were still at large. But many *what?* Convicted murderers? That was the clear implication, Brountas argued, and it was wrong and unfair. Nor, Brountas said, was the number of escaped convicts "at large" as substantial as the long lines moving through the turnstile visually implied.

Ailes denied that the advertisement was open to these interpretations. Ailes added, in the classic (lame) practitioner's defense, that the ad must have been fair and accurate because it had been cleared by the Bush campaign's lawyers.

Did Lee Atwater Deliberately Encourage the Use of the Willie Horton Story by State Parties and "Independent" Committees?

This was important for two reasons. For one, GOP state parties eventually went much further, and lower, than the Bush campaign in using Horton's story. Lurid brochures about the crime issue, showing a frightened white girl, were target-mailed by the GOP state party in Illinois, for example. And it was an "independent" committee, which purportedly had no contact with the Bush campaign, that made and aired its own, much more direct, spot about Horton, one that showed a scary looking mug shot of him and an interview with his rape victim. If they were taking instructions from Atwater, then their expenditures should have been counted toward the Bush spending limits. More important, Bush would have had to answer politically for the ads.

Atwater said that he had been worried from the outset about raising the visibility of Horton himself out of a concern that the Bush campaign would be accused of racist tactics. But in early June at a public meeting of GOP southern leaders in Atlanta, Atwater had publicly said—and had been quoted by *Washington Post* reporter Tom Edsall—that he wanted to make a "household name" of Horton. If Atwater had been so concerned about the visibility of Horton why, he was asked in Cambridge, did he not advise state party officials to limit their use of his picture and story? Atwater said that he had done so, but only after his speech in Atlanta. By then, participants in our session pointed out, the GOP troops and "independent" committees had every reason to think they knew the real Bush game plan.

Should Candidates Be Held Accountable for the Actions of "Unaffiliated" State Organization and "Independent" Committees?

Indirectly, our session raised an important new question: Just what *is* an "organization" these days? The growing role of so-called "soft" money is one reason why answering that question is difficult. More than $100 million in "soft" money was raised, mostly by the national parties, and redistributed for use by state and local parties in what were ostensibly "grassroots" efforts "unaffiliated" with the presidential campaigns. In fact these efforts essentially were controlled by the Bush and Dukakis campaigns themselves. To what extent, our session implicitly asked, should the candidates' campaigns be responsible for actions of the "unaffiliated"? The problem with "independent" committees is one of policing. These free agents, protected by Supreme Court decisions on First Amendment rights, can do as they please as long as there is no "contact" with the campaigns. But it doesn't take a clairvoyant to figure out some piece of nasty business a campaign might want done without getting direct instructions. Ailes, for his part, insisted that "independent" committees were a problem for all campaigns. Their Willie Horton ad in 1988, he said, had not helped the Bush cause. The Dukakis team, judging from the vehemence of their criticism of the ad, evidently didn't agree.

Was the Bush Campaign Guilty of Playing on Racial Fears?

This question, the centerpiece of our session, produced the most emotional moments of the Harvard conference. The transcript doesn't fully capture the heat and bitterness of the exchanges. Estrich shocked the symposium into silence by mentioning how her own rape had made her as qualified as anyone—if not more so—to discuss the "crime issue." She did not dispute the notion that the issue was a valid one to raise. Nor did the Dukakis staffers attempt to argue that there was something inherently immoral about "negative" campaigning. But the Bush campaign, in Estrich's view, had deliberately played on racial fears by using the Horton story to dramatize it. At the very least, she argued, the Bush campaign was guilty of a dangerously blithe and unethical disregard of the likelihood that Horton's story would play on racial fears.

The Bush campaign just as vehemently denied any racist intent or thinking. Atwater said that he had been determined *not* to use Horton's name and face in ads—to protect against accusations of racism. For the same reason, he and Ailes said, they had been careful to keep the number of blacks to a minimum in the "revolving door" ad. At Harvard, the Bush campaign countered with an accusation of its own. The Dukakis campaign, they said, had used the picture of an Hispanic felon in a spot that pointed up problems in a Bush-endorsed furlough program. The Dukakis campaign said that they ran the "Hispanic" ad only after extreme provocation from the Bush team. That was all Atwater thought he needed to hear. "I think that right there makes this whole thing a moot issue," he said. "You did it, we did it, let's close this off."

Did the Campaigns Have a "Special Responsibility" to Treat the Horton/Furlough Issue Delicately, If Not Avoid It Altogether, Because It Would Be Viewed in Racial Terms Regardless?

The Dukakis campaign was joined by Jackson convention manager Brown in arguing, in effect, that there really was no way to deal with the Horton story responsibly. That produced the only occasion in our session when a Democrat sided, however reluctantly, with the Bush campaign team. Fred Martin, Senator Albert Gore's campaign manager, noted that Gore had raised the furlough issue during the Democratic primaries, without knowing about Willie Horton, "because we believed that issue had some merit and ought to be debated. We raised it," Martin said, "without any imputation of race."

*   *   *

Behind these specific questions loomed a larger and, for the most part, unspoken set of issues. Does a campaign organization have any higher purpose than to win the race? Should they be called on to resist the sleazier features of the electoral and social environment? Are they supposed to raise the level of public debate?

Dukakis's staff implied that they had been hampered by their own—and their candidate's—values. They portrayed themselves as reluctant bathers in the muck, aghast at the morés of the Bush campaign. For most of the fall, Brountas said, Dukakis himself had insisted on an elevate-the-debate approach. This righteous portrait should have been eagerly applauded in Cambridge, home of "the L-Word People" made famous in Bush's demonology. But that wasn't the sense of the room. The blunt and roguish Ailes, the feisty and combative Atwater, more than held their own. Part of the reason was the audience, professional practitioners and observers of politics. It was a hard lot perhaps inured to grubby Realpolitik. No one was willing to call the Bush campaign a tasteful exercise. It was no Kennedyesque call to greatness. But pending further disclosure of damaging facts, it didn't set a record for perfidy, either. It was tough, nasty, and effective—high praise to many campaign managers. There also was a sense, expressed in private moments during the weekend, that the Dukakis campaign had forfeited the right to complain. This was not because its own ethical standards were low, but because it did not effectively fight back. And, despite its self-described high-mindedness, it was as devoid of tough proposals and grand vision as Bush's.

Who, if anyone, can ensure that the next presidential campaign (and the next Harvard seminar) isn't dominated by the 1992 version of the Willie Horton story? Electoral politics, we have to hope, will still contain its own self-correcting mechanism. As soon as enough voters decide they are tired of Hortonized campaigning, a candidate will rise by criticizing it. Even more optimistically, we can hope that the next crop of presidential candidates will have a more compelling "positive" message to sell. The surest way to climb out of the muck is to have something inspiring—and convincing—to tell the nation.

The Discussion

Howard Fineman: Delivering the message, or failing to deliver the message, was a lot of what campaign organization was about. We are talking about organization of two kinds: field organization—what was actually happening out there in voter land—and organization at headquarters. Organization at headquarters, as you know, was an oxymoronic phrase in a couple of cases.

I thought I would start out asking about the Bush campaign and how it decided to organize the shaping and delivery of its messages. I'm not so much focused on the five things you decided to hit on, but how you did it, and that leads directly back to Roger Ailes. I would ask Lee first, Why Roger Ailes?

Lee Atwater: He's the best is the short answer. To elaborate, I have been in politics for quite a while, and I have worked with everybody in our business in his area. He simply is the best. Second, Roger and I are soul brothers of sorts in terms of our approach to a campaign. We believe in really two things. One is the importance of staying on the offense, and the other is the importance of controlling the agenda. We can talk once a week, and we are in agreement.

I had a lot of turf and a lot things I was doing. Roger had a big amount of turf. I felt that the most important role in the campaign at the time when Roger came aboard was going to be his job. It was critical to have a person that I, as campaign manager, felt was like-minded to work with. Also George Bush was very comfortable with Roger Ailes and believes in Roger Ailes. And Roger Ailes believes in George Bush. That fit real well. Lastly, everyone else who was involved in the campaign, including Bob Teeter and Jim Baker, who was not in the campaign at the time but who I consulted informally on things of this nature, agreed with it.

Howard Fineman: Roger, one of the contrasts we saw from the outside was the extent of influence that you had most of the time. Clearly, there was a central figure controlling delivery of the message in your campaign versus many in the Dukakis campaign. What kind of authority did you want that made it possible for you to do this job and what kind of conditions did you set, if any, on taking the job?

Roger Ailes: In my contract with the campaign I insisted on direct access to the candidate whenever I needed it and insisted on being included in any meeting I wanted to be in, no matter what else happened during the campaign. Not that I would come to every meeting, but meetings could not take place without my being present if I wanted to be there. The second point was that I would clear the advertising with as few people as possible. As it turned out, the best thing that happened for George Bush was that the team around him all worked well together. I mean, when we had differences we argued, but we always went out of the room unified and we were never dinging each other.

I presented the advertising or my ideas about message or what have you to a group of four or five people. There were many times when I had to operate on my own, as in the Dan Rather thing, because we were isolated. The vice president was on *Air Force II*, there was a snowstorm in Washington, and we weren't able to hook up. I talked with the group that morning, and we tried to figure out the strategy. Basically, I had to call it in terms of how to handle that situation. I always had the feeling that Lee and the other guys would back me.

Matthew Reese: I know that in a campaign gossip is often overstated, Roger, but I want to ask if there is a germ of truth in what I heard repeatedly: that before [Jim] Baker came to the Bush campaign, really nobody could call a meeting and be sure the people that he wanted to have there would come. Is there any truth at all in that?

Roger Ailes: No, there is none. Lee or any one of us could call a meeting. Actually, it was a good feeling because any one of us could go on the road, knowing the other guys were going to have a meeting and that we were not going to be taken out or stabbed in the back. Usually, whenever possible, we were all hooked up by phone. If a meeting was taking place and one of us was out or if it fell in my area, Lee would say, "Let's not make that call until we get Ailes in the loop." And they agreed even if it was an immediate decision. So Lee did a very good job of holding us together, and we didn't have that problem.

I'm sure each guy felt that he was playing a very major role, but we understood the structure and how to work together. I think that's why we got through the primaries as effectively as we did.

Lee Atwater: My attitude was that when you're working with people like the Bob Teeters and the Roger Ailes—who, frankly, were masters of this game when I was still a teenage bumpkin—you don't try to throw around your title. The first decision I made as campaign manager was not to try to act like a boss, but to treat Craig Fuller, who was always a peer of mine in the White House, and Roger and Bob and Rich Bond as peers.

We did work as peers. But then in return they always deferred to me. I was *the* campaign manager. Ultimately, it was my responsibility. It came down to only three or four times that there were some critical decisions. They always deferred and they always backed me up.

Howard Fineman: There was a "Nightline" interview that took place with George Bush that I think was not one of your favorite events of the campaign. If this was all working so smoothly, how did that happen?

Roger Ailes: That was the one time it broke down, and it was the last time it broke down. It happened partly because I was on the road and partly because I had two roles. One was his public appearances vis-à-vis "Nightline" and Dan Rather and that kind of thing and the other was advertising. At a certain point I was pulled over to work on advertising, and there were some meetings going on regarding public appearances. I think somebody very innocently said, "Oh, fine, 'Nightline,' let's go ahead and do it, let's get it out of the way, it's going to be Iran-Contra."

The problem was, I think, they didn't schedule it very well. We had been in California, had flown back to Texas, came back to California overnight, and then back to Texas. He had a big speech at the Texas state convention that morning. Then he went out running that afternoon. By 6 p.m. that night he was worn out, and then he had to do "Nightline" at 10 p.m. Texas time. He was burned out. As we were driving into the studio, he looked at me and said, "Why are we doing this?"

Lee Atwater: There's one thing that you probably don't even remember. We were in the middle of a staff change.

Ailes: I was upset because I was overworked on advertising and this thing got scheduled. Once it's scheduled you can't pull out because it looks like you're running from it. So we had to go through with it. We had been in three or four different time zones in two days, and I knew it was not an optimum situation for the vice president.

Howard Fineman: As a general matter did you feel you had to—and did you, in fact—see what Bush was saying on the stump and in "free" media television appearances, or were you really focused primarily on paid advertising?

Roger Ailes: I was watching both the news, the free media, and the advertising. As we headed into the general election, I shifted more and more to advertising and only to the major events like the convention speech, the debates, and so on. I was more out of the loop once Sheila Tate came aboard. During the primaries, I was always trying to watch the free media projection as well as the paid media projection to see that they were the same. For the general election, I felt responsible to work with the press operation and make it seem similar.

Matthew Reese: How did you decide the targets and the message? Did you have a series of meetings? Did you work from a "brilliant memo" someone wrote? Did you go away on your mountaintop and come back and say, "The Lord has told me these are the four things"?

Roger Ailes: The Lord stopped speaking to me somewhere during this campaign. (Laughter)

Matthew Reese: Well, he's usually speaking to us. So he's busy. (Laughter)

Roger Ailes: I think Lee can answer that better. We all contributed. Obviously, we had ongoing polling; we had policy groups and ongoing research on the issues.

Matthew Reese: Did you meet, say every Tuesday morning, about messages and targets?

Lee Atwater: We met virtually every day.

Roger Ailes: Virtually every day we talked about what the message for the day was, what the message for the week was, and where we were going.

Lee Atwater: Basically, Bob Teeter, Roger, and I, and then Craig Fuller and Rich Bond met. But from the standpoint of most of the strategy decisions, it was Roger and I.

Matthew Reese: What part did the candidate have in this?

Lee Atwater: He played a big part in this. Well, he was an activist candidate in two ways. First, he was very aware of what was going on around him and in the campaign. Second, we respected his political judgment. I was talking to some people last night. He made some basic strategy calls in this race that we might have made differently. These calls made a difference in the race. For instance, it was his strategic call very early in this race on how to deal, in his role as vice president, with Ronald Reagan. That decision, which was a long-term decision for which he had the self-discipline to enforce himself and to keep us enforced, paid off very handsomely for him. We kept him very informed. All of us had ongoing access to him. We would meet with him daily, if he was in town, or one or two of us would jump on a plane.

Now the good news is that we did not play games with each other. I'll tell you who did a good job of representing all of our opinions—Craig Fuller. He was one of the most objective guys. For instance, in one incident Roger and I were pushing the vice president to accept a debate early in Houston, which ended up being the first debate. Craig had his own reasons for disagreeing. The point is that Craig disagreed with me. He was on the plane with the vice president. I had given him my very strong opinion on the issue, and Craig presented his position on that issue, as well as mine and Roger's. And the vice president went with us.

That was a big lesson to me about Craig Fuller. If you have a guy out there with the candidate who is willing to lose on a position like that, he's a pretty honest fellow.

Howard Fineman: So, basically, what you wanted the person on the plane to do was represent this message strategy as devised by the group back home. His basic job was to make sure that the candidate followed that to the letter.

Lee Atwater: Right.

Roger Ailes: If he agreed with it. You can't get Bush to do things he doesn't agree with. That's the problem and the opportunity. He has some options. Then he says, "I'm not going to do that, so come back to me again."

Howard Fineman: Is there a good example of a time when the cellular phone clicked on, Craig Fuller picked it up and told Bush what the plan was, and Bush said, "No way, I'm just not doing that"?

Roger Ailes: There were several times in the general election when we wanted to toughen the message and he wanted to ease up the message. He wanted a kind agenda.

The other time I can think of was when there was strong pressure for him to step away from Reagan earlier than he did. I think he had the convention in his mind—that at this point it would be legitimate for him to begin to articulate his views and take a separate position. We went into a black hole after we won our primaries. We couldn't get news coverage because the Democrats were commanding the news.

At this point we were trying to say let's start breaking away. We still have the major breakaway problem; if we don't do that now, we are going to have a major crisis. He resisted that. He decided to go on his own timetable. And ultimately he turned out to be right because people were more focused on the campaign at the time he did it.

Lee Atwater: I'll give you one—the Don Regan matter. Virtually every one of his aides and every one of his friends advised him very strongly to get involved in the Don Regan matter and advise Reagan that Regan ought to go. He refused steadfastly to do that for about four or five weeks. When he finally did do it, he insisted on doing it. He was the one who ultimately sat down with Don Regan and pointed out a few things to him, which ended up in Regan's leaving. He kept that totally quiet, and guys like me and Roger were saying, "Boy, you could really get some points."

Let me go back to the other point. Basically, our campaign organization was based on the simple premise that one person can't run a presidential campaign in this country. It's too big. There are too many components to the campaign. What you've got to do is get four or five people who are the best you've got and give them all the turf you can. Let those four or five people run the campaign. This means, in my particular job the single most important thing, until Jim Baker got there, was to keep everybody together, to be the guy to keep everybody pushing in the same direction. But the whole thing was based on people trusting each other, working together, having plenty of turf. And we had a candidate who did an absolutely excellent job in backing us individually, giving us self-confidence—myself particularly after Iowa—over and over again, even when things went wrong.

Roger Ailes: One morning after Iowa, he said he never saw five guys who thought they were pretty good, feeling pretty bad. He said, as I recall it, "Look, I have to take half the blame for this. You guys get some of it. I still think I have the best team on the field. We're not going to point fingers. We're going to win New Hampshire. I'm going to Kennebunkport and let's do it." That was the end of the discussion.

Matthew Reese: Susan and Paul, politicians outside the campaign said early on that the Bush campaign had much better and stronger control over their message than did the Dukakis team. How did you come to decide what was to be done? How did the candidate impact upon decisions? How did the acceptance speech become what it was? Who decided that? What was your organization structure? There were press stories about twelve hundred scripts. How many did you put in the drawer—which must have been the biggest drawer in Boston.

Susan Estrich: I'm giving them all to you guys. To begin with, I agree with Lee. It is impossible to run a presidential campaign, a general election campaign, by yourself. It's a lot easier to run a primary campaign yourself. For my part, when I took over the Dukakis campaign at the time of the Biden incident, I was advised by some people, "Delegate everything." Well, that wasn't something I could do at that point. I thought my most important responsibility was pulling people together and continuing onward.

It is a difficult transition. I think Bob Beckel and I probably are the experts here on the difficulty of that transition from a hard-fought primary campaign, and the Bush campaign had certain advantages over us. One was that they were institutionalized in Washington. Another was that they had a real head start. We kept winning every Tuesday, which was an advantage we had in the polls. But we were actually engaged in real politics every Tuesday as well, and that occupied us. So we didn't start as soon as one would have liked to in an ideal world to branch out and become a general election campaign.

We put a high priority on putting together a state campaign organization. We had existed from when we started through June with about eight or nine state campaigns managers. We moved them around the country throughout the primary process. We needed to expand very quickly.

One of the first assignments of Jack Corrigan, and Charley Baker, who is observing, was to build a national organization immediately. We went to the other campaigns—and I think we did this very effectively—to find their best state campaign managers and their best people and build a national organization. By the time of the convention we had close to 40 state managers in place and the beginnings of an organization. Frankly, however, they had a head start on us in many of the large states.

On the message, we didn't have a Roger Ailes. I wish we had. By a Roger Ailes I mean two things. First, a person of his talent because it's clear it doesn't matter unless you have his talent. But second and, perhaps, equally important a person whose judgment and relationship with the candidate is such that he has his trust and respect.

We were a fairly lean campaign in the primaries. We came out of the primaries with some major holes in our own organization. We tried to fill some as fast as we could. Mark Gerran had done an admirable job with the press alone. We brought in Dayton Duncan, who had done that for Mondale. We brought in Kirk O'Donnell in June to manage our day-to-day communications; Kirk had some real advantages, including the fact that he worked with Michael Dukakis some years before. He had the kind of relationship where he could hopefully manage that communication. We also made overtures to Ron Brown, but he had other responsibilities through July, and to Tom Donilon and to a number of others.

On the advertising side, we came out of the primary campaign having relied on two individuals to do our media. Neither of them had the kind of relationship with Dukakis that would allow them to assume anything approaching even half that of Mr. Ailes's role. So the question was, where do you go? How do you build something larger?

I have personal views which I'll share with you. I'm not sure Jack and Paul and others share them. We made a decision that there was no national media person who had the kind of relationship with Mike Dukakis that would allow him to step in and play a Roger Ailes role. We thought that reaching out to Madison Avenue, trying to put together a team using our primary talent but building heavily on commercial advertising talent, might be a way to achieve—and I'll say this in quotes—"break-through advertising." The kind of advertising that would be at some level different, better, sounder than political advertising.

Howard Fineman: Is it clear to you now that you needed an organizational model like theirs? Or was it obvious at the very beginning?

Matthew Reese: And do you think it was impossible to duplicate that organization?

Howard Fineman: You couldn't field an organization like that even from the start?

Susan Estrich: We had an organization. I mean, Kirk O'Donnell, working with Leslie Dach, Chris Edley, John Podesta, and others, had responsibility for daily communications, review of press, speech writing, issues, and policy. He had a weekly plan and a daily plan as to what we were going to say and do. There were daily communications meetings and weekly communications meetings, and that continued from June through November.

Now the substance of the message we can talk about later, but I think Kirk certainly had that half of Roger's job.

Roger Ailes: Can I make a brief comment? Keep in mind this kind of organization serves at the whim of the candidate. The Democratic party certainly has talent, certainly has people. Whether the candidate will allow a certain group of people to come in and play an important role in an area that he does not consider his area of expertise is another question.

Howard Fineman: Is that why you ultimately didn't go to work for Bob Dole?

Roger Ailes: Yes. I told Bob Dole I would like to be his third media consultant. I said, "You're going to fire your first two, whoever they are." (Laughter)

Howard Fineman: But you did have serious discussions?

Roger Ailes: I did, and I did, in fact, tell him that. I said, "If Bush is out by then, I would be happy to be your third consultant. Even if Darryl Zanuck comes aboard, you're going to fire him. So I think I would like to be considered third because by that time you will be scared enough to listen." I could see Dole was never going to let that happen.

Robert Beckel: Roger, and then, Susan, I'm going to ask you the same thing. Did George Bush have to approve every ad that went on the air or could you go on the air without his approval?

Roger Ailes: I think he knew every ad we were going to do, whether we read it to him over the phone or Lee described it.

Lee Atwater: There was not a single ad that he did not approve. I think in nine out of ten he saw them all.

Robert Beckel: Did he ever have to approve the ads from the scripts or could you go to production?

Lee Atwater: One or two times he did.

Roger Ailes: We could go to production.

Robert Beckel: In your case, Susan, did Dukakis have to approve every script?

Susan Estrich: Yes, until it got really hot in late September or October. I think it would be fair to say as the campaign really accelerated toward the end, it became logistically difficult, if not impossible. But Dukakis is a real hands-on candidate. That's one of his great strengths. It's a frustration when you disagree.

Roger Ailes: There's a difference in what you call positive or comparative advertising. If it's a noncontroversial ad, there's less reason to get candidate approval. If he's going to be questioned about this ad, he needs to see it. If it hits the air and he's asked about it the next time he gets off the plane, he has a problem. So you always make sure he sees it. But, you know, candidates don't necessarily approve all positive advertising up front.

Howard Fineman: I want to make clear that we want to stress here the organizational aspect.

I wanted to shift to the question of literally where Dukakis had his campaign. There is a lot of talk about how this campaign was an expression of the insularity of Boston. Let me ask a very simple, logistical question. Did you consider moving the campaign head-quarters down to Washington and, if not, why not?

Susan Estrich: It was not feasible because of Governor Dukakis. We didn't consider it for one simple reason: because Mike Dukakis was very serious about being governor of this state. So it was absolutely clear he was going to spend as much time as he could here in Massachusetts being governor. And given that, you can't have a candidate in one city and a campaign in another. As all of you know, the issue of how much time he spent as governor and how many days a week, et cetera, was one we lived with for many months. So there was no issue on that, Howard.

Let me just add, I think being a non-D.C. campaign had certain disadvantages, particularly in the general election when there was a perception that we didn't reach out enough. And we can talk about it. I think we reached out more than some people thought. It also had some advantages in that particularly throughout the primary process we were spared some of the Beltway back and forth, which you get trapped in. But it wasn't an issue any more than his resigning as governor was an issue.

Matthew Reese: I have been in primary campaigns and presidential primaries. It seems to me that in winning the primaries you have done the harder part of the project—even if you lose the general election. It's just such a miracle when you can come out of nowhere and get the presidential nomination. I know there's a natural reaction: hugging your friends and colleagues and saying, "By God, we did it, we showed those bastards." You feel that when you walk across the earth, it shakes from your own importance. I know that's how many of us felt with Kennedy in 1960, and I've seen it many times since.

But it seemed that you were more insular than usual, that you did not reach out nearly as much as other campaigns in the past did. The first reaction is very natural, but you didn't seem to adjust very much. People who were willing and able to help weren't pulled in, it seemed. The campaign seemed to be run by Boston pols, and there's a certain parochialism there. You brought Kirk O'Donnell from Washington. He's brilliant, but a Boston pol. You needed breath and depth you didn't seem to have. Is there any sense to what I'm saying?

Susan Estrich: Sure, there's some sense.

Matthew Reese: But not much, huh?

Susan Estrich: I would ask Jack to join in on this because I think we did attempt, in putting together a national organization, to reach out a little more broadly. There is a tendency in a group like this to focus almost exclusively on the people with whom you deal as press people, whether it's the Dayton Duncans or the Kirk O'Donnells and Susan Estriches, and to leave out some of the people who were running major states and the like. So I think that's a piece of it.

But I also think, Matt, there were talented people who came in August, who it would have been nice to have in June, and some who came in September who we could have used in July. But, more broadly, there is, I believe, a trade-off, a larger question, which is: Do you bring in people with no relationship to your candidate and expect they can win his confidence and take over major decision-making roles? That's one issue.

A second issue, I think a larger issue, is that I believe the Democratic party does pay some price for losing four of the last five elections, and that is, a lot of very talented people move on. A lot of the people who participated with Bob in 1984 and in the Carter effort in 1980 and 1976 did move on. I believe the Democratic party does have less of a permanent campaign establishment on account of our continuing losses.

After a winning campaign, you look back and say everything was worthwhile. There's a tendency—and I think some of my colleagues around the table from the primaries would attest to it—in a losing campaign to look back and say maybe it's time for me to move on in life. So those are at least two of the questions which we had to face.

Roger Ailes: I want to hear what Paul has to say about this. I don't know where all the people came from in your campaign. In our campaign it was interesting because Fuller's from California, Lee's from South Carolina, Bob's from Michigan, I'm from Ohio.

There was no hang-up about part of the country or education. All of us seemed to be sort of outside the Washington-New York Axis. I wonder if that had anything to do with it. I'm not sure about your campaign.

Paul Brountas: I disagree with the characterization of the campaign being run by Boston pols. I don't think Susan Estrich is a Boston pol. I don't think I am. There was an in-flow of fresh blood. The question is, should it have come sooner? Maybe it should have come sooner. Tom Donilon and Steve Engelberg joined us—Peter Adleman, Ted Sorenson to name just a few. I mean, there was a reaching out on our part. Susan had several meetings during the summer in which she invited key players in the party to participate.

John Corrigan: I have to say one thing. By the end of the campaign we basically had all the usual suspects of the Democratic party on board. And we did make an early attempt to give people specific roles. We felt strongly about having strong state organizations. We had Steve Murphy, who I thought was the best of an opponent's campaign managers. We had Tony Podesta running California, a very significant role in the campaign, not unlike what the Bush campaign did with Roger Stone out in California.

On the message side, I think basically we had every Madison Avenue person we could think of involved. There was no shortage of outreach. The problem was in the other direction. There wasn't a coherent, single person in control of the message. So we basically made mistakes in both directions.

Roger Ailes: Did you put one advertising person in charge of advertising?

Susan Estrich: We did. We put two different advertising persons in charge of advertising, one in the summer and one in the fall.

Howard Fineman: But there's a sense, looking back on it, that the Bush campaign had put together from the very beginning the team they were planning to have in place and in operation all the way through. When John Sasso was still around, when you started out, did you guys have the feeling at that point that you had the team that you were going to follow through to the general election, assuming you won the nomination?

Susan Estrich: We were a long-shot candidacy. They were the incumbent vice president of the United States, who was at least the front-runner in their race. When I took over I can say this. I spent hours on the phone with some of the usual suspects begging them to come join the Dukakis campaign in Boston. Not surprising to me, they said, "What? Are you out of your mind? You want me to give up a lucrative law practice [or consulting firm or the like] to go with your long-shot candidacy up in Boston, which is 6 percent in the polls? So, no, of course not."

That, I think, is one of the challenges we faced in a very different sense than they faced. They had their team in a very strong way from the beginning. We started out as a long-shot candidacy and maintained that cohesive team, and I think it was a strong team for the primaries. Then we were faced with the challenge, as a noninstitutionalized, non-Washington, D.C.-based candidacy, to grow in a very short period of time.

I think we did it quite successfully at the state campaign level, for which Jack Corrigan and Charley Baker deserve an enormous amount of credit. We did it fairly successfully at the political level, for which Chuck Campion, who was our political director, Bill Cable, Pat Griffen, and others deserve a lot of credit. And I think we did it least successfully in the advertising area, where we had all of Madison Avenue with shifting captains as time went on.

Roger Ailes: Did you make a mistake in getting rid of the two guys who got you through the primaries?

Susan Estrich: My own view of our advertising mistake was that the two people I knew best, who I felt most comfortable with and who I think are among the two best on our side, were not brought in early on to participate with us. I ended up working closely with them at the end. That is Bob Squier, who did the half hour for us, and Bob Shrum, who did the five-minute pieces for us.

But both of those people—it's no secret to anyone—had fairly complicated past histories with the Dukakis operation and with the governor. Neither of them was an obvious candidate for the job at the time. And I'm not sure Paul even today would share my view on that. I'm not sure the governor would share my view. But that's my own personal perspective.

Howard Fineman: Paul do you have anything to add?

Paul Brountas: No.

Howard Fineman: The Republicans are expressing a lot of healthy curiosity.

Frank Fahrenkopf: I have a question rather than a comment. On campaign organization, I think the difference in the process of the two parties between the primaries and the general election may have an impact on the effective nature of the campaign organization in the general election. What I mean by that is there are very, very few states on the Republican side in choosing delegates to our national convention that are not winner take all.

Our campaign operatives, whether it's for Dole or Kemp or Bush or Robertson or whoever it might be, go into primary states and caucus states realizing it's a winner-take-all ballgame. They go into each state with an attitude and approach to reach out and touch every corner that they can, realizing that if they win the nomination, they will already have in place an experienced team in dealing with a winner-take-all-approach—which the electoral college approach is.

So many of the Democratic primaries are proportional allocation of delegates. I think when you go into a proportional fight to win delegates you have a different mind-set and a different approach than in a winner take all.

So what may be an effective campaign organization for a Democratic candidate in the primaries may not be an effective campaign organization or may even be a defective campaign organization to meet the contest in the general election. You've really got to change, change dramatically.

Edward Rollins: Not to blow Lee's horn—and, obviously, after winning 40 states he doesn't have to have anyone blow his horn—I think a couple of things that went into place in this campaign are very, very important from an organizational perspective. There are only so many blue-chippers. As a college coach knows, a blue-chipper is one of the very best high school players. For 10 years Lee Atwater has been—particularly in the South early on and then, obviously, from 1984 on—both developing and training young political professionals. So when he started putting together this organization—and I know being on the opposite side in the primaries, trying to go out and find operators—they were all in the Bush campaign.

Ailes and Lee and Teeter have probably been in 20 or 30 campaigns—Senate campaigns, House campaigns—together. They know the skills. They know how to work together. To make one minor correction, we have won five out of the last six presidential campaigns. For most of the people who have been in these campaigns, it's their second, third, fourth presidential campaign. And the minute campaigns were over, Marc Nuttle was brought into the campaign and his organization was folded in. Bill Lacy, who ran California, gets folded into a campaign. Charlie Black of the Kemp campaign gets folded into the campaign. And even if we had a bitter primary—1976 was the last bitter primary we had—there was an attempt to bring in people.

It's just that continuity of having worked together that really pays off in maximum dividends. Obviously, your candidate has to perform; but no one had to question Ailes. They knew what Ailes could do. Teeter writes the script or Ailes writes the script or Atwater implements it. It's that ongoing thing that has been a 10-year process. Lee has been working on putting this campaign together for 10 years. George Bush was working for 10 years to put together a fundraising mechanism, and George was very effective at it. Money was never a problem. That pays off maximum dividends.

William Lacy: Let me follow up on something Ed said that I think is important. The day after Dole withdrew, Lee called me and basically said, "I want you to come by and see me in a week. I want you to decide between now and then whether or not you want to play a role in the Bush campaign." I went by the next week. He worked out an arrangement where I would advise/consult with him over the next couple of months. Then he called me up in June and said, "How would you like to go to California?" I said, "No way." Three weeks later I was in California. That is because of personal relationships and that's because of the fact we have all worked together.

The first thing I did before I went to California was to sit down with Ed Rollins because he knows more about California than anybody else. Ed gave me a lay of the land. Because I had worked for Frank Fahrenkopf as political director I knew exactly what resources there were at the national committee that I could bring to bear. As soon as I showed up in California, I was getting memos from Marc Nuttle, saying there were 300,000 identified Robertson supporters out there from their campaign. He said that if we would like to take it, we could have it. That's one of the strengths of the interconnections on our side.

Roger Ailes: I want to make one comment. I was the last to join the Bush group, the sort of inner circle. I signed on full time, I think, in July 1987 and had been doing some consulting prior to that. We all knew each other and had been working together for a number of years. We were a strong team in the spring of 1987—up and running with no problems.

William Carrick: I think I want to underline two comments, one that Susan Estrich made. I think the Democratic party institutionally suffers from a horrible deficiency. That is, we don't have the financial capacity to train our people and keep them in the business of politics and campaigns. Most of the people who participate in presidential campaigns professionally do it as a one-time experience or two-time experience.

We don't have the institutional wherewithal to keep people in the business of politics year in and year out, day in and day out. This is further exaggerated because we keep losing presidential elections and don't have the governmental positions to put people in. That's showing up more and more. There's less talent on our side than there has ever been. I think we found that from the recruitment of state campaign managers all the way up to top national positions.

The other point is what Frank Fahrenkopf said. I think that's a part of the puzzle. The Republican nomination process is designed to reach a conclusion much faster than ours. We have gone into the last three Democratic national conventions with unresolved major political conflicts between the first-place candidate and the second-place candidate. Even though the nomination may not have been in jeopardy, there have been contested political contests between ideological forces, philosophical forces, and tactical groups. There have been large political contests that have kept our campaign from coming together, moving forward and positioning itself for the fall campaign early on.

Robert Beckel: That's one point about this. I don't want to diminish the role of this great Republican juggernaut. Let's face it, Frank, you have $40 million or $50 million to keep all these guys working and a government to put them in.

Second, these guys had a winning campaign. I can tell you, we fought Gary Hart every step of the way needlessly. The Democrats have not had a clear running field like these guys have had. So it's awfully nice to say you reached out to the Dole people when you were beating them handily. By March, of course, you can reach out and be magnanimous and bring everybody together. But let's keep in mind the timing here. The Democrats have never gotten their act together.

And another good point: If we keep proportional representation, not only do we not win a state, but we have to stay in that state for months after a primary. This is why we have to do away with proportional representation.

Paul Brountas: I think Bob makes a very good point. You recall that Jesse Jackson started his bus tour from Chicago to the Atlanta convention to mount momentum for his support at the convention. So we went into Atlanta with a lot of pressure and a lot of tension which, fortunately, Ron Brown was able to resolve to a large extent. But we were fighting that battle right up until the opening of the convention. And don't forget we fought many primary battles throughout March, April, and May. People just didn't back off and say, "Okay, Governor Dukakis, here's a clear shot, here are our people, we want to work with you, let's go to work together."

Howard Fineman: In fact, isn't it true in Dukakis's case that he really did have the nomination locked up substantially earlier than, say, Walter Mondale did in 1984? And so wasn't the management task a little easier? In looking back on it now, do you think, Susan, that perhaps you spent too much time managing the Jackson relationship and not enough time looking ahead to the fall campaign?

Susan Estrich: Who knows, Howard. It was my view at the time—and, I think, Bob got into this as well four years before—that if that Jackson relationship was not managed well and if those last primaries did not reach a positive result from our point of view, then we were going to be in trouble come July. Whether you consider it finishing the primary process or getting ready for the general election, those are pressing problems that you have to deal with.

The Jackson relationship was difficult to manage up until the Monday of our convention. Ron and I go back a long way together, and I think we both agree on this. Had we not come together—and Paul played a very large role in this—our nomination would have been worth a great deal less. To explain that I was busy with outreach for the general election would have seemed a rather paltry explanation for a miserable convention that people watched for four nights on national television. There was also the factor that we continued to run in contested states and were concerned about Jackson.

Howard Fineman: Which state do you think Jackson would have won?

Susan Estrich: I didn't think he was going to win. They may have thought they were going to win. But there had been a tradition in the Democratic party of rejecting its nominee-apparent in one of the concluding primaries. And there was pressure on us to continue to make a strong showing in Florida, in California, in Oregon, in New Jersey. We took that very seriously. The governor took it very seriously.

Howard Fineman: You genuinely thought Jackson could embarrass you in one of those places?

Susan Estrich: We wanted to be sure he didn't. There was some concern about California. We had to make sure that we weren't embarrassed and that we didn't come into our convention (a) any more hobbled than we needed to be or (b) in a position where we gave Jackson any more bargaining power over us than he needed to have. So those were considerations as well.

We were out there in a mad skirmish for delegates. You in the press may have said, "Oh, they've got it wrapped up," but we weren't sitting on the required number of delegates until June 9. We were playing the super delegate process, which also was time-consuming. It may be a foregone conclusion, but it takes one hell of a lot of time. We were back in states we had won in February doing the follow-up and dealing with the Simon delegates and dealing with the Gore delegates and putting together that nominating majority in a way that would not appear to be a stop-Jackson movement.

All of these things that look easy now in retrospect were enormously time-consuming. And the truth is that on June 9 we did have the delegates, and, you know, we moved from there.

Lee Atwater: Reflecting on the point made earler, one of the earlier strategy decisions that we made—when I say "we" it was myself and the vice president in a meeting in his office on December 19, 1984—was the absolute necessity of winning the nomination early and winning it clean. When Ed and I got our jobs in the 1984 campaign we met with Dick Cheney for breakfast at the White House. I asked him, "What was the single biggest problem you had in the Ford campaign?" He said, "The biggest problem was you," pointing to Ed and me, meaning the Reagan challenge. About a week later I was sitting by Jody Powell at one of these fancy dinners, and I said, "Jody, what was the biggest problem you had when you look back on why you lost this thing?" He said, "Because of the Kennedy challenge."

The point is that if you're the incumbent, which George Bush would have been viewed as, and you are being challenged inside your party by the major player in the other wing of the party, what is happening to you every Tuesday is that you are facing two challenges: (a) people saying that this guy is not capable of leading the country, and (b) people saying that not only is he not capable of leading the country, he's not capable of leading this party.

My feeling, and the vice president shared this with me, was, in effect, to create a situation where you could put the nomination away so early you wouldn't have that kind of problem inside the party. What I outlined very early was what I thought could be done with the Super Tuesday configuration, particularly if we were able to position South Carolina appropriately. You would then have a fully united party by the convention. So it wasn't just a lucky break that we had something. That was one of the single, original strategic concepts we had in operating the campaign.

Howard Fineman: Ron Brown, you've heard how the Jackson campaign's insistence on collecting as many delegates as you could up to the end complicated various people's tasks. You were certainly entitled to use the rules as you did. Did the Dukakis campaign ask Jackson—I wanted to ask Susan this also—to quit his campaign, to stop his campaign and come aboard? Were there those kind of discussions and when did they take place?

Susan, did you ask that?

Susan Estrich: Ron, I will be interested in your response. The first thing that Richard Hatcher said last night was that Jackson made a decision at the very beginning that he was going to continue in this campaign until the end. That was certainly the message that was communicated to me by Gerry Austin, who at that point was my counterpart in the campaign, and the message that Jackson communicated throughout. It was the lesson of 1984 and past experience. So it was, from my perspective, never an issue.

Howard Fineman: How could it have hurt to ask?

John Corrigan: I believe we asked.

Susan Estrich: I believe we asked.

John Corrigan: I was in a meeting with Ron when the chairman of the party asked. Ron said no. I believe we were later criticized for presuming to ask that Jackson would drop out in the interest of the party. But I don't remember the exact circumstances.

Ronald Brown: Let me respond in a couple of ways, because we do want to keep some historical accuracy here. I think the simple answer to the first question about the Dukakis campaign's attempting to reach out or its success in doing so was that it could have done a lot better. What we are hearing here is that there were a lot of good reasons why it didn't happen. I agree with them. There were a lot of good reasons why the campaign didn't reach out more effectively. I became more convinced of that as a problem when I got to the Dukakis campaign.

One of my assignments was to reach out to Democratic leaders. We were still dealing with members of Congress who weren't on board and were feeling excluded. We were dealing with former party chairmen who hadn't been involved. We were dealing with a lot of people who hadn't been involved. But we heard all the reasons, and there were some good reasons why that did not take place.

I mean, it was not that folks were sitting around on their hands doing nothing. They had other problems, some of which were caused by the fact that there was a contested contest right up through the convention. So I think to deny there was an outreach problem is just not correct. To say there were some very good reasons why it didn't take place as effectively or efficiently as it could have is also correct.

I think it was clear that Jesse Jackson was going to be a candidate all the way through. There were a whole set of dynamics that started right after the California primary. One of those dynamics was the whole talk about VP, and the stakes being increased on that and how you play in that. Frankly, it all started that weekend at the La Costa retreat when the press was focusing on that issue. Then the Dukakis campaign had to make a decision about how to deal with that issue and how to grope, work their way through that process. Paul was in charge of that.

Jack is correct in that there was a meeting I had with Susan, Jack, and Paul in Susan's office where a direct question was asked about Jackson dropping out. Susan's assessment of that is right. I don't think there was a remote possibility of that happening at that time. Jack is correct as far as my response was concerned. Knowing there wasn't a remote possibility, I said that wasn't going to happen.

Part of this was tied up in that whole super delegate thing. Here was a guy who did very well during the primaries and caucuses, won 13 states, finished first or second in 46 of the 54 contests, and he had virtually no super delegates. He won a lot of states, yet almost no super delegates from those states were for him. I think that he and others associated with the campaign felt particularly offended by this outcome. It was certainly something they were very concerned about.

If you talk about having some impact on American politics, playing some meaningful role, doesn't it matter that you won in South Carolina and Georgia or wherever and not one single senator or congressman, not one single governor from those states, was going to be for you at the national convention as a super delegate. So that was part of the drive as well. There was a feeling you've got to go out and talk to these guys and say, "Gee, what's the story here, fellows? Let's be fair." So there were a lot of considerations driving this process.

I am very sympathetic with the problems that the Dukakis campaign faced, but just because you say there were reasons for what happened doesn't mean some things didn't happen that shouldn't have happened and couldn't have been done better. They could have been done better.

Susan made a comment a little earlier, and I just have to respond—I don't want to, but I have to—about my own involvement in the Dukakis campaign and efforts to get me there that were widely reported. I have a little different recollection of what actually took place. The fact is that Susan did talk to me shortly after the convention, and at that time there was a perception that there was some hesitancy to have some of Jackson's people involved in the Dukakis campaign.

My position at that time was that I was not going to be involved until I made sure that the Jackson people for whom I was responsible were taken care of—meaning that they had some meaningful involvement. I did not think that the perception that the guy who had negotiated the agreement at the convention jumped up the day after the convention and took some high-level position in the Dukakis campaign when no other Jackson people had been included was a very good position to be in. And I said I was not prepared to do that until there was some meaningful involvement of Jackson people with the Dukakis campaign.

Susan also said to me at that time that she would like to have me involved by participating in some regular meetings in Washington with Ann Wexler and Dick Moe and others. For some reason that involvement never took place. It wasn't until sometime after Labor Day, when Sasso came back, that there was ever any discussion with me about coming to join the Dukakis campaign. That is what happened. Those are the facts.

When I was asked after Labor Day, I made preparations to go to Boston. I got there somewhere around the 20th of September. I don't mean to personalize this, but I don't want it left on the table that somehow Ron Brown was begged to come to the campaign and was too busy practicing law to join the campaign. That was not the case.

Howard Fineman: Do you have any reply?

Susan Estrich: I didn't mean to suggest that, Ron. I think we faced a problem, and Jack can talk about this as well. Some of the Jackson people we brought fairly easily into the state campaigns and state organizations. But there was some sensitivity in doing the kind of consolidation with blacks who had worked for us since the very beginning and felt a very strong interest—they had been there with Dukakis at a time when it was not popular in the black community to be with Dukakis. There was some sensitivity in terms of how you take this group, who had been with you from the beginning and felt it had an interest in going forward, and bring in a new group and where the marriage comes. That's always true as you go from a primary to a general. But I think there was particular sensitivity there.

Ron was in a somewhat different category, not simply because he had negotiated with us, but because he had a long-standing relationship with Dukakis, with me, and with others, which made it more sensitive for him until we could resolve some of our other people.

Howard Fineman: You both said the whole vice presidential selection process added cross-currents. I wanted to ask Paul if you or Dukakis ever considered telling Jackson, in effect, he would not be considered for the vice presidency.

Paul Brountas: We did not. We never told any other candidate who was being considered that he would not be considered or that he should be excluded from consideration. It would have been unfair to take one of eight or nine candidates and treat him differently.

Howard Fineman: Did anybody ever say, "Wait, let's just cut this off now so we are not spending the time from June 6th until the convention with Jesse Jackson out there running a vice presidential campaign"?

Paul Brountas: Again, we did not think that was prudent to do. And, in any event, I don't think it would have been effective, so why do it? It was pretty well known that in June and July Jesse Jackson was encouraging the prospects of becoming the Democratic vice presidential nominee. There was a very strong group within the Jackson organization that felt he was entitled to it. I don't know whether he believed initially he was entitled to it, but as we approached the convention we certainly believed that Jackson wanted the nomination. Ron can comment on that.

Marc Nuttle: There's an interesting epilogue to be stated here. That is, how the two major parties managed diverse groups in the 1988 election cycle. Bob Teeter presents a treatise in which he advocates that in 1972 the Republicans all looked alike, dressed alike, ate alike, and, in fact, were alike. From then to 1988 the party began to expand to other groups—evangelicals, economic conservatives, foreign policy libertarians. The GOP had to learn how to manage those different groups as one election unit.

George Will, in an article in *Newsweek*, described the Republican party as dispeptic, an ulcer condition from being too full. Well, we took our Maalox and the components of that were two things. One, the relationship between the people running the various committees and campaigns at the top was very solid. I was a field counselor for Reagan/Bush in 1984. I worked with Ed Rollins and Lee Atwater. They protected me against moderates within their own organization when they tried to purge me from campaign access. Frank Fahrenkopf gave all campaigns access to every tool and resource that the Republican National Committee had available. There was trust in regard to the various committees' motives. Before I made any tactical move that would in anyway embarrass the Republican National Committee, I would call in and allow for a quick committee opinion.

But, the second component is more fundamental, that is, the issues. There was very little disagreement among the candidates on the key issues. Presidential campaigns are candidate driven, event driven, or issues driven. Voters were motivated by issues in this cycle, particularly activists and conservative group voters.

The ease by which conservative organization groups were able to endorse George Bush is a credit to Roger Ailes and Lee Atwater and others who developed the Bush message, theme, and image. They understood what is important to the GOP base. In fact, right now the Republicans, in my opinion, are doing a better job of managing diverse groups than the Democrats, which is a major switch in 50 years of the American two-party system.

Howard Fineman: Since we have Lee Atwater around for only a few hours, I want to swing back over to the Bush campaign. You guys put together a very large opposition research organization very early on that, I think, was unprecedented in presidential campaigning.

That's my way, from an organizational point of view, of asking you about your basic attitude toward running for President, running George Bush for President and the famous "40 percent solution" you talked about in your unfinished thesis on "negative campaigning." Tell us what you thought about the campaign from back to front, even before you knew who the opponent was going to be. And am I correct in surmising that that the big opposition research staff you set up to find out everything you could about the others bespoke your basic plan for the campaign?

Lee Atwater: We had a little bit of an unusual organizational chart. The only group that I was very interested in having report to me—and they also reported to everybody else, but specifically to me—was opposition research. At the head of our operation research was someone who has been with me for many years—a guy named Jim Pinkerton. Pinkerton is a very, very bright person.

I'm a very simple person. It was clear to me—particularly in the spring when the one miscalculation we made was there was not going to an opponent left after Super Tuesday—that opposition research would be important. It was also clear to me that the

Dukakis campaign—and I never figured out whether it was the right decision or whether it was conscious or not—was going to try to, in effect, create an issueless campaign and use incompetence and all that sort of stuff.

So I brought Pinkerton in the first week in April and said, "Look I want you to get the nerd patrol." We had about 35 excellent nerds in the research division. And I told Pinkerton, "We need five or six issues, and we need them by the middle of May, because it's going to hit the fan by mid-May." What I thought would happen was that they would be getting easy wins every Tuesday and would be looking better.

Howard Fineman: Five or six issues," I assume, did not include restructuring the Third World debt.

Lee Atwater: Actually, I gave him a three-by-five card and I said, "You come back with this three-by-five card, but you can use both sides, and bring me the issues that we need in this campaign."

Howard Fineman: Are you being facetious?

Lee Atwater: I carried it around with me.

Howard Fineman: I saw the note card afterwards. I was just asking whether you ordered it put on that to begin with.

Lee Atwater: That's about all I can handle, Howard. So anyhow, I said, "You all get to it and see what you come up with." Now, by the way, opposition research is just one component of the campaign. They came back with enough data to fill up this room.

Frank Fahrenkopf: Let me stop Lee for a moment. We had over 125,000 quotes from 436 different sources on computer.

Howard Fineman: Just on Dukakis?

Frank Fahrenkopf: No. That was the total on the candidates.

Lee Atwater: But, anyway, they had enough information to fill this room. I said, "Look, I'm quickly being confused. You take about a week and come back in here." So he came back and, sure enough, he had found seven or eight issues. Some of them got famous; some of them didn't.

Howard Fineman: Are there any that we haven't heard about?

Lee Atwater: There was one talked about behind the scenes. It was never used in the campaign. We had to contain Roger on this one issue.

Roger Ailes: By air time, we went down two points. I said, "Now I've got something." (Laughter)

Howard Fineman: For the uninitiated who haven't been reading the various accounts, including the *Newsweek* special election issue, we're talking about some obscure laws on the Massachusetts books. Bestiality is what we're focusing on.

Lee Atwater: Basically, we had a tight set of issues that we felt were important. The other thing I told Pinkerton was "Here's a three-by-five card. What I would like to be able to do is get this three-by-five card, draw a little line in the middle of it, and put three things on top and three things on the bottom." That's basically the campaign plan. So I said, "We got to have two things. I want two three-by-five cards, one with the issues on it—opposition research issues, one small component—and the other, the three things on top of the line and three things on the bottom of the line." So that was done.

Now the next thing Bob Teeter did—and this will show you how our whole organization was integrated—was to put together a series of eight focus groups to test out quite a few things. One of the things we wanted to check was these issues. The first testing was Paramus, New Jersey. It was a very fortunate set of circumstances because, number one, we had a three-day strategy session after that already planned. We had a lot of time together and a lot of time with the vice president. And, number two, all of us went to the focus groups—Roger, myself, Nick Brady, Craig Fuller, and Bob Teeter.

People are laughing about the Paramus thing, but the fact of the matter is it was a very important evening to us because three facts came out of the focus groups. Number one, it was very clear to me that, despite what anybody said, the voters in this country were not particularly familiar with either candidate. It was almost startling how little they knew about either of the candidates. Number two, it was an issueless campaign. Voters were not focused on any one or two or three issues. The issues that were popping up were issues like drugs, moral-fabric-type issues.

Roger Ailes: Twenty minutes in, somebody mentioned something about the economy, but mostly it was values and what we were going to do about these kids on drugs and how we were going to deal with it. There was a lot on social fabric and very little on the economy.

Lee Atwater: The third point concerned the eight or nine comparative issues. The group, by the way, consisted of conservative Democrats who in 1984 supported Reagan but in 1988 were supporting Dukakis. The woman moderator was very good. After her 40-minute discussion on the issues in one of the groups we watched, 40 percent switched from Dukakis to Bush. In the other group, 60 percent switched. We had time to sit down over a three-day period and use those results, along with a lot of other things that were going on, to, in effect, fashion strategy.

Now let me say this. George Bush felt very strongly about a couple of these issues, particularly the pledge of allegiance. He jumped on the pledge of allegiance issue before anybody else in the campaign did. He felt very strongly about it. He believed that it was a legitimate difference between himself and Dukakis. I remember, Roger, and I'm sure you do, too. He was amazed. He just said, "This guy is just wrong on this."

He believed in basically all of these issues. What I was worried about, I think we were all worried about: It was obvious that the Dukakis campaign was going to try not to allow issues to drive the campaign, to try to make competence or some other obscure issue drive the campaign. If they were able to do that, they would have won.

Why? Two reasons. Number one, the swing vote in almost every state or certainly in enough states to get over 270 electoral votes was conservative, populist—to use the cliché, Reagan Democrats. And if they didn't see any differences or particular differences between the two candidates, guess what? They would have gone back and been Democrats again. They're always looking for an excuse to be, because they are Democrats. So if we were to allow the Dukakis campaign strategy to unfold and not get on these issues, they would have prevailed.

Second, I do believe in this whole notion of historical cycle. We have been in eight years. We had a Republican President for 2 four-year terms. They would say, "Look, there's not a lot of difference between these two candidates. It's time to give the other party and candidate a chance." We made a conscious decision. Our decision was to stay on issues—don't use red language, be factual, be truthful. If we did that, regardless of the cacophony that would come out of the other campaign and to a certain degree the media, the voters would not buy it.

And I remember making the statement that, "Look, the good news is that we do not think the other side will plug into this." They would not recognize that these were salient issues because, we believed, they didn't have populist people in the campaign—guys like Roger and me who went to Newbury College and all that. It would take them a long time to figure out what was going on, but that when they did it was going to hit the fan.

Roger Ailes: We also had the feeling that the candidate—Dukakis—would dig in and defend from a legal standpoint issues that the American people just had an instinctive feeling about, i.e., the pledge. His personality profile, which we took a look at, was of a guy who said, "I'm right, you're wrong, and here are the reasons" with no regard to how or why people responded emotionally to an issue. In other words, he may be right technically, but the American people react instinctively to issues like the flag, not technically.

William Carrick: One quick question: After the focus groups, what did you see as the principal issues?

Lee Atwater: Taxes, national defense. We all felt that national defense was really a sleeper issue. One of the things raised by the focus groups that wasn't one of the issues was the fact that since peace and prosperity weren't being discussed, our theory about the attention span of voters being very short this year was true. We were going to get an added boost after Labor Day, because peace and prosperity would become part of the thing.

The pledge of allegiance was in there. The death penalty was in there. The mandatory drug sentence was in there. The furlough issue was in there.

Roger Ailes: We tested with Boston Harbor.

Lee Atwater: I think those were the main ones we tested.

Howard Fineman: I wanted to quickly get a response of the nonpopulists.

Susan Estrich: I want to talk about one of the issues, and I want to focus a little bit while Lee is here because I think it's important. We can talk about the pledge and death penalty later, but I do want to talk about this furlough issue and Willie Horton in particular. Lee, I may not be a populist, by your definition—and I did go to Wellesley College—but I happen to have been a rape victim and taught about rape and wrote about rape. I saw that one coming right between the eyes. We tried to deal with it as an issue about crime. We tried to deal with it as an issue about furloughs.

But my own sense all along was that it wasn't ultimately about any of those things. We weren't going to deal with Willie Horton by emphasizing our crime record in Massachusetts, for goodness sakes, let alone the federal furlough policy or Ronald Reagan's furlough policy. All of that was fine and all of that we put out there.

But my sense—and I want to do this while you're here—is that it was very much an issue about race and racial fear. Whether it was so intended or not, the symbolism was very powerful. It was, at least to my viewing of it, very strong—look, you can't find a stronger metaphor, intended or not, for racial hatred in this country than a black man raping a white woman. And that's what the Willie Horton story was.

I talked to people afterward, men and women. Women said they couldn't help it, but it scared the living daylights out of them. We're talking about the association of Dukakis with rapists. Nobody likes to talk about race, so they just talked about rapists. But I would have to add that this is America, let's be honest, with black men who come in and rape and beat and stab white women. I talked to men who said they couldn't help it either, but when they saw the leaflets later and the ads and the like, they couldn't help but thinking about their wives and feeling scared and crazy.

And I think Dukakis very subtly, whether it was intentional or not, became associated in value terms. I mean, Democrats are vulnerable to being "soft" on crime. That's just part of what comes with the Democratic label. If you add into it that you're from Massachusetts and against the death penalty, the case is stronger still.

But it seemed to me that on furloughs we were dealing at a much deeper level of values of hatred, racial prejudice, of fear. Tubby Harrison, our pollster, tested it—I think, before Paramus, New Jersey. And we had that as a terrible vulnerability on our part. We put it on our polls, tested it five different ways, and there was nothing we could dream up or make up about George Bush that hurt him as much as furloughs. The various ways we asked the questions, both in focus groups and in polls, hurt us. So it wasn't surprising to us that you used it. We saw it there.

Maybe we didn't deal with it right. In hindsight I can think of all kinds of ways to respond that may have been better. But there are much larger issues than the tactical construction of your ads versus our ads, and of negative campaigns, and whether we should have fought back six consecutive days rather than switch subjects in midstream. I know I talked to Reverend Jackson about this. I know he spoke to the vice president about this.

There was certainly a perception, even among those of us who call Harvard home, that this was a very damaging and devastating attack, but an attack that went far beyond conventional terms of debate when you come back with your crime rate or come back with the federal furlough program or come back with Reagan's furlough program.

Lee Atwater: Good. I'm glad you brought this up while I'm here because we needed to get out in the open—the whole story about this issue.

When I first heard about this issue, I didn't know who Willie

Horton was. I didn't know what race he was. I was told a story about a guy—I didn't know the name—who had gone to a gas station. There was a 17-year old kid there who was trying to work his way through college. The guy stabbed this kid 24 times, cut his sexual organ off, stuck it in his mouth, cut his arms and legs off, and stuck the guy in a trash can. This guy was then thrown into jail and received a furlough under the Massachusetts furlough program, went out on furlough, and raped and brutalized a woman.

You know, it was sickening to me, but what was sickening was that it defied common sense. Let's think about it. Our specific quarrel with the furlough program was the specific situation in which murderers with no chance of parole got to be furloughed. That was the issue.

What bothered me about it—as a simple man and I really am and don't pretend to be more—is it defied common sense. Why would you let a guy like that, who had no chance of parole, out for a weekend with no supervision? Number one, Dukakis was against the death penalty. Why should the guy come back? What incentive did the guy have to come back? And, number two, what incentive did he have not to do what he did when he was on the furlough? Because if you don't have the death penalty, when you go back nothing worse can happen to you. That right there was what made the furlough issue click in my mind.

Howard Fineman: When did that come to your attention?

Lee Atwater: Well, the first time I heard about the furlough thing, I guess, was when Gore raised it in the primary. Pinkerton or one of his guys told me the story.

Howard Fineman: Was this before or after you sent Pinkerton to come back with this note card full of issues? Did you already have furlough on the card?

Lee Atwater: I think it was before that—when Gore raised the issue.

Frederick Martin: April 12th. It came to our attention, Lee, in what I took to be your campaign press organ, *The Washington Times*, which did a story about the furlough issue about a week or 10 days before or two weeks before. So I assumed this was well known to you.

Lee Atwater: No. The first time I became conscious of it was in April, in the Gore campaign. Our group didn't come back until sometime in May.

Howard Fineman: But you had already heard this story that made no common sense to you.

Lee Atwater: Yes. That was the first time I heard about it.

Finally, obviously, when it came to our attention that Willie Horton was black, we made a conscious decision—Roger was there at the meeting when I took the lead—not to use him in any of our paid advertising, on television or in brochures. We figured at the time that we would have to try to police other people. There were so many groups, just as there were all kinds of groups out of the Dukakis group. I still have all these posters of Bush with "Hitler for President" and Bush with a moustache. I never blamed you all for that because I know you didn't do it.

The second decision we made was that the day we found any kind of brochure or television ad from an independent committee, we would denounce it publicly right off the bat.

By the way, let me clear up one thing. One of these public committees said that the proof we "collaborated" with them, was the fact that they didn't get a letter from Baker until three weeks later. What they did get was—a very strong letter—from me one day later. They wanted to hear from Baker. So the only reason they heard from Baker three weeks later was because they didn't accept my letter, which had come three weeks before.

Robert Beckel: Was that the Americans for Bush crowd?

Lee Atwater: I can't remember. The point is that I personally mentioned Willie Horton's name one time in the entire campaign, and realized it was a mistake to do that.

John Corrigan: How often did George Bush mention it, just for the record?

Lee Atwater: It doesn't matter.

John Corrigan: I think your point is you dropped the Horton issue.

Lee Atwater: I was trying to make two points. Number one, I am a white southerner and anytime I said anything I was accused of being a racist. The only time I brought up the three-headed troika was in response to an interview with Willie Brown, in which Willie Brown was proudly crowing about their three-man ticket. I said, "I agree with Willie Brown." That was used against me as racism. So I personally stayed totally out of that issue for that reason.

But Willie Horton—there was nothing racial about Willie Horton. We resent the fact that it was used racially in the campaign because we certainly didn't, and we were very conscious about it. I think the furlough issue was a very important issue in this campaign. I think it was symbolic. I think it was a value issue, and we didn't back off at all from using that issue in the campaign. We are very sorry if anyone took it racially, because we had a concerted effort in our campaign to make sure that race was not used in any way, shape, or form in the development of this issue.

As a matter of fact—this has never been told before—when we first shot the furlough spot of the revolving door that we used on television, we used regular prisoners. Roger and I looked at it. It was a totally natural thing in the prison. Frankly, we worried there were too many blacks in the prison scene, so we made sure that on the retake there were but one or two.

Paul Brountas: Did you ever make the statement that is attributed to you, "By the time we're finished they're going to wonder whether Willie Horton is Dukakis's running mate"?

Lee Atwater: Yeah. I said I made one statement one time. I apologized for it publicly the next day. At the time there was nothing racial about it. I never even mentioned Willie Horton.

Let me tell you something else about Willie Horton. One thing I did every month in that campaign was to go to some out-of-the-way place with the family. I never told anybody who I was or what I did. We'd just sit around, listen to people, talk to people. We went up to Luray, Virginia, on the 4th of July weekend because I read they were going to have a convention of motorcycle drivers—middle-class motorcycle drivers.

We went to Brown's Chinese-American Restaurant, which is a great place in Luray, Virginia. In a booth behind us were two couples, a black couple and white couple who owned motorcycles, talking about the *Reader's Digest* which had just come out. The two women were talking, and it interested me because, obviously, we had a gender problem at the time. So I turned around and started talking to them about it. They got all upset about the thing.

Before it was all over, everybody in the restaurant was over there talking about the thing. The waitresses closed the restaurant, and we sat around talking about this whole furlough thing all night. I said to myself this issue has a real life, this issue counts to Americans.

I reported this to Teeter, and he said, "You know what's interesting? We just had a focus group in Alabama. A woman in the focus group started talking about the *Reader's Digest*. She almost had it memorized verbatim. And the whole focused group shifted." And let me tell you something. I couldn't back off. If people out in this country feel strongly about something like that, it's an issue. I don't give a damn what the echo chamber is saying. Every now and then, just for novelty, if nothing else, we ought to humor the voters. If they are really concerned about an issue, they think it's an issue, then by God it's an issue, and it ought to be treated as an issue. That's the way we felt about the furlough program.

Roger Ailes: I want to point out that the Bush campaign never used Willie Horton's picture in any paid advertising. At the same time we were being accused of racism, the Dukakis campaign produced an ad with an Hispanic on camera with a woman in a body bag, cutting to George Bush next, and implying somehow he had something to do with this woman's rape and murder. If it was not an issue, you folks certainly seemed to think it was an issue when it came to the Hispanic and the woman in the body bag.

John Corrigan: The point of running the ad about the federal furlough program was to essentially make the point that George Bush was being hypocritical for making the whole issue because there was a federal furlough program—for eight years—where a rapist had escaped and had murdered someone.

Susan Estrich: He was a drug trafficker.

John Corrigan: George Bush never said word one about it.

Roger Ailes: The difference is that in Massachusetts you don't have a death penalty.

John Corrigan: You said the Bush campaign never used Willie Horton's picture. Every piece of literature that we complained about in the course of the campaign came from a Republican state committee. It's my understanding, and I'd appreciate it if Mr. Fahrenkopf would clarify this, that all of the RNC executive directors, all of the state party executive directors, are on the RNC payroll. Is that correct?

Frank Fahrenkopf: Totally false. Absolutely false.

John Corrigan: There's no coordination between the state parties?

Frank Fahrenkopf: There's state coordination. We don't pay the executive directors' salaries. We have no control other than what we did, for example, in Illinois when this garbage piece appeared. As soon as that hit, we were on it quick. At both the campaign and the Republican National Committee, we got on Piper, one of the individuals out there, and we shut it down as quickly as we could.

Robert Beckel: For the record, they were using your money on that. Now that money went straight from the RNC to state parties.

Frank Fahrenkopf: That's what I'm saying. It stopped.

Lee Atwater: Look at it from a commonsense standpoint. We knew that stuff hurt us. We weren't trying to do that. The second we knew about it we shut it down.

Howard Fineman: You knew the potential of it, Frank and Lee. If you knew the potential, did anybody say, "Let us handle this, you stay away from it, state party and other people out there"?

Lee Atwater: Yes.

Howard Fineman: But at the same time you were quoted at one time down in Atlanta in June saying you were going to make a household name out of Willie Horton.

Lee Atwater: I said it once. I said I was sorry I said it and apologized for it. That's the only time I mentioned it.

Jack Corrigan: Was that at a meeting with state parties?

Lee Atwater: No. Again, there was no reference to what race he was or anything else. I don't think many people in that room knew what race he was at the time because the issue had just developed.

Paul Taylor: You knew you didn't have to talk. Given the state of racial fears in this country, all you had to do was put it out there. Surely, you had conversations at that time.

Roger Ailes: If the media thinks "wimp" is an issue, they certainly should have thought Willie Horton was an issue. So you were a part of this.

Susan Estrich: And they did, Roger. My point is that although you may not have mentioned Willie Horton by name in your furlough ad, George Bush mentioned his name regularly in his speeches.

Let me finish on just two points. Each time he did—or at least often when he did—it would lead to network stories. We would have a little network recap that would show a picture of Willie Horton and newspaper stories that would show a picture of Willie Horton. We both know—sometimes to our frustration, sometimes to our delight—that getting your candidate, if your candidate is willing, to say X will make it into the news cycle.

Roger Ailes: That's like talking about the Ayatollah.

Susan Estrich: This was not a debate, Roger and Lee, with all due respect about furlough policy. I mean, there are very few things I'm quite certain I can beat you on in a debate, but if you want to talk about the operation of the Massachusetts furlough program and whether, in fact, it was any different from the federal program and the other 26 state programs, the answer is no.

Roger Ailes: In one instance you're saying George Bush had nothing to do with the Reagan administration. On the other hand, you're saying I wouldn't trade arms with the Ayatollah. Which is it? I mean, did he?

Susan Estrich: I'll do arms to the Ayatollah in a minute. Let's stick with the furlough issue.

Lee Altwater: The American people do not think that it's racist to mention someone's name. That's why that charge never went anywhere. That is why *The Washington Post* and many other publications in most states wrote editorials saying it wasn't a racist campaign. The American people are very fair-minded. Again, I basically trust the American people as a group. They strongly rejected the notion of racism.

Let me tell you something. As a guy who has been in southern politics for 20 years, there's no question in my mind that Republicans, Democrats, blacks, and whites all reject racist politics. If there were any racist politics in this campaign, it would have backfired on us, on the party. That was a spurious charge, and the voters treated it as a spurious charge.

Roger Ailes: If Willie Horton were white, we would have used the furlough program.

Lee Atwater: We might have used pictures of him.

Susan Estrich: Let me respond to that. The point of our ad was very simple. Two sides can play this ugly game. You want to play to fear, you've got your ugly story of a black man raping a white woman. Well, we'll tell you an even uglier story. It happened to be an Hispanic man who left a woman to die, in front of her two small children. Yeah, two people can play this ugly game. We resisted, maybe to our ultimate detriment, playing the ugly game until late October. I mean, we resisted playing it. We resisted playing it because we felt wrongly, rightly—our candidate felt—that was not the tone he wanted to set.

The only purpose of that ad which ran for a week or so at the end was to show, "you want to play this game? You want to debate furloughs? Fine. You can come up with an ugly story on our side, we can come up with an ugly story on your side. What does it prove?" George Bush, we were making the point, is a hypocrite. There's been a federal program that is very, very similar to that Massachusetts program; this man happened to be a drug trafficker, but murderers were also furloughed for up to 30 days. And we hadn't heard one word from George Bush about the federal program. Not a criticism. Not a concern. Not a complaint. Not an expression.

The criticism we got was why didn't you do this in September.

Well, Mike Dukakis wanted to set a different kind of tone for his campaign.

Roger Ailes: I had 22 negative commercials against George Bush on my desk by then. The idea of setting a different tone is baloney.

Paul Brountas: The Dukakis campaign never prepared negative ads like those the Bush campaign prepared and ran. The Bush ads contained mistruths and lies. For example, the Horton ad said there were 268 escaped Massachusetts convicts who fled after parole, giving the impression they were all first-degree murderers. The Horton ad had to be the lowest kind of campaign ad that we have ever seen in presidential politics.

Roger Ailes: That had been scrubbed by five researchers, three lawyers, and nobody in the media could tell you that was really untrue.

Lee Atwater: Wait a minute. I want to respond to Susan because I hope everybody in this room clearly focused on what she just said, because it's the most amazing thing I think I ever heard. She just said three things. One, they did use something we didn't do: We never used Willie Horton, but they did use an Hispanic in their ad. Two, she clearly inferred that they realized consciously it was racism, but, three, it wasn't wrong because we had done it first and because we did it more than them. I can't believe it.

Susan Estrich: No, I did not.

Lee Atwater: Everybody just heard you say it.

Howard Fineman: Let's do this one person at a time.

Lee Atwater: I'm just saying everybody in this room just heard Susan say they used an ad with an Hispanic in it. She, in effect, said they knew what they were doing but it was not wrong because we had done it first. I think that right there makes this whole thing a moot issue. You did it, we did it, let's close this off.

Howard Fineman: Before you close it off, Paul wanted to say something.

Paul Brountas: Clearly, we used that ad to demonstrate what Governor Dukakis was saying for weeks about the Horton ad, that it was hypocritical and cynical and was using a terrible personal tragedy for political gain. And Vice President Bush never did denounce or disavow that ad, never responded to the criticism and continued to run the ad. He knew full well that similar ads were being run by private organizations with Willie Horton's picture and knew full well that those ads were damaging to us.

What we did was run our ad to show the hypocrisy and the cynicism of the Horton ad—to tell the public that there were federal parole programs and a California parole program, that there were 37 other programs that permitted parole of convicted felons, and this is what happened under one of those programs. That was the purpose of the ad, and that is what we intended to show.

Robert Beckel: I want to talk about a couple of things, factual things. I think it's important for the record. I think, Lee, you can understand, even though these guys weren't associated with you, but I would really recommend that somebody look at the Americans for Bush stuff and look at their contributors. They're your contributors, Frank, of the RNC, and, Ed, they contributed a lot of money to Reagan/Bush in 1980 and 1984.

I don't believe those guys conspired with you, but the money that went into that thing was substantial. Willie Horton's black face was on the air for 10 weeks. It was paid for by a committee called Americans for Bush, funded by not just right-wingers but by a lot of people who were contributing to the RNC and Ronald Reagan and George Bush for years. So you can assume when they look at this thing that some people will conclude there was a lot of Republican money behind this.

Roger Ailes: That's a lot different from saying the Bush campaign did it. Anyone in here can do it. This is America.

Robert Beckel: It wasn't just a bunch of leaflets.

John Corrigan: If we used that answer, you would accuse us of being legalistic and elitist.

Roger Ailes: We can't stop independent expenditures any more than you can. I hate them because they mess up your media plan.

Ronald Brown: Listen, we are all grown, sophisticated, fairly knowledgeable people who know the issues which polarize our fellow countrymen. It seems to me, particularly on the race issue, that we all have a very special responsibility. I think that's what Susan was trying to point out. I think that's what Beckel's last comments were addressed to.

About an hour or two ago I was talking about why Jesse Jackson wasn't really in the mix on some of these other issues. I said I thought the reason was that he had an overriding impediment, so he never had to deal with some other issues, and that overriding impediment was his race. Everybody around the table said I was right, that that was the overriding impediment. Now we get into talking about whether race is a factor. Lee is saying, well, we trust the will of the American people. I know I trust them, too, but there's a lot of racism out there. We know it, and we know the kind of divisions it caused in our society.

It just seems to me that it is clear, whether the Bush campaign did or didn't do it, the Republican National Committee or somebody didn't meet their responsibility in dealing with this issue. You knew what it was causing. You knew what was happening. Maybe you couldn't control everything, but nobody stepped up to the plate and said, "It's devisive, it's dangerous, it's wrong."

Roger Ailes: So you're saying that because he's black, we can't use the issue.

Ronald Brown: I didn't say that, but there were a lot of things going on.

Roger Ailes: Despite the fact he was a murderer and rapist, you're saying he should have been given special treatment because he was black.

Ronald Brown: I'm not saying anybody should have been given special treatment. What I'm saying is very clear.

Roger Ailes: Maybe he should have.

Ronald Brown: What I'm saying is there is a special responsibility we all have. I think somebody failed to step up and meet their responsibility on this issue.

Lee Atwater: Let me ask you a question, Ron. Do you agree with Susan's point that because we had done it, it was justified for them to use an Hispanic in an ad to teach us a lesson?

Ronald Brown: I didn't take that to be Susan's point.

Susan Estrich: That wasn't the point. Let me clarify. Perhaps, with all due respect, I didn't make myself clear enough for you.

Lee Atwater: I though it was very clear.

Susan Estrich: Well, let me clarify it because what you're saying is not a reflection of what I was intending to say or what I thought I said. In the interest of being absolutely clear let me say it one last time.

The purpose of our doing the final ad on furloughs was to make clear the hypocrisy of George Bush who had, as vice president of the United States, been in a position to act or to take steps or to speak out on a federal furlough program in which exactly the same thing as he was complaining about in Massachusetts was going on for six years.

I agree with Ron on this issue of intention. At some point it became clear what was going on here and no one did step up. And for 10 weeks we did see his picture on TV, and we saw state party after state party after state party using it.

I know how we used our money. We had substantial influence on what state parties did, Frank. We asked some people who had been thinking of forming independent parties not to in our case, so at least there was a power of persuasion.

After 10 weeks of the furlough ad we felt—some say the time was long overdue—it was time for us to call George Bush on his hypocrisy in attacking a program and an isolated incident in Massachusetts when there were exactly comparable isolated incidents at the federal level, as there were also in California. So we played an ad which did just that.

Lee Atwater: Why did you use an Hispanic in that ad?

John Corrigan: That was the case.

Lee Atwater: That's the exact answer we have. Why is it different?

Susan Estrich: The difference is that in August we did not go out and say that that's an issue we can use against George Bush to play on values, et cetera. Let's find ourselves an isolated incident to use on the offense against George Bush.

Lee Atwater: The second question is what state did you use that ad in? What state did you show it?

Susan Estrich: A number of states.

John Corrigan: Not Texas.

Lee Atwater: Does anybody here know anything about Texas politics? And you use an Hispanic in an ad like that?

Susan Estrich: We did not use his name. We did not use the ad in Texas.

John Corrigan: We never used the person's name. We used his picture.

Lee Atwater: What state?

Jack Corrigan: We ran it in California. We ran it in every state where you ran the furlough ad. We did not run it in Texas.

Roger Ailes: You already lost Texas. That's why.

Howard Fineman: I have some other people impatiently waiting to ask questions. I think Fred Martin was one and then E.J. and Susan.

Frederick Martin: Roger said something that I think is important. Al Gore raised the furlough issue, not knowing there was a Willie Horton, not knowing there was a race issue involved, because we believed that the furlough issue had some merit and ought to be debated. We raised it without any imputation of race. I do reject the notion, at least as it applies to the Gore campaign, that we were subtly trying to raise a race issue by raising the furlough program.

William Lacy: Let me bring up something. Susan, you talked about how you tested your research on the furlough program and how devastating it was every time you tested it. I didn't see your research, but the first survey we did in California when I arrived on the scene tested the furlough issue and had nothing to do with Willie Horton by name or his race. It simply asked if people would be more or less likely to vote for Michael Dukakis if they knew that he had approved or had supported a program that allowed murderers— convicted murderers—out on weekend passes.

I have seen hundreds of polls in my career, and I have never seen an issue cut against a candidate like that. It had nothing to do in that polling with any of those other factors. It was a powerful issue in and of itself.

E. J. Dionne: One observation and two commonsense questions. The quick observation is I don't think we are debating whether furloughs were a legitimate issue. I think we are debating something else. Two commonsense questions are: If you cared so much about not using Willie Horton's face, then why didn't you tell your state parties ahead of time before they used his face not to use it? The second question: I have heard recently that there was a second case similar to the Horton case, where the facts were more devastating to Governor Dukakis—where somebody was pardoned and then murdered someone. You never used that case, and it appears that the guy is white. First, why didn't you tell the state parties not to use his face, and is the second thing true?

Lee Atwater: We did repeatedly, through our field organization and people in this room, particularly Ed and Bill and Marc. We did it very early.

Howard Fineman: Is this before or after you said you were going to make a household name of Willie Horton?

Lee Atwater: Right after. Because I saw the fact that it was being used as a racial situation which was not my intention. We made it so that we ought to just cool it on Willie Horton at that point.

E.J. Dionne: Have the state parties ever so massively disobeyed your orders?

Roger Ailes: I have been in this business for 20 years. You've got guys out there printing it. You can't control it.

Lee Atwater: I don't think anyone I talked to in any one of our meetings knew it, because when I talked to them about it they stopped.

The second point, E.J., about what you just said. I learned about that case after the election. Frankly, had I known about it, we would have been smart to go with that and never mentioned Willie Horton. In other words, if the guy was white, there would have been zero question about our intent.

John Corrigan: Is there anybody here who worked for George Bush in 1980? If he felt so strongly, why didn't George Bush raise the issue against Ronald Reagan?

Roger Ailes: We didn't have the 35 nerds.

Edward Rollins: If you tried to raise the issue on Ronald Reagan, that he had furloughed a cop killer, the issue would not have worked. The reason the issue worked and worked so effectively was not because Willie Horton was black, not because of the severity of the crime. It reinforced the negative impression that people had about Dukakis, that he was a Massachusetts liberal who was against the death penalty and soft on crime. Willie Horton in many states in this country would not have been a problem because he would be executed for the initial crime, as he probably should have been.

Susan Casey: I wish we could take this just a little bit beyond whether we did or didn't have this intention, or whether we could or couldn't control the states, or whether we really meant to do this or not. What happened was, as you said, a very powerful match lit a fire that was very effective against Dukakis, but that fire spread much wider, which is what I think Ron was referring to. It lit the racial issue. That was very clearly what happened.

The question I think that we all ought to ask ourselves is, when that happened, was there some special responsibility to step back and say this is not something that is good for our country and let's step back from this? You had many effective tools to beat Mike Dukakis. Let's step back from this because we do not want that devisiveness in this country.

Beyond what you intended, what you did, what you couldn't control, when it came to that point, then perhaps we all ought to examine, in terms of our roles—the press and candidates—whether you could have stepped back and maybe taken some responsibility for ending it.

Howard Fineman: I'm interested in what you thought when you heard about that issue, when you realized Willie Horton was black, when you saw the problems associated with it. Did you think that, even if you didn't use his picture in an ad, you were going to have to deal with politically inspired accusations of racism? Or were you concerned that it really would be, as Sue said, a match that would light off a conflagration? Or did you simply dismiss it as opposition criticism?

Lee Atwater: I don't know from what advantage she's looking, but if you examine George Bush sitting down with Jesse, I don't think we were in a racial strife. If you examine what is going on in this country, if you examine exit polls and everything else, I don't agree with her premise at all.

Susan Casey: It wasn't just looking at the data; I was just looking at what is going on in America.

Lee Atwater: I watch what is going on in America. I think we did a pretty good job of that in the campaign. I saw that group was politically trying to use that issue against us. I didn't think it had salience with black or white voters because I think they were more concerned with the furlough issue. I think that if we did any type of focus group or data today, my point would prevail over yours because I do not think there was an issue of racism, because there was no racism in the Bush campaign. I do not think that people thought that the use of the furlough program was an injection of racism in this campaign. I have yet to see any data anywhere, in any shape or form, to sustain that.

Roger Ailes: I think the American people are color-blind when it comes to crime.

Lee Atwater: I have never seen a poll yet in which blacks—and I have seen cut-outs on blacks—that the blacks did not agree with George Bush's position on the furlough issue.

Susan Estrich: The history of the administration of criminal justice in this country is a history of racism. We should be clear when it comes to crime that Americans are not color-blind. It's long been the case that blacks have paid much more severely. If you look at the crime for which Willie Horton was subsequently punished, it is a crime for which black men have been executed time and time and time again in this country and for which white men have almost never been executed.

Roger Ailes: Is your point it should not be because he's black?

Susan Estrich: My point is I think we are kidding ourselves. The question is what obligation a presidential campaign has when it flames such fires. But to pretend that America has somehow overnight become a color-blind society is ridiculous. I go back to Ron's point because it is so telling when we talk about Jesse Jackson. We immediately talk about the impact of race as the first, central, and most basic factor of his candidacy. Then we come to talk about criminal justice and you talk about it as if race is not a factor. It is.

Terry Michael: Did you have a white furloughed rapist option?

Lee Atwater: No. You have to understand when this issue was developed we didn't know Willie Horton was black.

Howard Fineman: Let's try to close this up now that everybody has accused everybody else of being a racist.

A couple of questions. Lee, when you got that original list with the furlough issue on it, is that something that you discussed with George Bush? Was there a discussion with George Bush about the possibly very controversial nature of this attack, especially on the furlough issue? I'm trying to get a sense of whether you knew how explosive it would be.

Lee Atwater: We didn't think it was controversial. We did discuss it. We went off to his home in Kennebunkport. We don't maintain it's non-controversial. It's controversial with the political component.

Howard Fineman: Susan, you said there were a lot of things you thought you could have done, perhaps, looking back on it now. One thing has been suggested, even by some of the Bush people in conversation here. Let me ask it in quick form. Was there a way for you to have changed the subject entirely, to have gone the hard populist route, gone some other attack route, rather than to respond by making an Hispanic ad? In retrospect, is that what you think you should have done?

Susan Estrich: It's a much larger question. The real question concerns their little three-by-five card of how they were going to run the campaign negatively against us—should we have adopted the same kind of approach? Not the same issues obviously. Our issues would be different against them, but it would be the same kind of negative campaign. We did the same polling and focus groups they did. We made a decision, however, to run a positive campaign on a different set of issues. That may have been a mistake, but our approach was not the same as theirs.

Howard Fineman: We have two more minutes here if anybody else wants to make a comment.

Roger Ailes: I think Lee left the impression we only were working off a negative theme. We weren't.

Lee Atwater: I said it was a very small part of the campaign.

Roger Ailes: The fact that you didn't focus your ads, limit them, and run the hell out of them, is different from the idea that you didn't have them and wanted to run a positive campaign.

Howard Fineman: One last comment from Dave Gergen.

David Gergen: Is it the view of the Dukakis campaign that the Bush campaign should not have raised a question about furloughs at all because Willie Horton was black?

Susan Estrich: No. My position, I suppose, is twofold. First of all, that whether intended or not, the furlough issue played to, ignited, stimulated, and was effective in part because it underlined racial tensions. And I'm sorry, Roger, "whether intended or not" is a phrase I think I have used each time I have said this because I don't know if you sat down and planned it. I have no idea. But whether intended or not, personalizing it in terms of the Willie Horton story did ignite that kind of a flame.

Would being soft on crime be an issue for Mike Dukakis? Absolutely. Was it a more telling issue and more troublesome issue to respond to because it was personalized in this story? In my judgment, it was. And so the second question on the table is: Did that impose an obligation on the Bush campaign to somehow handle it differently, deal with it differently, make sure in this case, unlike others, your state directors didn't disobey you because it was so important?

I never heard George Bush call for the Americans for Bush ad [on Willie Horton] to be taken off the air. You and I do know it wasn't technically a Bush ad, but looked a lot like a Bush campaign statement. Should he have stood up and said, "I want to take the ad off the air because it personifies this in a racial way"? Maybe.

Chapter 4

THE MESSAGE: ADVERTISING, SOUND BITES, AND REPORTING POLLS

Introduction by Judy Woodruff and Edward Fouhy

Since the 1950s, television has grown into an increasingly critical player in presidential campaigns, to the degree that now it is the means by which a majority of voters receive their information about the campaign. But television in both of the forms that impact on a national political campaign—local and network news reporting and paid commercials—became a significant player at a surprisingly early stage in 1988. Starting in January, long before the first caucus-goer in Iowa had registered his preference, George Bush made a combative appearance on the "CBS Evening News" that began to dispel the "wimp" image some had labeled him with. A few weeks later in New Hampshire, a Bush television commercial critical of Senator Robert Dole's stand on taxes became an important factor in Bush's victory in that state's primary.

In the Democratic primaries, another commercial focusing on the alleged flip-flops in policy positions taken by Representative Richard Gephardt badly hurt his effort, which had, ironically, been helped earlier by a TV ad featuring a mythical $40,000 Hyundai.

Even before the paid commercials and news coverage became factors, many of the candidates had their staffs do extensive polling and conduct discussions among so-called "focus groups," preselected small groups of voters interrogated at length on their attitudes toward the candidates and issues. One manager acknowledged that virtually nothing was said by his candidate until themes and positions had been tested with the voters: Almost nothing, he said, was done on the basis of the candidate's own ideas or feelings. Other managers acknowledged the same, suggesting their messages had been derived carefully based on what would play well with the voters. A few insisted they had not done this; in fact, the representative of the Senator Paul Simon campaign said if it had been done, Simon might not have run in the first place.

The 1988 campaign had been termed the most negative and issue-poor ever by many observers, long before the managers gathered in Cambridge. The advertising strategies of the two candidates were dissected and scrutinized throughout the fall campaign, and particularly in the final weeks—some said at the expense of news coverage of the issues. News organizations assigned reporters to do nothing but cover the development and production of television commercials, and some of the managers felt this enhanced their impact to an inappropriate degree. In addition, the words "handlers" and "sound bites" entered the lexicon of the public, not just the political insiders, thanks to an unprecedented amount of reporting—both print and broadcast—on the process of the campaign, as opposed to what the candidates were saying. Handlers even became the theme of one of the Dukakis campaign's most controversial television commercials.

The campaign managers differed sharply in their views of the impact of their own advertising and that of their opponents in the general election campaign. There is a spirited difference of opinion between the Republicans and Democrats, especially the Bush and Dukakis managers, about the frequency, accuracy, and subtext of the negative ads. What they did agree on is that both George Bush and Michael Dukakis started their fall campaigns largely unknown to the voters. Their polling turned up a remarkably blurry public vision of the two men, and a deeply rooted reluctance on the part of the voters—early on, at least—even to focus on the campaign.

The Bush forces made a decision in late spring, following sessions with focus groups, to stress elements in his record which they felt would undermine public confidence in Dukakis's record as governor on such matters as prison furloughs and the condition of the Boston Harbor. But it wasn't until after the personal ridicule of Bush by speakers at the Democratic National Convention that the gloves came off and the more negative campaign began. It was a highly successful campaign, and the lesson from it, according to former Reagan campaign manager, Ed Rollins, is that "tough, hardhitting, negative commercials" are here to stay in presidential campaigns. Rollins said, in his opinion, no matter which side fires the first volley, the other side must fire back immediately or risk serious, even fatal damage. And this applies, not just to paid commercials, but to comments by the candidate and his surrogates and staff that will appear in news coverage.

As for the news media, the managers (Roger Ailes, in particular) differed in their views of its role in the general election campaign. But they generally agreed that in order to meet the demands of the daily news cycles, there must be a theme of the day—every day: something fresh and new, or sharply pointed, that will catch the attention of newspaper editors and reporters, and television news producers and correspondents and their vast audiences. Some observed that the appetite for news has grown so, and the news cycles have accelerated, perhaps with so many different news outlets, that stories had a much shorter shelf life than in any previous campaign.

Some managers observed that news reporting of the campaign is the major factor in shaping public opinion, insisting that paid advertising merely provides a sort of background music for the war of images and sound bites waged on TV news programs. The major dissenter from this view was Rollins, who said the Bush television commercials made paid media really matter for the first time in a presidential election.

Most of the participants, as well as observers not attending the conference, have criticized the news coverage of the campaign in 1988 for not stressing sufficiently issues and the records of the candidates. Many outside observers have blamed the campaigns and the candidates for that; the managers here tended to put the blame on the media. It is probably accurate that because of the limited time and space the news media must live with, and with television's need for attractive visuals, a major casualty is context. If a candidate is doing well in the polls, the odds are that his coverage will be more favorable, no matter what he says. Moreover, the shrewd media manipulators realize that once a critical television news report is made—that is, taking a candidate to task for exaggeration of misrepresentation—it will probably never be repeated. Thus it is easy for the candidate to take one hit and then just keep coming back with more of the same that he got criticized for in the first place. George Bush's campaign mastered this technique in 1988.

Another problem with television news is its inability to say, "Sorry, folks, we have no news tonight. Candidate X only did photo opportunities, which have no bearing on the race." To the extent television feels it *must* report on a candidate, no matter how inconsequential his comments or actions, it will continue to be manipulated by shrewd politicians.

As for polling, it seemed to increase by exponential amounts in 1988. Whatever the total number of polls, they were an inescapable factor throughout both the primary and general election campaign. Virtually every national news organization published its own sampling of public opinion. During the primary period, a low standing for a candidate meant less news coverage. That in turn led to fewer campaign dollars, and even lower poll ratings, a vicious circle for the struggling candidates at the back of the pack. One poll, in particular, during the general election, was singled out for being overplayed: the ABC–*Washington Post* poll done on the eve of the second presidential debate.

The news media were, not surprisingly, on the receiving end of a lot of the criticism as the political professionals gathered. Journalists complain that when a politician wins an election, he says he did it on his own. When he loses, he blames the press. But it is the voters in both instances who have rendered the judgment, the news professionals say, not the press, which is just trying "to report the facts, ma'am." The political practitioners have something Roger Ailes of the Bush campaign called the "orchestra pit theory" to discredit the "just the facts" defense. Ailes reminded the group that if two candidates are on stage, and one says he has a solution to the Middle East crisis, and the other falls in the orchestra pit, the latter will be on the evening news.

Clearly, the flawed campaign of 1988 has brought the reformers out in full cry. They turn to the media as an easy target, to look for changes. Some suggest a ban on political advertising as a solution. Lifting equal time restrictions on broadcasters in return for regularly scheduled, prime-time hours for the candidates' free use appeals to others. An agreement between the candidates, long before the campaign begins, to debate a minimum of four times between Labor Day and election day and to hold open, televised press conferences once a week during the campaign period is a popular idea.

In defense of the media, it is fair to say that all aspects, including television, probably did a better job in 1988 than any previous election. But so did the campaigns do a better job of manipulating the media. So maybe there's a standoff. In any event, there are two groups that make a major miscalculation: those who say the media has no impact on the process, and those who claim it has a determinative impact. This election wasn't won by CBS or *The Washington Post;* it was won by George Bush. And it wasn't lost by NBC or *The Wall Street Journal;* it was lost by Michael Dukakis.

The Discussion

Edward Fouhy: We are going to be focusing on the paid and free TV aspects of the campaign, although we intend not to let the print press off the hook. A great deal has already been said about paid television, but it does leave us room to talk about some of the crucial primary and general election ads—"Dukakis in the Tank," "Dole and Tax Policy," and so on. We want to get you all to talk about why you bought the time, where you bought it, what strategies you had in mind as you made your ads and made your buys. We also want you to tell us how you framed your message so that it would get attention on the evening news and what was new in the way that you manipulated or tried to manipulate the press and television: what the effect was of the more so-called cost-effective ways the networks were covering the campaign, particularly the primary campaign; and, finally, what was the impact of the media's seeming obsession this year with polls and poll-driven reporting.

Judy Woodruff: We are going to do all that in 90 minutes. We want to split this up arbitrarily, into maybe 40 or 50 minutes worth of primaries, and the rest of the time on the general election.

I want to throw out, first of all, maybe what sounds like a fairly naive question. Earlier today, Lee Atwater was quite candid in saying that the Bush campaign did focus groups and polls to try to determine what was on the minds of the voters. The assumption was that what was on the minds of the voters would become the legitimate issues for the Bush campaign. My question is—again, we are focusing on the primary period, so all of you are involved in this—were there any campaigns that were so naive as to think, "We've got something we want to tell the American people about the way we think this country ought to go, and we are going to focus our campaign on that" and then proceed to make a series of statements or appeals based on that, rather than doing it the way the Bush campaign did: going out and polling and finding out what it is that people want to hear about and then talking about that?

Susan Casey: We were very naive, if that is the way we are going to judge things. Gary [Hart] felt that he had something to say, that he had something to offer, and that's what his campaign would be about. We did not have a pollster yet, though we were talking with some. We had not done focus groups. We, in fact, had battles among the staff. A couple of staff members were very much in favor of focus groups so that we could find the one or two things we should focus on. I shouldn't say battles. It sort of came up and was quickly dismissed.

But there were foreign policy issues and there were domestic issues. Those were the ones that needed to be laid out in a presidential race. There were at least one or two other candidates in the Democratic party running who had similar feelings. And we thought if we could—maybe it was naive or silly—change the political dimensions so that issues could matter in a presidential race, that's what we ought to try to do.

Judy Woodruff: Is that naive? Any other campaign want to confess that it was?

Frank Fahrenkopf: To be fair, Sue, Gary Hart had been a candidate in 1984, so he had been through the war, and Gary had some very specific ideas. I don't know the degree to which they changed after the 1984 campaign, but he had been out there. He had been with the people for a period of time during the 1984 campaign. It's a little different from someone jumping in who had not been involved.

Edward Fouhy: Jack Kemp certainly had a message.

Edward Rollins: I was about to say that in spite of what the polls and focus groups said, Jack Kemp obviously had a message. He was going to talk about goals in Iowa and everything else. Obviously, he convinced an awful lot of people.

On our side, being fair, there wasn't much of a differential among the candidates. All of the Republican candidates were pretty much on the same wavelength. They were all for SDI, for no tax increase, for tough law and order and tough on drugs. So we didn't need to spend a lot of money on polls or pollsters, but we all did.

Allan Hubbard: Du Pont did not. We did no polling and we actually did a focus group just to figure out exactly how to present the social security ideas.

William Lacy: We actually contemplated doing that in reverse order. Looking at all the surveys, we saw exactly what Ed saw—and what the Bush campaign and Roger saw—and came to the conclusion you had to look for a way to distinguish among the candidates. We saw Dole do that through the biography, through the leadership issue. But we also toyed with ideas, never really unveiled them, never really went with them—things such as calling for a constitutional convention for a balanced budget and others like that which would have been very novel.

Judy Woodruff: Why didn't you do that?

William Lacy: We didn't do it because we never came to the conclusion it would really benefit us.

Ronald Brown: I don't think anybody would use the term "naive" for Jesse Jackson, but from what I know of that stage of the campaign there were no focus groups, there were no polls. Part of the reason was the same situation as with Gary Hart. He had been out there and done it once before. But part of it was that he had his own focus group—that is, calling people at three and four o'clock in the morning and asking them what they thought. It seemed to work pretty well as far as developing a message that was clear and concise and understandable.

He had four years since 1984, three years before moving into the cycle, to feel the pulse. He was—at least from conversations I had with him at that time—absolutely committed to broadening his base and to appealing to a broader constituency than he had heretofore appealed to. That excited him and determined a lot of the focus of his outreach.

Terry Michael: We didn't have an exploratory phase of any sort. In fact, if the candidate had an exploratory phase and listened, he probably wouldn't have run. The whole rationale—the "not neo-anything, just a real Democrat" strategy—stemmed from Paul Simon's belief that there was a void out there on the issues he believed were important. I don't think it was naive to pursue those issues because, in fact, it was our political positioning strategy. Ours was a strategic decision to go with what he really believed in. That was our strategy, to present Paul Simon as a guy who was standing up for things he believed in and which our party believed in, wherein nobody else was doing well enough.

Roger Ailes: Let's face it, there are three things that the media are interested in: pictures, mistakes, and attacks. That's the one sure way of getting coverage. You try to avoid as many mistakes as you can. You try to give them as many pictures as you can. And if you need coverage, you attack, and you will get coverage.

It's my orchestra pit theory of politics. If you have two guys on stage and one guy says, "I have a solution to the Middle East problem," and the other guy falls in the orchestra pit, who do you think is going to be on the evening news? (Laughter)

One thing you don't want to do is get your head up too far on some new vision for America because the next thing that happens is the media runs over to the Republican side and says, "Tell me why you think this is an idiotic idea."

Judy Woodruff: So you're saying the notion of the candidate saying, "I want to run for President because I want to do something for this country," is crazy.

Roger Ailes: Suicide.

Frank Fahrenkopf: I want to say that our candidates—the seven Republicans—didn't really have to go out and do any polling. What I did—because I knew as party chairman I would be in the middle of seven people running around—was to start meetings in the late spring of 1987 with those individuals. I asked each candidate to designate someone. As you know, I polled monthly for the White House. I would share the polling data with the representatives from each campaign, and we met monthly to make sure that problems wouldn't develop. They had the opportunity to look at that data. Now if they wanted to take something they saw there and expand it by going out and doing their own, they could do it.

Jack Corrigan: I want to say that the cynicism in this discussion is getting way out of hand. Most of the Democratic candidates, certainly Michael Dukakis, held strong views and very firm convictions on what kind of country this ought to be.

Roger Ailes: Good jobs and good wages.

John Corrigan: Michael Dukakis took very specific positions on all of the issues. Your candidate had fundamentally flip-flopped on basic values, in particular on the abortion question and on what he once called "voodoo economics."

Roger Ailes: He flip-flopped years ago on that.

John Corrigan: On off-shore oil.

Roger Ailes: You guys did a little flip-flopping there on trade and some other issues. Dukakis changed his position dramatically on military weapons systems.

John Corrigan: That's not true. The positions, as you characterize them, are not correct.

Roger Ailes: What you're saying is your guy had a brilliant message envisioned in . . .

John Corrigan: What I'm saying is he ran on his values. He ran on a firm set of beliefs.

Roger Ailes: I don't believe that at all. He ran to the right. He ran as a moderate. He didn't run as a liberal.

John Corrigan: You can't imagine a different world view than your own.

Roger Ailes: Don't attack me personally. There's no need for that. The point is everybody felt that he was moving further to the right.

John Corrigan: We just listened to Lee Atwater talking about Paramus, New Jersey, focus groups. You discovered these issues, you took them to George Bush, then he found strong views on the subject. He didn't have a position on furloughs before you took a focus group on it. None of us believes that. He had a position on off-shore oil that flip-flopped 180 degrees after you polled in California. He flip-flopped on abortion inside of 12 hours.

Roger Ailes: You had a pollster in your race. You were running on purity?

John Corrigan: Sure we had a pollster.

Paul Brountas: You see, the important difference is what Lee Atwater said and did. He took the opposition research, then we went to Paramus, New Jersey, in May or thereabouts and he started devising a campaign which was essentially negative.

Roger Ailes: He never said that.

Paul Brountas: You asked the question whether people are naive enough to think they can run for President of the United States without going to focus groups. That probably is the wrong question.

Judy Woodruff: I meant without basing their campaign on what they find.

Paul Brountas: You do base the campaign on your findings, but if you have some values of your own and some standards and principals of your own, you use them and apply them even though they may not be derived from focus groups. It is also important to determine what positively impacts people, rather than what influences only negative reactions.

John Corrigan: We used focus groups and polls to gauge our political progress. We never used it to decide what Michael Dukakis was thinking.

Howard Fineman: When did you first start doing them? Did you ever do them before he announced?

John Corrigan: No. Iowa maybe.

Roger Ailes: You never tested your themes to see if they would work?

Susan Estrich: Yes.

Roger Ailes: That's all we did.

John Corrigan: Howard asked when. I said after he announced.

Judy Woodruff: Continuing in the primary period and looking just now for a moment at paid advertising, when and where did paid advertising, if anywhere, make a real difference for any of you in Iowa or New Hampshire?

Edward Rollins: One place: New Hampshire. Roger Ailes's straddle ad.

Judy Woodruff: Explain what you mean.

Edward Rollins: First of all, everybody in Iowa ran bio ads. They didn't really change the chemistry. The only ad that really made a difference in the primaries was a very effective commercial Roger put together. First, there was a pretty good commercial put together by the Dole people, the "no footprints" ad. And then the Bush campaign came back, reacted as quickly as they needed to, with what they called a straddle ad that basically depicted Bob Dole as someone who was straddling on the major issue that Republicans care about in New Hampshire, which is taxes.

Judy Woodruff: Was there any disagreement in the course of the campaign about that ad or was that just a natural thing to do?

Roger Ailes: We knew they had a footprint ad because it was out there floating around. We didn't know when or where they were going to spring it. We thought that Dole was most vulnerable on the position of straddling on issues. If you watch his language, he's very careful and very precise how he says things so that he can have it both ways. And there were two or three issues—I don't remember exactly what they were—where he did straddle. So we had the research done, and we had the capability of doing the ad overnight. When we decided that it was a dead even race in New Hampshire, we took it to the vice president. The first straddle ad we made was cut, not because it was inaccurate, but because the vice president thought it was unfair. I think there was a word he [Bush] didn't like. Then finally on Saturday morning, he said to go with it.

Judy Woodruff: What did you all do in reaction?

William Lacy: It was very difficult for us to react to the ad once it hit the air because it was hitting the air at a time when TV stations had supposedly closed down. I think what happened or didn't happen before that is much more important. I think that there are a couple of important points to make before going into that.

First, we knew something like that was coming or we should have known. We had done quite a bit of thinking about what the Bush campaign would do. I know Lee very well and had worked with him for quite some time. I knew the way that he would approach things and knew that at some point we were going to see that. I expected it in Iowa, but it came in New Hampshire, so we should have known it was coming.

Second, we were dealing with a problem that all campaigns have after a big win. We saw this massive shift in our tracking in New Hampshire. We saw it shift much more among character attributes and different personal dimensions than we did actually in the ballot. But with this great swing, our pollster was calling Dole "Mr. President." Bob Dole told me that himself.

I think the environment was bad for us at that point. We knew what we had to accomplish after Iowa. We had a very good week. Dole had a very good week on the stump in New Hampshire. We were taking advantage of our momentum and knew we had to do something to preempt Bush on taxes or on straddling because we knew something like that was going to come up. There was actually a spot done. There was actually an attempt made to do an even better one because the first attempt was shot on a bad day for doing shots and came out poorly.

Edward Fouhy: Did John Sununu really have the telephone number and home addresses of the television station general managers? Is that how he got that spot on the air?

Roger Ailes: No. What happened was that I knew they [Dole campaign] would not be able to react. By the time we got it sold to the vice president, which was Saturday morning, the station logs were closed. I was able to get it on a Boston station, and Lee and John Sununu personally went to Channel 9 in New Hampshire and got it in the rotation. So it aired on only two stations, one station in Boston and on Channel 9.

Edward Rollins: Equally important, as good as that commercial was, Pete Du Pont the next day in a debate shoved the [no tax increase] pledge in Bob Dole's face, and Bob Dole did not react to it effectively. That just reinforced once again the straddling. I was in the hospital for surgery while watching that. I thought Dole literally would not take the *no tax* pledge. I was amazed afterward when I found out that on Tuesday he had said he would take the pledge.

Judy Woodruff: What about on the Democratic side?

William Carrick: I think we started an ad campaign in Iowa the day after Christmas. Nobody else was on the air on either side. We basically started with a bio spot to tell people who Dick Gephardt was and what he had done, that he had been a leader in Congress and whatnot. We went from there to a 60-second spot which basically was the famous $40,000 Hyundai, which moved numbers. We started at 6 percent and in 10 days we were at 28 or 29. So it probably moved numbers faster than any other spot I know of, at least in the primary scene. We had some other spots that complemented it, but that was basically a very strong ad that crystallized Gephardt's message on trade and competitiveness. In a way, it was very understandable to the average Democratic caucus attender.

Edward Fouhy: The first ad that—I think Dan Payne produced it—seemed to have an effect in blunting the Hyundai ad was the flip-flop ad. Would you agree with that, Susan?

Susan Estrich: We had two negative ads. Both of them came well after New Hampshire. What you guys did to Bob Dole in New Hampshire, they did to us in South Dakota—which is to say, an ad appearing on a Saturday in a state where we lacked the ability to open up TV stations and make an instant response. And it cost us very dearly.

We showed Dukakis the ad afterward. Up until that point he had been resistant to negative advertising. But when he saw that ad he made the decision—we all made the decision—that he had to be ready should it show up again. So we produced two ads. Dan Payne produced the flip-flop ad and Ken Swope produced the PAC ad. We made the determination that if and when Gephardt went negative on us for Super Tuesday—and I think the ad we ultimately responded to was that little congressional ad of the guys on the steps attacking both Dukakis and Gore—we would respond with those two ads. They were quite effective.

In Iowa, I think Gephardt's was the only advertising that really made a difference. We had a problem in Iowa not so different from the problem we had in the general election—that for a variety of reasons, people perceived Michael Dukakis as somewhat like an ice man, as lacking in passion or caring about people like us. We tried to use his commitments on homelessness and Central America and the strong emotional feelings he had about those issues to address it. I think it helped a little, but nothing on the scale of Gephardt's.

William Carrick: I don't think the Dukakis ad did anything to blunt the Gephardt message on Hyundai. It basically raised questions about Gephardt.

Roger Ailes: In retrospect, the win in New Hampshire for Bush was big enough that the straddle ad may not have won it. He was campaigning much better that week. He did a half-hour program which was very good. He had a normal base of support in New Hampshire anyway. He basically said no new taxes, period. And Dole was, I think, sitting on his lead a little bit. By Friday afternoon his people had pretty well decided they had put it away and didn't work as hard over that weekend as they could have.

William Lacy: I think you're being modest. I think it was effective and hit us real hard. I think in retrospect, if we'd gotten an ad on the air over the last few days that would have preempted an attack on either straddling or taxes, we would have been in better shape.

Susan Casey: Can I ask a question on this? How much impact do you think the actual ad had versus the reporting on the national news about the new ad? My question throughout all of this was this: The Hyundai ad was a good ad, but maybe it was even better because it was on national news for a week. I think it was the reporting of the ad.

Roger Ailes: You get a 30 or 40 percent bump out of it by getting it on the news. You get more viewers, you get credibility, you get it in a framework. But even if the reporters trashed them, which they started doing toward the end, it is negative trashing.

Susan Casey: It starts to frame it somehow?

Roger Ailes: The ad still works. Consequently, I think, you get a big bump out of a very creative ad.

William Carrick: That was an almost unique phenomenon started in this campaign: Paid advertising as news and the unveiling of paid advertising started to drive the nightly news. Everybody's ads were being reported, particularly something new and different and unique.

Susan talked about the negative ads that were used on us—the PAC ads. That ended up not only being on the nightly news, it drove a lot of stories and it became a real instrument in driving the free media story for them against us negatively.

Edward Fouhy: But that is a legitimate story for the media. If you're spending 60 percent of your campaign budget on television ads, shouldn't they be reported on?

Roger Ailes: It might be better to put it in the news somewhere, like the weather, rather than make it the lead story in America tonight. I think you give more importance to it than it has and just makes you more a part of the process.

Judy Woodruff: Were there any other ads during the primary season that really made a difference—that were really pivotal in anybody's campaign—that you think were important for somebody else?

Marc Nuttle: There was one unique situation. There was a discussion earlier about having to get in the arena of credibility to be acceptable as a candidate. We weren't. All of our TV ads, many of our major expenditures in the fall of 1987, were a little different. We bought inserts in the Sunday newspapers introducing Pat, just like IGA sells groceries. These introductions were followed by 30-minute perspectives that aired in the appropriately targeted areas. Cable was also an important ingredient in reaching our targeted audience base and congressional districts.

It was interesting to note in our tracking that in Iowa, the only place where we made a break into the establishment Republican vote, we got a tremendous response from the full-page newspaper ad comparing Pat to John F. Kennedy. The religious comparison and issue ad that played well in Iowa did not necessarily play well in New Hampshire.

Edward Fouhy: Two items that I wanted to clean up before we leave the primaries. We talked a little bit about the Bush-Rather confrontation this morning. Do you want to tell us who your source was at CBS?

Roger Ailes: I want to protect my sources.

Edward Fouhy: The other, it seems to me, signal event in that period was Bob Dole's interview with NBC News' Tom Brokaw on the night of the New Hampshire primary. Did that have a negative impact?

Roger Ailes: I think it was "good night, Bob."

William Lacy: It was anyway. The bottom line in our assessment was that if we didn't win New Hampshire, there was really no way we could come out on top.

Judy Woodruff: That was the "quit lying about my record" comment made by Bob Dole.

William Lacy: Right. We were able to come out a week later and win Minnesota and South Dakota but the victories were totally ignored. Then we went South and got clobbered. So I don't think Dole's comment was pivotal in terms of the campaign. I think what was pivotal was the fact that George Bush beat us.

Linda Wertheimer: I wonder about the effectiveness of the sort of—I've never seen it done before—time-shifted commercials that Robertson ran in Iowa where everybody was getting audio and video cassettes in the mail.

Marc Nuttle: Well, it was all coordinated, paid advertising—the video and audio cassettes and direct mail. The video was partially made from out-takes of the perspective programs, the themes, the speeches, the words. The vocabulary was all carefully chosen so that when you got a piece in the mail, saw Pat on TV, read the insert, played the tape, it all fit.

Linda Wertheimer: Did that make any difference? That's a very novel kind of advertising to do.

Marc Nuttle: We came in first or second in the first seven primaries. That is the base procedure that we set throughout the South, throughout those early states. You bet it made a difference. It dropped the negatives from 50 or 55 percent to 32 percent, sometimes as low as 28 percent in some key spots—very manageable numbers. We could track the show and the receipt of the videos and tapes with the increase in our vote in Iowa.

The reason we didn't get a bump from the Iowa surprise showing to New Hampshire was there was no base in New Hampshire to attract. There was no constituency to go to, and it had never been there in the northeast corner as a region.

William Carrick: I learned one lesson early on—and I think this is particularly true in the Democratic side, maybe not so much on the Republican side: It was essential to lay a positive foundation for your candidacy before you did anything in advertising. You know, the basic bio ads were not exciting, didn't get on the nightly news, but they were extremely important to a virtually unknown candidate. We had good bio ads, and when we were able to use them early, they made a big difference.

In terms of Iowa, we were doing it the day after Christmas in places where we were able to lay an early foundation with the biographical ads. You could pivot on that and go to tough issue ads on trade or whatever else. I think the same thing was basically true with Dukakis, who had an excellent bio spot that laid a foundation.

Susan Estrich: We used our bio spot everywhere. Just a funny story: Our New York people said that under no circumstances did they want this bio spot. They wanted a special ad for New York and whatnot. So we put together a focus group and showed them all our spots and all of everybody's spots. The spot they liked best was the bio one because, I think, it conveyed information and because we were in a race, as Bill said, of unknowns, none of whom except for Gary had been around the track. We used that bio spot all the way through.

Judy Woodruff: You're talking about the key primaries?

Susan Estrich: Yes.

Terry Michael: We used it in New Hampshire in November. I think we were the only Democratic campaign other than Dukakis to buy any early New Hampshire time to develop a base. We think our bio spot there really helped us move to early development of a base in New Hampshire.

William Carrick: Our other point relates to Super Tuesday and our previous discussion. I think we ended up on Super Tuesday with basically a 96-hour campaign. There wasn't really any time to develop any large themes or anything. It was very, very tactical. I know we suffered from our inability to lay a positive foundation on Super Tuesday and then pivot off that. I think the Gore campaign and the Dukakis campaign had the same sort of problem. We were there one day and we were gone the next. My fundamental belief is that Super Tuesday very, very badly served the voters.

Judy Woodruff: Susan, you said you ran the bio ad in a lot of places. If that's the case, why then did the Bush campaign focus groups find so many voters who didn't have a sense of who Dukakis was?

Susan Estrich: It's a drop in the bucket, Judy. What did you spend, Roger? I don't have my numbers. You spent $5 million?

Roger Ailes: Five million. That's a drop in the bucket.

Susan Estrich: It's an absolute drop in the bucket in terms of providing information.

Judy Woodruff: You mean you were doing it, but you weren't reaching that many people?

Susan Estrich: The general election is a substantially different one in some of these states. What you're trying to do in the primary media buy is focus in on those people who are paying attention and provide them some information. To agree with Bill, many never became engaged in most Super Tuesday states because there were too many states and the candidate would zip from one state to another. You would lay in media in the hopes of raising your profile somewhat.

David Gergen: Before we leave the primaries, I wanted to return to an interesting comment by Lee Atwater. He said voters were so disinterested this year that essentially an event would have a political life of about 72 hours. So the momentum out of Iowa disappeared in 72 hours. That, of course, is in direct contradiction to the old conventional wisdom that your candidate should get a major lift out of winning a key early state like Iowa. Are we now into a new age?

Roger Ailes: I had a sense of acceleration this year. Maybe I'm getting older, but I had the sense that events were accelerating and things had a shorter life span. You had to come up with new stuff faster. Things were wearing out quicker and the news was losing interest in an event faster and looking for more things to happen.

Susan Estrich: We didn't find that in our campaign. (Laughter)

Roger Ailes: I'm sure it felt like a long time that week. But I did have a sense—I don't know whether anybody else did or whether it was just me—of acceleration.

David Gergen: So the effect of Dole's victory in Iowa began wearing off by that Friday?

Roger Ailes: It became a new soap opera. At that point you were reading everywhere the political obituary of George Bush, and then by Friday the question was, "Is he dead or isn't he dead?" So there's that kind of language.

John Corrigan: One other subject that I think is important is the competition between news organizations was such that the race to declare the winner was so intense, that a lot of momentum that some candidates might have gotten out of early victories, they got out of polls. It first happened with Simon when he went into the lead in the Iowa polls. He went up in New Hampshire in *The Boston Globe* poll. Dick Gephardt was predicted to win in Iowa. He got exposure on the national news for two weeks before Iowa and his victory became an afterthought.

William Carrick: There was a lot of coverage in the two weeks before Iowa that ended up being shown extensively in New Hampshire, particularly with a Massachusetts candidate on the Democratic side and the extensive Boston TV coverage. There was a tremendous news bounce from Iowa to New Hampshire. Any event that happened in Iowa got covered right here in Boston. So a lot of the momentum actually happened before the caucus night.

Edward Rollins: There's a special history on the Republican side, at least relative to the New Hampshire. Anyone who is running a campaign in New Hampshire on the Republican side has to run a campaign until Wednesday noon, the day after the election. There's a long history going back to 1976 with the Ford-Reagan battle. Reagan left four days early and basically lost his whole momentum. In 1980 George Bush had tremendous momentum coming out of Iowa. He went back to Houston to lie by the pool, and the last weekend is when he made it up. In 1984 Mondale left the state early, and Gary Hart basically moved forward.

In 1988 Bob Dole literally quit on Friday night. That was my impression. Dick Wirthlin told him he was 8 points up. And not only that, he got an endorsement from Al Haig that day. There was nothing else on the network news that night, and he went up 7 points. Al Haig never had more than 2 points during the entire time he was in New Hampshire, and how Dole went up 7 points is beyond me. But the bottom line is Dole quit campaigning for all practical purposes, and Bush accelerated right on through to election day. And I think that's what changed the momentum.

Frederick Martin: While it's true there was not much of a bounce coming out of Iowa and it didn't last as long as formerly, we also had a totally different calendar. A month elapsed from Iowa to the 8th of March. It's a very hard thing to try to sustain momentum for one month. Also, never before had 20 states voted on one day. There could be some voters in those states who had decided they were going to make a joint decision, or who at least felt part of a single process that was occurring on that same day.

It has been said here that the campaign for Super Tuesday only lasted two days. That's true for some campaigns. It certainly wasn't true for ours. For the month you were in Iowa and New Hampshire and South Dakota and elsewhere, we were in the South, and we felt very much engaged. We also steadily watched our numbers climb from the 8th of February to the 8th of March.

Judy Woodruff: One other thing before we go to the general. That is, the networks made a decision very early on, partly because there were so many candidates and partly for financial reasons, that they were not going to be able to put a correspondent, producer, or even a crew with many of the candidates who were running in the primaries. Can any of you talk about the effect that had or didn't have on the conduct of your campaign?

Terry Michael: We didn't really think in terms of network news for most of those months in the fall. That wasn't our target; CNN to some degree was, because they had the "Inside Politics" show every night. But there weren't any network crews in Iowa at that early stage. We didn't see much early network news coverage of this fairly equalized group of candidates. There was no big-foot front-runner there to cover, so there was no major personality to command airtime—and that's what the network news concentrates on, big personalities. I think that's the big difference between 1984 and 1988 in Iowa. In 1984 Iowa was selecting a competitor to the de facto nominee, Walter Mondale. In 1988, there's was not a probable nominee, just a whole group of smaller personalities—from the news perspective—competing with each other.

Daniel Mariaschin: Certainly for Du Pont and Haig, there were two front-runners out of six competitors who were receiving most of the attention: Bush and Dole. Then there was Pat Robertson, who for various reasons was of interest to the papers and the networks. Jack Kemp had his small share, very small share, of network time. For us it was really a matter of scratching for coverage. It hurt us badly in terms of establishing even a presence. I can't recall, but I don't think we had network TV with us more than five or six times during the course of our campaign. It was frustrating to say the least.

Judy Woodruff: Did it have an effect on anybody else?

Edward Rollins: Without reporters you had film crews and producers making judgments elsewhere. And you were very dependent on *The Washington Post, The New York Times,* or whatever to ask the questions, to follow the stories. I think the networks basically went more into the mode of just looking at the fancy pictures as opposed to really covering stories of the campaign. They did themselves a great injustice. Whether they did the campaigns a great injustice, I don't know.

John Corrigan: We made an assumption based on an article in *The Post* in December or January where Paul Taylor and David Broder said they were going to cover Jackson, they were going to cover Robertson, they were going to cover two other candidates in each party, that's the maximum. So we assumed they were going to be covering the winner of Iowa and New Hampshire.

Marc Nuttle: One thing we could do, in reference to issues and to receive press that would be beneficial to our campaign, was to speak with specificity on key issues to our base. We picked locations where we could draw cannon fire from liberal elements to show exactly where we stood on those key issues. A problem with that tactic is that it's really arduous to implement when half the American public can't spin the globe and put their finger on Canada. Under such circumstances, it's really hard to explain to that section of the public the difference between Galbraithian and Friedman economics. You play the hand you're dealt. As managers we have to do that.

Judy Woodruff: I want to move onto the general election. The Dukakis and the Bush campaigns had to change focus from running against candidates in their own party to running against the guy in the other party. Susan, Jack, anybody else who wants to jump in, how much of a problem was it for the Dukakis campaign to shift its message?

Susan Estrich: Let me try. I'm not sure I know. Obviously, you turn to George Bush, and there are real differences. We had, I think, a number of problems. And I was struck by a comment Lee made about how many times you have been around the track. Most people who have been successful in the general election have run for President before and have a base. It goes not only to the candidate's skill and the skill of his staff and his team—and, believe me, after you have been through it at top level, you learn a lot—but it also goes to your acceptability to the American people and to the imperatives of building a foundation for yourself. This was a known and considerable task that Michael Dukakis faced on June 8.

I think I alluded earlier to the fact that on June 8 we had our party's nomination. We had some politics left to do of a fairly substantial nature in preparation for the convention. We also had no foundation underneath us. We had a superficial sense of Michael Dukakis as a winner as a result of those consecutive Tuesday primary victories and a George Bush who disappeared off the scene. I think all of us recognized this could not endure. So our challenge was to create a foundation under Michael Dukakis.

Now I suppose there are two schools of thought. Bob Beckel and others were in meetings with me in June and July as we discussed this. One school of thought would see the problem as building the foundation under Michael Dukakis. I think I discussed earlier the three elements of that foundation from our perspective: Cares about people like you; making the case for change; and leadership character. The other way to approach it was to say that we were never going to build a full foundation under Michael Dukakis, but our approach would be to make sure that a superficially weakened George Bush never recovered. Or to quote Lee Atwater, "to keep beating." He used the analogy of sitting in your boat and keep beating the other guy before he gets into your boat.

There were many people inside the Democratic party who felt that the way for us to win was to keep Bush on the defensive the entire time—to try to find the equivalent of Lee's six issues and beat George Bush day in and day out for six months. We decided not to do that. Hindsight may be 20/20. Perhaps we should have. That doesn't mean we didn't run negative commercials along the way.

Edward Fouhy: Who is "we" in that decision?

Susan Estrich: I'm not going to do that. I view "we" as the Dukakis for President campaign with our candidate and our campaign.

Edward Fouhy: Is that one decision that is made in one room at one time?

Susan Estrich: No. It's a decision made over time but a decision that reflects the character and nature of both our candidate and our campaign. It's a decision that was made well before the convention and was remade over time. So our challenge was to come up with an affirmative strategy. I think I outlined the elements of that. But it was a matter of Michael Dukakis shifting in that positive way, understanding that along the way there would be negative ads back and forth, but that the essence of the strategy would be to attempt to make this case for change, to build on leadership and character and to make the case that Michael Dukakis cares about people like you.

Judy Woodruff: Is that what you think you went on to do?

Susan Estrich: We tried to do it. As I said last night, I think we did "cares about people like you" very effectively. I think, we didn't succeed in the argument for change, and character emerged as a very different issue than the one we had planned.

Roger Ailes: "Cares about people like you" from our standpoint looked like class warfare: "You were born rich, I wasn't, so, therefore, you should vote for me." That's what we thought you basically laid out at the convention. In other words, it's like punching somebody out and then saying, "Well, we don't want to fight." At the Democratic Convention you said, "Where was George?" That's footprinting. You made a joke of him personally. You said "silver foot in his mouth," "rich boy." You even said "wouldn't sell arms to the Ayatollah." That's where you laid out your negative theme.

What are we to think? Here they come, folks, with all their negatives, and they're coming down on us. And didn't they think we would figure that out and decide that the campaign was going to be in the negative?

Susan Estrich: First of all, it may be a distinction without a difference, but Michael Dukakis didn't do any of the things you just said.

Roger Ailes: Oh, he was surprised by all this stuff?

Susan Estrich: Ann Richards did them, Ted Kennedy did them, and others did them. Roger, I'm not sure—and I speak for myself on this—that the question of who started it is one that we sitting around this table should debate.

Roger Ailes: If you throw the first punch, the other guy is going to punch back.

John Corrigan: The difference between the two campaigns and the way we presented this issue—I alluded to it earlier—is between truth and fiction.

Mr. Ailes: Oh, come on.

John Corrigan: Hold on a second. The Saturday before the Republican Convention somebody brought up George Bush's war record. On the same day Michael Dukakis said that has no place in American politics.

Roger Ailes: I thought that was a good thing for him to say.

John Corrigan: Around the same time someone—a Republican senator—accused Kitty of burning the flag. George Bush still has not said word one about that.

Roger Ailes: Well, he has. He's disavowed that publicly on several stations, including the David Frost show. I know he disavowed it once publicly, and he was asked about it again and said, "I already disavowed it publicly."

John Corrigan: It had nothing to do with the coordination of the Pledge of Allegiance issue, right?

Roger Ailes: Absolutely not. But that's like saying, as you just told me, that you had no coordination with Teddy Kennedy saying "Where was George?"

Susan Estrich: I didn't say that.

Edward Fouhy: I think we covered this ground. I would like to move on.

Frank Fahrenkopf: I think something happened regarding advertising before we actually got into the fall campaign that was different this time. In early June I was on a long airplane ride to Tokyo. I had in my lap a brand new poll that had been done by Richard Wirthlin for the White House. That poll scared the hell out of me because it showed at that point in time a majority of the American people thought that Michael Dukakis and the Democrats could do a better job of keeping unemployment down, interest rates down; could do a better job in managing the economy; and "the gap" between women and men voters was something like 25 to 27 points. I had always felt that this whole gender issue was economically driven rather than by some social issues.

I came back from that trip and called Roger and Atwater. I said, "I'm going to do something that isn't usually done, but we are going to do it," meaning the national committee. That is, between the two conventions, we ran generic advertising very specifically targeted. I spent $4 million on two ads; one of a little girl with a coloring book; and a black and white one, which was a lot of fun, with the song "I Remember You." Our buys were very, very carefully pointed at our intended audience, and we ran those between the conventions.

Edward Fouhy: Who were you aiming them at?

Frank Fahrenkopf: We were aiming them primarily at women because we felt that was a problem area economically and also because there was a feeling out there that people had forgotten the comparative on the economy. That's also why every speaker the first two nights of our convention in New Orleans made a now and then comparison on the economy and on foreign policy and dealing with the Soviet Union. It was very carefully laid out.

That was something that had never been done before. But we were out there with a $4 million buy during that period of time. In fact, we did $13.5 million in generic advertising in this campaign. As far as my recollection, that's never been done before.

Edward Fouhy: Does anyone have a comparable figure for the Democrats?

Robert Beckel: It's never been done by the Democratic party.

Susan Estrich: We did a small amount.

Robert Beckel: Frank, you never took into account before you put those ads on that these guys [Bush campaign] were out of money and were not getting any airtime for the entire spring? They were getting killed in the polls and you're saying you put that $4 million up just because you were worried about the gender gap, not because you were worried about them sinking out of sight?

Frank Fahrenkopf: I wasn't just worried about the gender gap. I was worried about the whole perception of where we were in the economy.

Roger Ailes: Who was responsible? What we perceived to be a good economy, you guys perceived to be a bad economy because of the deficit. What he was worried about was our national issue. It's like taking the environment away from you guys. Taking the economy away from us was not something we wanted to have happen.

Susan Estrich: That's right. But you were going to get it back.

Edward Fouhy: During the period of July/August, you were on the air in the South and on the coast primarily, I think, with the harbor ad. When did you first go on the air with the harbor pollution ad?

Roger Ailes: The harbor ad came after we got hit on plant closings in Texas in August, I think.

Susan Estrich: My memory is you didn't have any money until after the convention. Then you were involved with Quayle for a good week to 10 days, and nobody was advertising. The only advertising I recall from the summer was the generic "tell them I remember" spots. We advertised in the summer and the Americans for Bush advertised in the summer. These guys didn't start until after Labor Day.

Edward Fouhy: Your first ads were on after Labor Day?

Roger Ailes:　I think so. We decided to take the bounce out of the convention. We may have done some specific state stuff, but I don't think so.

Edward Fouhy:　How long had your advertising group been together and what was the planning process during the summer?

Roger Ailes:　The planning process had me doing all the ads personally in the primary. I brought in one group from New York, which was a Madison Avenue team that had worked together in 1984. My theory of putting together the advertising team was not to look for the biggest names on Madison people but to find some creative people.

I had an original advertising meeting. I just started making phone calls, working on it for about a week. I found a black agency in San Francisco where a woman had done some pretty creative work, and I had some people submit some material to me. I found a very creative shop in Milwaukee and some guys in New York. But they were never the superstars. They were the people who I thought I could get the best work out of. I wanted to be able to get all the egos in one room when I needed to and keep the train on the track. So my theory was not to go for big names.

So when it was announced at that stage that they had a super cavalcade of stars on the other side, I got a lot of calls from people on our side saying, "Hey, can't you do better than that?" But I knew I had some creative people.

Judy Woodruff:　What kind of ads were you trying to make?

Roger Ailes:　We knew all along that our strategy was simply to define ourselves and define the other fellow. In our case we had to redefine ourselves, thanks to *Newsweek*.

Judy Woodruff:　After the convention you still had to redefine yourselves?

Roger Ailes:　We had to continue the redefinement. The convention certainly helped, but we had to stay on that track. What you do with advertising is you define yourself and you define your opponent. You can do that as a person or do it based on issues. Throughout the campaign the media was asking for a vision from somebody, anybody. They didn't care who. Am I right?

Frank Fahrenkopf:　You're right.

Roger Ailes:　And contrary to what my friend here says, I didn't know what the Dukakis vision was. I remember Kemp had one. Neither Dole nor Bush were terribly successful, quite honestly, with coming up with a national vision or cluster of issues that seemed to be something that would galvanize the country. We read that partially to mean that people weren't that unhappy. We did see that they wanted some change, but we read that to mean they wanted some change from Reagan, but they didn't want any radical change. We knew the definition of Dukakis would be to take change too far and risk the economic growth and recovery they had. We needed to re-create that. We needed to say Bush was going to continue the best and get rid of the rest of the Reagan policies.

So in terms of the advertising, going back to tactics, I started interviewing these people. And around convention time I put together six diverse advertising people—as I said, one from the Midwest, Jim Weller from California, another group from New York. I set up a fax machine in my office and gave everybody the number. I said, "Every time you have an idea, I can't get on the phone with you because I can't get my work done. So just feed in whatever you guys have. If it's about today or tomorrow, something you think we ought to be saying, if it's related to the news, ideas for a script, feed it to me." I would get the information a couple of times a day, work on ideas, and decide what spots needed to be done.

Edward Fouhy: Did the fact that the Olympics were going to be on a month late and that the writers' strike probably was going to cut the audience for the networks figure in your strategic time buy?

Roger Ailes: Yes, it did. I don't remember exactly how. (Laughter) All that sort of thing came into play as we negotiated for the debates—the Olympics, and the World Series, and all that. With regard to the buy itself, we were always trying to maximize our dollars because we decided we wanted to have plenty for the end. We wanted to keep a certain amount of contingency and we didn't want to have to go dark from Labor Day on at any time. Then we had to make a decision. We saw them going to the networks and starting to go spot buys. Then you announced an 18-state strategy. Lee made the decision to keep an air cover nationally that would hold our base in the South and other places and strategically buy key states we needed. We knew we would take Texas and Florida and hold the South. We knew we could go without New York and California.

Judy Woodruff: When are you talking about?

Roger Ailes: We had a must-win list, obviously, so we kept a certain amount of air cover on the network almost all the way and then targeted our key states: Michigan, Ohio, New Jersey, Illinois. We were actually prepared to pull all our advertising out of California at one point and write it off. We elected not to do that.

Susan Estrich: But you didn't tell Lacy this, right?

Roger Ailes: Once we sent Lacy to California, we didn't need to do that.

William Lacy: We had a unique situation in California with all the initiative advertising in 1988 where we probably had over $100 million spent on initiative advertising. That did figure with the way Roger bought the media in our state, in the sense that we made a fundamental decision to go on early and stay on all the time and spend some money early rather than concentrate everything very, very late. We felt we could run in the clear a little bit more early on, rather than get caught up in all the clutter.

Edward Fouhy: There was a story that you spent about $100,000 on CNN in the month of September and ran all of your ads on CNN primarily to reach the nation's newsrooms. Is that story correct?

Roger Ailes: Not quite that crystal clear. I'm not sure we ran all of our ads. We kept the bio ad. We kept positive ads on cable. We kept the positive presence on the air almost all the time, and we were using cable because the positive ads were better in the 60-second forum, which is where we would get a more cost-effective bio.

Judy Woodruff: What was your most frequently aired ad?

Roger Ailes: I don't know. I would say the workhorse for us was the actual original 60-second bio we did in the primary. We were still airing that in November in places. We had another 60-second ad with the kids. We had a 30-second family ad. We used the harbor ad a lot, maybe too much in some places. We ran the furlough ad, the revolving door ad, and the tank ad just a short period of time. But that was the workhorse cluster on the advertising. We then had tactical ads for states.

Judy Woodruff: What percentage of the ads would you say were negative and what percentage were positive?

Roger Ailes: I have no way of knowing, but we stayed positive more. We got all the publicity with the negative, but we ran more positive than negative. We got a lot more out of the news with the negative.

Edward Fouhy: Susan, can you do the same scenario with the Dukakis people?

Susan Estrich: We started in August with advertising. We did a convention/biospot because we made a decision that our lack of foundation—which I have referred to over and over—the lack of any information about Michael Dukakis, was really of deep concern to us. So we made the decision to start buying—we started in California and Texas—before the Republican Convention, and we did this basically with "the new era" spot. We had a 60-second version of it and a 30-second version of it.

We did not buy further in August, although we had considered it, because—and I'm sure we will talk more about this later—the selection of Dan Quayle and the controversy surrounding that and the press efforts and the like so dominated the news in the next 10 days to two weeks that it was our judgment that to spend money at that time was to waste money. The Quayle thing had to resolve itself. I think it resolved itself in a way that helped George Bush, but that is for later.

In August, well, who was in charge? We made a decision—I mentioned it earlier—while using some political talent to reach out to the commercial world. In August, Scott Miller and Gary Susnjara were in charge. In September when John [Sasso] came back—and he had an expertise in advertising—he reviewed the inventory.

We spent much of August not so differently from you—except, I think, ultimately to less success—coming up with scripts that were intended to do two things basically. The most important was to establish Michael Dukakis on these strategic themes, which I have mentioned. A good deal of time was spent on that. The second was to look at Bush vulnerabilities to see if we could come up with scripts on that. The third was to anticipate our vulnerabilities, particularly furloughs. We spent some time working on scripts to anticipate that.

From September on, David D'Allesandro of John Hancock was in charge.

Judy Woodruff: What happened when you started seeing the ads the Bush campaign was running?

Susan Estrich: This is post–Labor Day then.

Judy Woodruff: Let's move into that period. What happened when you saw the negative ads they were running, the furloughs, for example?

Roger Ailes: You made a decision to go to the handler ads at some point.

Susan Estrich: My sense is they had three very strong ads that were the workhorses for them: furloughs, Boston Harbor, and George Bush kissing his granddaughter. And George Bush kissing his granddaughter provided cover; I heard it was running at most 20 percent and the others 70 percent. I have no idea if that is correct.

Roger Ailes: Those changed by state and by week.

Susan Estrich: Yes, by state and by week. What that one did was soften him up enough and provide enough of a positive base that you could hammer us on furloughs and Boston Harbor. When we saw those ads, we decided our first response would be the handlers' ad. It's a very controversial ad, but a decision was made that we were seeing in our focus groups a reaction to the manipulation of this campaign, to the role of handlers.

I think it is certainly true that handlers received unprecedented coverage in this campaign. I think the fair way to describe it is that the packaging ads were intended as a soft anti-Bush approach to try to turn furloughs and turn the environment. One was done on furloughs. One was done on the environment.

At the same time or shortly thereafter, Judy, there was a concern that perhaps we needed something a little more straightforward and traditional in terms of political advertising, given the barrage of negatives. Another series of ads were made that were more straightforward and conventional.

Judy Woodruff: How long did it take you to turn around, to get your tougher ad on?

Edward Fouhy: And was your decision poll-driven, or was this a visceral feeling?

Susan Estrich: No, no, no. Nothing is visceral. Let's be honest. You make mistakes, but you research them carefully before you make them. (Laughter) Very little is done viscerally here. We polled. We had extensive focus groups. You know, you still can go wrong, but you don't go wrong for lack of trying—at least in the general election we were polling constantly. We were focus grouping their ads probably as much as they were.

The handler ads took a while to produce. The straightforward negatives were much quicker; maybe they looked different. A losing campaign always seems to have more ads running than a winning campaign. The answer is very simply that you're always trying to look for something that works maybe a little bit better and hoping to come up with something that is stronger. I think our most successful ads in responding to furloughs and ultimately to your tank ad came at the very end when we did that furlough spot, which we did very quickly. Bob Squier did it for us.

Judy Woodruff: Why did it take so long to come up with an effective response?

Susan Estrich: First of all, we did run a furlough spot much earlier than that, in Texas. I'll be honest. It had no impact whatsoever. We did not win the crime issue on account of it. I think part of what made the later furlough ad and the tank ad ultimately effective was not so much their contribution to a debate or defense but rather that they accomplished two other things at that point. One was "Fighting Mike." Mike Dukakis looked like he was fighting, and there had been a perception that he wasn't.

Second, fairly or unfairly, Roger—because I know you don't like this—but by that point George Bush had begun to pay the price of what was perceived as a negative campaign. By the third week of October our polls were showing by about 46/24 in terms of who was running a negative campaign—George Bush. So we had finally succeeded.

Roger Ailes: The media helped that a great deal.

Susan Estrich: It imposed the added price on him, and the ads were effective not on furloughs, but on flak.

John Corrigan: The ads that were most effective were basically ads that reinforced things that were fact-based or news-driven. The reason the furlough ad worked was because it was a very persuasive argument about furloughs. The handler ads changed that and erased it to some extent. They were less effective with voters than they were in turning the focus of the race back to credibility and back to a factual response to furloughs, a factual response to the harbor. They served a limited purpose in getting out. But after that the dynamics of the race changed somewhat—not enough obviously— back to a discussion of credibility, what people were saying.

Judy Woodruff: Do you agree with that, Roger?

Roger Ailes: Yes. I was hoping that you would keep running them all the way through. They were changing the dynamics so much.

Terry Michael: I want to ask a generic question of Roger about paid versus free media and their impact on this campaign. A lot of Democrats feel it was your negative ads that did us in. And I have a feeling that most political reporters have this almost radical infatuation with using paid media as an indicator of how skillfully a campaign is doing its job. What would you be willing to concede percentagewise—if you quantify it this way—delivery of the Willie Horton message by free media as opposed to by your ad?

Roger Ailes: First, we never did a Willie Horton ad. There was never a Willie Horton ad.

Terry Michael: Then the furlough ad.

Roger Ailes: Well, that's a separate issue.

Terry Michael: Did they need you in the campaign is what I'm asking?

Roger Ailes: I tried to convince them they did. (Laughter) I think that free media drives presidential campaigns much more than the paid media does. This year they may have had a little more impact because of the spectacular lack of knowledge of both candidates—even the vice president. After seven years as a vice president, he was very much unknown. Both candidates were very much unknown. So, therefore, paid media did tend to flush them out more than usual. However, I still think that the free media drives presidential campaigns.

Edward Fouhy: What are some of the free media stories you can say really had an impact, Susan or Roger, or both?

Susan Estrich: I can think of lots of them—for one, the mental health story—8 points right around there. George Bush was unknown but not in the same respect Michael Dukakis was unknown. I mean, George Bush was the incumbent vice president of the United States. However little people knew about him, he was, as Lee said earlier, within that zone of acceptability before he even began.

We were, I think, very badly hurt by a story that in part was triggered by the President's statement at his news conference: "I'm not going to comment on the health of an invalid." That had every local television show in American television news saying, "Dukakis not crazy. More at 11." What do you do with that?

Edward Fouhy: Any other story you can think of?

Roger Ailes: There was controversy about the vice president having a relationship which, apparently, caused the stock market crash. We just told people there was a fear he might not be President and the stock market went down. But there was about a four- to five-minute piece on CBS news that night in which they never called it the adultery question or anything else. They just wrote about the controversy surrounding the vice president, and by the end I was sure he was dying of cancer or had some terrible problem. They never said what it was, so you went away with a very sick feeling. It was a clear Dan Rather hit, but we took it and just said, "Hey, we know where they're coming from; let's try to recoup tomorrow."

Susan Estrich: Even our recovery at the end, when we came back very strongly, I would love to say was due to targeting our media to the states where we came back. But we were coming back in states we had pulled out of or suspended our operations in weeks and months before.

Roger Ailes: There were actually minuses for both candidates, for example, the Koppel interviews—remember the night
he [Bush] kept calling him "Dan."

Judy Woodruff: Aside from Roger getting a lot of credit for
his ads, he and the Bush campaign got a lot of credit for delivering
the sound bite of the day to the networks. How did you in the
Dukakis campaign approach that whole question? Did you realize
going into the general that you would have to have a message of the
day?

Susan Estrich: Of course.

Roger Ailes: Standard eight-second.

Edward Fouhy: But you have been doing that since 1968,
and the networks really haven't changed their method of coverage.

Roger Ailes: As we understand it, the sound bite went down
to eight seconds this year.

Edward Fouhy: But does it have any real impact?

Susan Estrich: We understood. You know, Roger might
have a better way with words than Kirk O'Donnell but I don't
know. I think Kirk O'Donnell has a pretty good way with words.
We understood that we had a job every morning to come up with a
sound bite for the night. I think here of your story earlier about the
guy who falls in the pit.

One of the realities of network coverage was basically there were
three ways to make the news, three sound bites you were looking
for: Either you attack your opponent or you respond to your opponent's attack, or you lay out a 19-point program on health care. You
can only do a 19-point program on health care so many nights. We
did a lot more of that, frankly, than you guys did—the bullets and
the points and the like. But you can't do it every night. So the
reality of the sound bite coverage was attack or respond to attack.
Michael Dukakis was not attacking every day. Maybe we were
wrong and he should have been.

Judy Woodruff: Let me interrupt you. You're agreeing with
Roger then that you can't talk about issues in the campaign.

Roger Ailes: Not for the evening news sound bites.

Susan Estrich: The only time we got coverage talking about
issues is when we had major policy proposals. And I don't mean a
paragraph in a speech. I mean, you know those blue and white
things, those of you who covered it, with the seven bullets. Those
things take a lot of time to work on. We felt very strongly about
them. The governor felt that a series of such specific proposals

would be an important cornerstone of his campaign. We did them once a week, but you can't do them seven nights.

Roger Ailes: We had hundreds of them, too. Nobody knows any of them. The Dukakis camp did a terrific job of getting their issues together. They had programs, but nobody knows anything about any of those things. You know, there's this sort of vision and there are themes, there are issues, there are slogans, there are sound bites. (Laughter)

Susan Estrich: There's a long trek from one to the next.

Judy Woodruff: I want to ask you what lesson you learned from that.

Edward Rollins: Four years ago we sat here and I made a statement, and there wasn't a political manager who sat around this table who argued with me. That was that it wouldn't have mattered one iota whether we spent one penny on paid television. The paid television in general elections really doesn't matter. It matters in Senate races. It matters in gubernatorial races. In this election, however, paid media mattered. Paid media became a very, very crucial part of this election cycle and changed the game forever in presidential politics.

Judy Woodruff: What part of the paid media?

Edward Rollins: The tough, hard-hitting comparative ads.

Judy Woodruff: The Bush ads? Is that what you mean?

Edward Rollins: The general election.

Edward Fouhy: Are we ever going to go back to a kinder, gentler television campaign?

Roger Ailes: Not if the television people have anything to do with it.

Judy Woodruff: Are we mixing apples with oranges?

Edward Rollins: What I'm saying to Bob, and he might disagree with me—as much money as we spent in 1984, nobody ever moved the entire course of the campaign. There's no presidential campaign in the age of television where one ad or a series of ads really made a difference. I mean, people will go back and argue that the Lyndon Johnson and the daisy plucker ad made a difference. The truth is that ad was run once on network television.

In this particular campaign Roger's ads worked just as Roger's ads worked in a Senate race or gubernatorial race. We have now come of age in presidential campaigns with tough, hard-hitting, negative commercials in the arena. They will be from here on.

Judy Woodruff: You're saying they were tougher and more negative than what they were in 1984?

Robert Beckel: Just one point on that. In 1984 combined we ran about 5 to 7 percent of our money combined on negative ads. That is a huge distinction from 1988, whether you want to call them comparative or negative or not. You ran one and we ran two.

Frank Fahrenkopf: But there's a difference. Most Americans knew who Ronald Reagan and Walter Mondale were. I think the important point here that Roger pointed out is that all of the way along there was a real question in the minds of the voters about who George Bush really was and what he stood for and who Mike Dukakis was and what he stood for. So there's a difference in the climate depending upon the stature of the two candidates and what the American people know of them.

Edward Rollins: That's true, but a threshold has been crossed, and we are never going back.

Larry Eichel: I'm not disagreeing that the paid media was important. But if you look back at the campaign, by Labor Day George Bush was 8 points ahead and had laid out his basic comparative case already with very little paid media. Certainly, the paid media reinforced that.

Edward Rollins: The difference was the holes he put in the side of Michael Dukakis at that particular time, when the polls were going back and forth. You began with a base. Both parties had a base of 41 or 42 percent—and George Bush being at 34 or Mike Dukakis at 55 is rubbish. The bottom line is they had a base of about 42. The bounce that keeps moving, that 18 points, is really which commercials move people one way or the other.

The truth of the matter is with the convention and the whole bit, Bush getting back on top or moving his campaign forward was a very important part of it. But the more important part of it was the damage Ailes did or George Bush did. Roger's efforts, the damage he did, basically ended this campaign about a month out, because no matter what Dukakis did, the negatives had been driven up so high that there was nothing he could do to convince a majority of that 18 points.

Judy Woodruff: A combination of paid ads and what Bush was saying on the stump, is that what you're saying? Or are you saying primarily the paid ads?

Edward Rollins: The ads led the way. The message on the stump reinforced what the ads did.

Judy Woodruff: Anybody disagree with that?

Roger Ailes: In the final analysis, the people vote for President for a couple of reasons. They vote for somebody they think is a strong leader. They vote for somebody they like better than the other person. There's a "like factor" in there. These are your sort of independent swing voters, I think. We know that it's comparison shopping when they go into the voting booth. We knew if they looked at it and said this fellow is a taxer and this fellow isn't, this fellow wants to give the death penalty to drug kingpins and this fellow doesn't, this fellow has experience in foreign policy and this fellow doesn't, this fellow's a little bit more likable than this fellow, then we probably would win the election. And that's how people think. We think, frankly—and anybody who knows George Bush knows it's true—there's a very much a kinder, gentler side of the guy. That kind of vision did catch on to some degree. We saw it in our tracking.

Judy Woodruff: Do you believe you could have won the election with fewer negative ads, less negative talk?

Roger Ailes: Yes. You see I always contended when I saw the Dan Quayle ad, when I saw the plant closings ad, when I saw the handler ads, when I saw some of their other negative ads—and I have a reel of 22 negative ads they produced against us—that how negative do you have to be? The fact is, is it quantity or quality? We had three you can remember: tank, revolving door, and the harbor. We ran the hell out of them. To my count I had 22 negative ads produced by the Dukakis campaign. They didn't quite have the same impact. Who was more negative is my question? The one who had 22 negative ads or the one who had 3 that worked?

William Carrick: In Atwater's absence, I think I'll defend or give due recognition to my fellow South Carolinian. The Bush campaign had the same fundamental strategic foundation of every campaign Lee Atwater has done since Lee and I first met each other 18 years ago. I mean, it's the same thesis, which is if you drive the other guy's negatives up high enough, he won't be a credible candidate and you can blow by him. It's the same thing he has done in race after race from his first encounters in county council races. It's a theory that he has developed to a science. It worked for the first time in a presidential campaign.

Judy Woodruff: You all in the Dukakis campaign should have expected that.

Susan Estrich: We did.

Roger Ailes: Let me go back to the Democratic Convention. I tell you this honestly. We assumed after the Democratic Convention, "Holy cow, these people are taking the gloves off and they're coming at us with everything they've got and what they've got is Iran-Contra, Noriega, drugs, incompetent, fool, rich." I mean, they were coming at us.

Edward Rollins: You had a great theme to run a campaign, whether you knew it or not.

Roger Ailes: My point is once you get punched, you punch back.

John Corrigan: On June 12 there was a press conference with all of the other Republican candidates. They spent all their time attacking Michael Dukakis. I think the focus group was at the end of May.

Roger Ailes: I'm not saying you started it. That isn't my point. I'm saying for four nights of network television we watched you guys attack, and we figured "Hey, they're attacking."

Edward Rollins: To be perfectly honest, I don't think Roger ever expected his ads to be as effective as they were. We always expected some response. It's like running off tackle. You put a game plan together, but you've got to run off tackle four or five times. If you do it the first four or five times and its works, why quit?

I think what happened here is that Roger's commercials worked so effectively and Dukakis never responded effectively to them. That's why they worked so well, so why stop them.

Edward Fouhy: On that note, let's move on to polling. It seems there's a perception that polls influenced or, perhaps, drove news coverage by newspaper and television more than ever before. On the night of October 12, the day before the UCLA debate, ABC ran a poll that indicated that George Bush was ahead in every state but the District of Columbia. Was that the only story that had an impact that was poll-driven? Were there other stories that had the same sort of impact? Bigger? Smaller?

Roger Ailes: Coming down the home stretch, I thought that the polls were closing. At one point the ABC poll showed Bush was actually getting a little bigger lead in the last 10 days, and yet the networks were all reporting the race was tightening. One night CBS had a graphic on the screen showing the margin widening. They reported—and I think you know this because Teeter called Dan Rather on the set—that the race was tightening. We thought that was a little bit of hype. But that was the only one I can think of.

Susan Estrich: I agree with Ed [Rollins]. Summer polls showed a wide fluctuation, and I think many of us recognized that none of it was very stable at that time. Yet they create dynamics of their own which can be damaging to a campaign. I think it was damaging to the Bush campaign for a while in July, when there was a perception he was way behind, and suddenly everybody was second-guessing everything he did. They obviously were damaging to us at various points, and I think the ABC poll was particularly irresponsible. That was a night before a major debate, at a time when the overall horse race, according to them, was at 5 points. They were on, I think, for five or ten minutes, and they had state after state wrong. Their methodology was off. They were calling states no matter how many people were in the sample.

Judy Woodruff: Does anybody want to respond? Dan.

Dan Balz, National Editor, The Washington Post: As everybody knows, we polled with ABC. It was a joint project. But we decided as we were going through the project that each news organization would interpret the poll on its own. So, essentially, once the results came back there was no real communication to figure out how we were interpreting. We knew they were doing it differently. We knew they would probably interpret it somewhat more aggressively.

We decided because of the sample size of the poll, in part because it was taken over a several week period, that it made more sense to use this as a base, but not to use it exclusively in doing the story. Paul [Taylor] wrote the story on it, and our interpretation of the poll was more conservative.

Edward Fouhy: Can you add anything to that?

Paul Taylor: No. I tell you there is institutional pressure. You spend a lot of money on polls. You get a set of numbers back. The numbers have a reality of their own—a reality that in this ambiguous world we live in can be a very comforting thing. For us, we had these numbers, but, frankly, for about half a dozen states we thought they may be fishy, and so we decided to put together a double map that showed, for those states, numbers different from our own. We used other polls and on-the-ground reporting instead.

Robert Beckel: ABC spent 15 minutes on that poll. You know that was wrong. That was, perhaps, the worst poll done in the history of American politics.

Paul Taylor: You can attack the poll on a methodological level. That's easy enough. But that poll, for all of its problems, even the way ABC presented it, reflected a fundamental reality of that race in mid-October. Even though the standard horse race polls being done tended to have Bush ahead by a range of 5 to 8 points, it was the sense of most of us in the political community that the race was not really as competitive if you looked at it through an electoral college analysis. Dukakis was not nearly as competitive. That poll was an effort to bring that analysis to bear. I think it was a legitimate form of journalism.

Edward Rollins: There were 100 national polls taken in 1984. There were 144 national polls taken this time, not counting all the local radio stations that did a nationwide sample of 200 persons and all the local newspapers that felt they had to have their own polls.

Terry Michael: Isn't that the real difference between 1984 and 1988, too? I don't remember all that much more reporting or percentages of numbers of polls by television in 1988 over 1984, but what stands out in my mind from the 1988 coverage is all that red on the map for Bush and that little bit of blue for Dukakis, representing a presumed electoral vote landslide. And isn't it that aspect of polling stories which uniquely impacted on the voters this time?

Judy Woodruff: Did the reporting of the polls have a material effect on anybody?

Terry Michael: The electoral college graphics had an effect.

David Gergen: But look at the way undecided Democratic voters broke in the last two weeks after that red and blue went up on the screen. Many broke for Dukakis, which suggests this analysis was wrong.

Comment from the Floor: In point of fact, Ailes seemed to think there was no move toward Dukakis.

Roger Ailes: There was. I'm simply saying that doesn't make up for the fact that you had a graphic showing it widening and it was closing.

Edward Rollins: Let's talk about what was left in the last couple of weeks of the campaign and the undecided voter. There were a lot of Democrats sitting up there, and that's really what was happening. I mean, our base was getting pretty solid. Republicans come home. Independents come home. The voters who were undecided were mostly Democratic voters, whether they were going to break for us or for you.

There's a certain psychological voter who wants to be with the winner. Whether that vote comes in the last three days or within the last month when they think it's over and start defending their position, the bottom line is you get a better closing. So a lot of your Democratic voters dropped in. But that doesn't mean there had been a 4- or 5-point differential that had already taken place.

Judy Woodruff: Your point is what? That people do pay attention to the poll results?

Edward Rollins: Sure.

Susan Estrich: Otherwise, we are all wasting a lot of time because Roger in his campaign and our campaign spent a lot of time, notwithstanding that we trust our own pollsters for the numbers, dealing with that ABC poll.

As for the electoral college—and I'll be brief—my own view was that had we been able to close up the 5 points in the gap, we would have won. If we couldn't, we would lose. A number of states would have come to us. What has it been, over 106 years, since the electoral college has decided an election? So the enormous prominence given at a time when the race was by ABC's own admission within 5 points, the suggestion it was somehow nonetheless over, was damaging to us.

Howard Fineman: Did you actually see any effect from that?

Susan Estrich: It's impossible to know because the debate was the next day, and after the debate we definitely went down.

Judy Woodruff: Dan can respond, and then we're going to have to stop.

Daniel Balz: People, news organizations, our own included, and the networks had been doing electoral college projections for this election from Labor Day on. Nearly all of them suggested that the electoral college lock for the Republicans was beginning to form again. Why was the night that ABC put their own poll on the air so much more devastating to you than all the others that were being done weekly or whatever?

Susan Estrich: Sheer weight of it. Fourteen minutes.

Paul Brountas: The timing of it. Apart from the methodology and whether there were mistakes in the methodology, you had the second presidential debate coming up in the next day or so. It had a significant impact on the second debate. It said to the voters that Dukakis had to hit two grand slam home runs in that debate in order to come out even. That's impossible.

Judy Woodruff: A lot of people were paying attention.

Comment from the Floor: I respect *The Post* a lot for being much more cautious. We actually did a poll on the effect of polls. We asked people two questions: Do polls affect a lot of people? and Do they affect you? It was something like 26 percent were sure they affected a lot of people, but only 2 percent admitted they they themselves were affected, and they were split on either Dukakis or Bush.

Judy Woodruff: I want to get this straight. Aside from this ABC/*Washington Post* poll, you're saying that the sort of drum-beat constant reporting of polls really didn't matter?

Susan Estrich: No.

John Corrigan: If someone goes back and does an analysis of the network news, you're going to find every network had a poll every week. Every network had an electoral college story every week. Usually they reported on each other's polls, if they were sufficiently dramatic. Basically that eats up the time and space on the evening news in a year when the sound bite dropped from 14 seconds to 9 seconds. It makes it much harder to get our message out.

Roger Ailes: We spent a lot of time saying how devastating the negative ads were. We did have two presidential debates. And there were three media events that may have affected the election: the Dan Rather issue, the primary debates, and the convention speeches. I think they all had a tremendous impact.

Judy Woodruff: Thank you all very much.

Chapter 5

MONEY AND THE CAMPAIGN

Introduction by Larry Eichel

Presidential elections in the United States are not cheap. According to Herbert Alexander of the University of Southern California, perhaps the nation's ranking expert on campaign finance, the final bill for the 1988 campaign amounted to nearly half a billion dollars.

By reason of sheer magnitude alone, money was a major factor in determining the outcome of the 1988 campaign. In the presidential saga, as in most political races, those candidates who did not pass a certain financial threshold never won the right to be taken seriously or decided not to run at all. And the candidates who had the most money—Michael Dukakis and George Bush in the nomination fights, Bush in the general election—turned out to be the winners.

This is not to say that money was the controlling factor—despite the staggering amount involved—or even the dominant factor. The outcome of the two nomination struggles cannot be explained simply by looking at financial bottom lines. Nor did Bush defeat Dukakis in the general election simply because the Republicans raised more money to supplement Bush's efforts than the Democrats did for Dukakis; in fact, the gap between the two parties' financial performances was far narrower in 1988 than in other recent elections.

But money matters. One Republican, Pat Robertson, could run because he had his own private fund-raising base, which he had developed during his career as a religious broadcaster. Another Republican, Paul Laxalt, withdrew when he found money less available than he had thought. And in both parties, during the long months before the nominations were locked up, the campaign managers operated with the knowledge that their political strategies, no matter how brilliantly conceived, would not work unless there was enough money for brilliant execution.

Such was the focus of the campaign managers' discussion on money: How financial concerns influenced strategy. Much of the discussion centered on the Democratic party, largely because there was more of a gap between the haves and the have-nots on the Democratic side and more of a correlation between money spent and votes won. In the first half of the primary season, when the Democratic field was large and the race relatively diffuse, the biggest spender turned out to be the winner in 14 states—New Hampshire, Minnesota, South Dakota, Washington, Maryland, Florida, Texas, Missouri, Tennessee, Arkansas, Oklahoma, Kentucky, North Carolina, and Nevada.

The Democratic primaries also provided the most obvious case of a candidate whose demise was hastened by money problems—Representative Richard A. Gephardt of Missouri. By late February, after victories in Iowa and South Dakota and a second place in New Hampshire, Gephardt was being touted as Dukakis's most serious rival for the nomination. The congressman from St. Louis had developed a hard-edged populist message and a top-flight campaign organization. And he seemed to have good prospects in the large midwestern industrial states that had yet to vote.

What he did not have was money. Without it, he could not get his television commercials on the air in sufficient numbers to make an impact. And so, as the pace of the fight quickened, Gephardt become all but invisible. In an instance the Gephardt campaign was all but over. With money, he could have been a contender; without it, he became a footnote. Months after he dropped out, Gephardt admitted that he had made a mistake. He was wrong, he said, to have spent over 100 days campaigning in Iowa. He should have spent those 100 days raising money.

The Democratic primary also provided the anomalous case of Jesse Jackson, whose performance had no connection whatsoever to the state of his campaign war chest. In fact, Jackson ran better when his campaign was proverty-stricken than when it enjoyed financial health.

The focus on the significance of money in the 1988 campaign began long before 1988 arrived. In 1987, the year before the voting, each candidate's ability to raise money became a key measure of his credibility and viability. This was particularly true for the Democrats. Unlike years past, they had no preliminary events—no straw polls at state party conventions—to test their respective strengths. With the contenders so little known, early public opinion polls were highly suspect. And the creation of Super Tuesday required candidates to seek votes in 20 states simultaneously.

All of which led many politicians and commentators alike to treat the candidates' financial reports to the Federal Election Commission as the single best indicator of candidate support. These reports, which showed just how effective each campaign was in raising and saving money, led a lot of members of the political community to take Michael Dukakis very seriously very early.

Their judgment was vindicated by the results. That is not to say that Dukakis won the nomination because he raised the most money. But money provided him a cushion to help him absorb the inevitable bumps along the way. And it gave his managers the precious ability to treat the campaign as a long-term project rather than a day-to-day exercise in survival. Dukakis's aides could open offices in key primary states and plan their purchases of television and radio time in advance—without fear that a single disappointing primary would plunge them into sudden austerity.

The basic rules governing the financial side of the 1988 presidential election were fairly simple, albeit not widely understood. In seeking the Democratic and Republican nominations, candidates operate under a system of partial federal financing, with the government matching all or part of the contributions candidates received. To qualify for matching funds, a candidate first had to collect at least $5,000 in relatively small contributions from each of 20 states. Having done that, he was entitled to receive a federal match for every contribution received, up to a maximum of $250 per contribution. In addition, he had to abide by various stipulations, the most significant being these: an overall spending ceiling of $27 million in seeking the nomination; specific restrictions on how much could be spent in any one state; and a $1,000 limit on what any individual could contribute.

As indicated in the discussion that follows, many campaign managers believe the $1,000 limit—set in 1974 and never adjusted for inflation—has become unrealistically low and could be doubled, tripled, or quadrupled without damaging the balance of fundraising power built into the system. In their view, the current system forces candidates to devote far too much time and effort to raising money, an activity many candidates find unpleasant and demeaning. Said Fred Martin, who managed the campaign of Democratic contender Senator Albert Gore, "We used to have a property qualification for voters in this country. We now have a property qualification for candidates. If you're not able to raise $20 million, you won't be the nominee."

The managers also have little use for the state-by-state restrictions, which came into play only in the Iowa caucuses and New Hampshire primaries. In Iowa and New Hampshire, the managers made a mockery of those restrictions. In Iowa, the first of the major contests, the spending limit for 1988 was $775,000. But the limit was full of loopholes. For example, if a campaign rented cars in Illinois, that didn't count against the Iowa spending lid. If campaign workers slept in South Dakota, their hotel bill didn't count. If commercials were bought on a Nebraska television station, much of that didn't count. If those commercials concluded with an explicit fund-raising pitch, they might not count at all. And if a candidate limited each Iowa visit to four days, none of his travel expenses counted.

Tim Ridley, who worked for Democratic Senator Joseph R. Biden, Jr., confessed that the Biden campaign would have spent more than $2 million in Iowa, had it not folded more than four months before caucus night. Other campaign managers said privately they actually had spent in the $2 million range. Some of the Republicans may have spent more.

Once a candidate gets nominated his life is supposed to get simpler. At least, that is the intent of the federal campaign finance law. In keeping with that statute, Dukakis and Bush each received checks for $46.1 million from the federal treasury following their nominations. By accepting those checks, they agreed to spend only those dollars on their campaigns. And yet, throughout the month of September both candidates appeared at fund-raising dinners night after night. For whom were they raising all this money? Themselves, more or less.

This money was dubbed "soft money" in the curious jargon of political fundraising. It was used to finance field operations around the country, operations which are technically separate from the presidential campaigns and which were supposed to work on behalf of the entire party ticket, not just Bush or Dukakis. Such activity was perfectly legal, permitted by the Federal Election Commission under the rubric of "party building." And each side had its own army of lawyers to make sure the activity stayed legal.

But these field organizations were very much part of the presidential campaigns. They were directed by individuals handpicked by the presidential campaign managers and were paid directly out of the national campaign headquarters. They operated out of the same offices. While there was nothing secret about them, they amounted to a shadow campaign, raising and spending money with few restrictions. About all they could not do was publish a brochure or produce a commercial proclaiming "Bush for President." They could, however, seek support for "George Bush and the Republican ticket."

The amount of soft money raised and spent was enormous. In 1988 the Republican National Committee raised nearly $97 million, while the Democrats raised $56 million. They did so without having to concern themselves with all of those regulations from the FEC. When it came to raising soft money, the rules did not apply.

The net impact of the influx of soft money was to undermine the public finance system imposed in 1974 after the Watergate scandal. Some campaign managers think that it is no big loss; they argue that the system deserves to be undermined. In their view, strategists had to find ways to raise the extra money because the amount the campaigns got from the federal government was not sufficient to run a national campaign. With candidates for senator or governor often spending $10 million or more in a single state, they ask how can someone run nationally for $46.1 million.

Reformers, though, look at what happened in 1988 with utter disgust. Said Fred Wertheimer, president of Common Cause, "the spectre of large private political donations with the ability to buy access and influence with the President of the United States once again casts a shadow over the American electoral process." Veteran Republican strategist Ed Rollins, no reformer he, dismissed "the whole shooting match" as "absurd."

But the job of the campaign managers was to operate within the system, not reform it. And that was the focus of their discussion.

The Discussion

Larry Eichel: I would like everyone to keep in mind that we're not talking about how you raise money, but how money influences the campaign and how it influences strategic decisions.

I thought we would deal basically with three topics here. First of all, I want to deal with the campaign for the Democratic nomination, particularly the early period, the period in which the field went from seven to two. Money obviously was a key factor in campaign decisions—on where to compete, how to compete, and when to leave the campaign. Second, I want to talk a little bit about the money on the Republican side and what influence that might have had. And, third, I want to get into a discussion on the whole question of independent expenditures, soft money, and all those things we don't understand very well but which added an awful lot to the final bill of this campaign.

Robert Beckel: I want to make a couple of points. I'm going to ask some questions that are very specific, based on my own experience in the use of campaign finance law. It may appear as if I'm trying to trap you into a statement that you broke the law. Of course, I don't believe anybody did that, but it's important for us to talk about how we creatively use the finance rules and regulations to benefit campaigns.

Larry Eichel: I thought we could start with Bill Carrick, who described the Gephardt campaign as the campaign that was eaten by Iowa or something like that. But, anyway, by your strategy, you chose to spend the limit and, perhaps then some in Iowa, and to go hard in New Hampshire. You came out of New Hampshire in a situation that in some ways looked very competitive, but you had money problems.

I wonder if you could talk about the money you had then, what kind of bounce in terms of fund-raising you got out of the early events, why it wasn't bigger if it wasn't big enough, and how, knowing that you had a limited amount of money, that affected your approach to Super Tuesday. Obviously, Super Tuesday and money are kind of linked in this process.

William Carrick: Well, where do we begin here? The bottom line is we raised $6 million pre-Iowa, not counting the matching money. In the course of that we ended up spending the limit in Iowa. We ended up spending close to the limit in New Hampshire. In terms of the momentum factor, we didn't gain any bump financially. There wasn't (a) enough time to collect the money bump if there was a bump, and (b) I'm not quite sure there was a bump.

I mean, it was the same thing that happened in terms of competition for the story coming out of Iowa with the Robertson second-place finish, the protracted battle for first place in Iowa with Simon, and the fact that Gephardt basically was a single-digit candidate in Iowa until December. We came on so fast and so quickly that there wasn't any sort of financial momentum produced before the Iowa victory. So we didn't get any bump.

Larry Eichel: It's February 17 or whatever and you're looking at Super Tuesday.

William Carrick: The way we always looked at Super Tuesday throughout the calendar pre-Iowa, or whatnot, was we had large pockets of support in Florida and in Texas. All across the South we had all these congressmen more than willing to share their advice for how to carry Florida, Texas, Alabama, Mississippi, Georgia, et cetera. I had eight congressmen in Texas tell me how we were going to win Texas—and seven in Florida and four in Georgia. So the strategy had always been to run a very ambitious Super Tuesday game plan.

Well, we ended up with $1 million to spend on media for Super Tuesday. We spread it all over the Super Tuesday states. We tried to compete both in Florida and in Texas. I think Fred made a more disciplined decision than we did about Florida. The Gore campaign spent a lot less money in Florida than we did. We were just spread too thinly. Dukakis made the shrewdest strategic decision about Super Tuesday. From the beginning he developed a game plan for survival.

I think it's fair to say that probably Gore and Gephardt both had a much more ambitious plan for Super Tuesday and that was to win a more substantial body of states and delegates all across the region. We were competing in literally every state from Oklahoma to Florida, Arkansas, all the Super Tuesday states. One million dollars doesn't go very far spread over those many states.

These are the kind of things that you never have an answer to. In hindsight, however, we probably should have had a strategy that put us almost exclusively in Texas, where our polling data held up until very late in the game, or maybe in Texas and Oklahoma where we were also fairly strong. But we were just spread too thin financially, and we got blown away, particularly as we got caught in the cross fire of negative ads from both Gore and Dukakis. The Gephardt campaign was the focus for Gore and Dukakis on the negative advertising side. They targeted much of their advertising resources to defeating Gephardt on Super Tuesday.

Larry Eichel: You tried to run a $2 million strategy with $1 million.

William Carrick: I think we tried to run a $4 million strategy with $1 million.

Robert Beckel: Bill, let me ask you a couple of questions. You raised $6 million. What was your match rate when you got your match check?

Larry Carrick: Forty percent, something like that.

Robert Beckel: When did you have to go to the bank to borrow against your match before Iowa?

William Carrick: We started borrowing against the match in October or maybe in September.

Robert Beckel: When you got your check, you had about $8 million or $9 million raised?

William Carrick: Yes.

Robert Beckel: You came out of Iowa, and your match caught up. You had about $1 million to spend after Iowa and New Hampshire—you had about $1 million to spend on Super Tuesday.

William Carrick: We basically had spent the match before it arrived. The $1 million was basically what was raised, and we again borrowed against prospective matching money that would come in.

Robert Beckel: I have a question for you and Fred. The question for you: Exclusive of headquarters expenses and fund-raising expenses, what did you spend on Iowa up to that point, and what percentage of your available dollar do you think you spent in Iowa on the Gephardt campaign?

William Carrick: We spent the legal limit.

Larry Eichel: Susan, did Super Tuesday come down to a question of who spent their money the most wisely in terms of media markets? I think, if you probably went through the spending reports, that you would find—I'm not suggesting this was a cause— a correlation.

Susan Estrich: We spent about a $1.6 million on television on Super Tuesday, which is not that far different from our rivals. We had two advantages. One, we had money going in. In December Jack and I—Charlie was in New Hampshire at that point—and others sat down and allocated funds. We were opening up Texas and Florida organizational operations at a time when Bill was having to close down organizational operations because he was out of funds. So I think one issue is total amount spent.

But I think an important thing for us as far as the fund-raising operation was the freedom and flexibility Jack had early on to make spending commitments in Texas, Florida, the State of Washington, and in Maryland. Those were our four corners for Super Tuesday. We worked to get an organization on the ground in those states so that if we won New Hampshire we would be in a position to capitalize.

Second, once it came to media, we polled extensively for Super Tuesday. We were tracking constantly and were able to move money on a daily basis based upon polling data. As soon as we knew Florida was certain—and there was a point about a week to 10 days out when Tubby, who is cautious, told me that Florida was going to be fine—we pulled substantially back in Florida to a minimal buy and were able to move our $1.6 in that respect. Maryland was one state we went in and made a preemptive buy to make sure no one would challenge us. So we spent a good deal of time where our spending was dictated completely by Tubby's polls.

Robert Beckel: You obviously made a decision not to spend a lot of money in some Deep South states, although you left the impression, I think, that you all were running everywhere.

Susan Estrich: We went in and played.

Robert Beckel: But you basically pulled out of Alabama, Mississippi, and Louisiana early, right?

John Corrigan: One qualification: All of our early spending plan was largely based on delegate performance. There were states where you knew Jackson, just by the proportional representation system, was going to do real well. We made a fairly straightforward formula-driven judgment about where we could win the most delegates. That led us to Texas, Washington State, Maryland, North Carolina, Massachusetts, Rhode Island, obviously.

Susan Estrich: It led us out of Alabama, Mississippi. We did some buys in some of the Deep South states, but they were very small. We played Alabama for a couple of days to see if we could convince anybody that we were going to play in Alabama. But by and large, as Jack said, we did not make substantial media investments in states where we did not feel there would be a substantial delegate return. We did go, for instance, to Kentucky, on Tad Devine's suggestion, as I recall. When we were able to cut back in Florida we made a decision that while we didn't think we could win in Kentucky, we thought an expenditure in a flat race there could boost our delegate count. So we went into Kentucky to get some delegates. The only place we didn't succeed was North Carolina, where we made a much larger investment than our ultimate delegate return.

Robert Beckel: Of the $1.6 you spent, how much of that was spent on anti-Gephardt commercials?

John Corrigan: Not that much.

Susan Estrich: We ran our workhorse position spot the most, and that was running 60, 70 percent.

John Corrigan: We ran that where Gephardt was on the air.

Robert Beckel: Fred, you ran negative ads against Gephardt in the South. Did you put some of your resources into that?

Frederick Martin: We ran negative ads against everyone in the South. We put about 10 percent of the media buy into those ads, and 90 percent was positive.

Robert Beckel: What was your budget for spending for Super Tuesday states?

Frederick Martin: On television and radio you mean? It was roughly $2 million. We began the buy on the night before the Iowa caucuses, the 7th of February, and continued for one month. We were on the air in about 25 to 30 markets in the South.

We had essentially two goals with this buy. One was a state strategy and the other was a delegate strategy. It was uncertain going into the year what was going to be the measure of success on March 8. It's still uncertain when you look back what was the measure of success. We hoped to win five or six states if we could. We hoped to win 200 to 300 delegates. We ended up with about 318 delegates on that night, and we won six states.

We bought media time in states we knew we could not win. That is, we made a buy, a substantial buy, in the panhandle of Florida for the purpose of getting delegates, and we got some. We made a very large buy in a few markets in Texas for the purpose of getting some delegates, and we got quite a few. The same in Louisiana, which we didn't think we could win. The same in Mississippi, which we didn't think we were going to win. So we were attempting to pursue a two-track strategy, and that cost us about $2 million.

I think we probably outspent all the Democratic campaigns on media in the South but not on field operations. If you were to combine the expenditures on field operations in Super Tuesday states and media costs, we were outspent by Dukakis—I'm quite sure of it.

William Carrick: The biggest problem I had, as Susan Estrich alluded to, was the ability to plan for what we were going to do. We had developed a computer model based on delegate alloca-tion per market, and we knew what we would buy. But it all depended on what money came in that day. Then we would make the buy for the day. We had to make some judgments based on the tracking numbers. And the lack of available money led to decisions that were not always based on research.

So early on there were things that were sensible decisions then, like buy in Florida, where, even if we finished second to Dukakis, we would have gotten a lot of delegates. These were terrible deci-sions in hindsight because the political climate changed so dramati-cally in the course of that 10 days. So trying to do things in some sort of intelligent manner without sitting on the money and not having the cash flow was almost impossible. There were too many variables. We made a lot of very bad strategic decisions as a consequence.

The other thing was an incredible cat and mouse game going on among Gore, Gephardt, and Dukakis. You know, one day we would call up and ask for avails all over Atlanta. Then that day we would place an order for every market in the state except Atlanta and see if we could get them to buy. And they'd call and get avails for every market in Alabama, and our media would call back and say, "The Dukakis people are buying Alabama." Then it was Gore. It went on and on. They called one day and ordered a ton of avails for Oklahoma. I don't think you [the Dukakis campaign] ended up buying.

Frederick Martin: You spent some money on Oklahoma and Kentucky.

Robert Beckel: Ron, Jackson spent his first media money in the South, right?

Ronald Brown: To tell you the truth, that was before my time. My understanding is that about $200,000 was spent for Super Tuesday.

Robert Beckel: A lot of radio.

Ronald Brown: Mostly radio.

Larry Eichel: I would like to ask one general question. I think our understanding of primary politics is that with few exceptions most candidates are in a situation where they have to be spending money very quickly as it comes in and that you do events in the primaries where you spend money to raise money. Was there any event in this whole primary season on either side that produced a sudden flow of money for anybody?

John Corrigan: Yes. *The Des Moines Register* poll.

Terry Michael: Our best fund-raising month seemed to be in the period after we lost Iowa. I don't know how much impact *The Register* poll made after we began that period, but we had a $1 million month in February. A lot of that money came in after February 8. I don't know how much of it I could assign to *The Des Moines Register* poll.

I've got my own theory on why we got that money. It's strange. We didn't get much of a money bump after being number one in *The Des Moines Register* poll in the middle of November. That may have been simply poor fund-raising. But we got a bump from losing in February. I think part of that was because we had a small donor base which said, "This is the guy carrying our torch; we've got to help him out."

Robert Beckel: Simon was reasonably successful in direct mail.

Terry Michael: I think we may have had the best ratio of matching funds to donations. We had $2.8 million in matching funds and $6 million in donations. I think we had a 50,000-small donor base. I think that had something to do with the connection those donors made with the personality of Paul Simon and the connection they made with his message.

Larry Eichel: Is it fair to say that all the Democratic campaigns at some point assumed that Dukakis would be a finalist in this process simply because he had such a good fund-raising base?

William Carrick: I think it's fair to assume the Dukakis campaign was the only campaign on our side that could make rational, long-term planning decisions. Everybody else was dealing with emergency and contingency decisions. Their decisions about Florida and Texas, putting together extensive field operations, were very important decisions. They were based upon their financial resources.

Terry Michael: What do you mean about a finalist? You mean all the way through?

Larry Eichel: I mean one of the three candidates who would be standing after Super Tuesday.

Frederick Martin: That was one of our assumptions later, yes.

Susan Estrich: Money is important precisely for the reason Bill says, I believe, in that it allows you to do the long-term planning you need to do rather than raise money hand-to-mouth after victories. But if we had lost New Hampshire, all the money in the world wasn't going to take us south.

Terry Michael: We assumed we would be the liberal-of-choice in the South if we won New Hampshire, regardless of Dukakis's money.

John Corrigan: There's sort of an underlying assumption in this conversation that there's a cause and effect. Money drives the strategy. The reason people give money to candidates is because they believe in them. The reason we were able to raise a lot of money is because a lot of people believed in Governor Dukakis. He had a strong basis of support within the party; he was an attractive candidate. Therefore, he could raise money. Therefore, he could rationally plan and make decisions. The way that we talk about it, it's like money bought the election. That's hardly an accurate assumption.

Larry Eichel: Would you say, Jack, that lack of money is more of a symptom of a failing campaign?

John Corrigan: Lack of political viability. But you can spend all the money, run out of it, and then cause your own political viability problem. But if you're an attractive candidate, people support you and you're viable.

Frederick Martin: I disagree with that. If the Gephardt campaign had the money, they could have been a colossal problem for Al Gore and our campaign in the South. I think if you [Bill Carrick] had gotten your message out on television in the 25 same markets where we placed media, with equal volume, we would have had a hell of a problem.

John Corrigan: Dukakis was a very, very strict candidate. We only took individual donations. A lot of donations from Massachusetts were rejected because of potential conflict of interest.

Frederick DuVal: I'm not sure the reverse is true, even with $5 million in the bank. If you had been a more distant third in Iowa or a fourth and then not won in New Hampshire, I don't think any amount of money could have brought you back because I don't think there was a safety net there for you.

John Corrigan: We had a plan.

Robert Beckel: But it is true, Jack. You had a bigger base here than other campaigns. But it's also true that all of you as campaign managers in the year before—absent straw polls which brought us up so much in 1983—did use money as a sign of health of your campaign. I remember whenever the filing thing came out, you all were very quick, if your had money, to rush to everybody who was doing public opinion and say, "Here's our money." And very much of the Dukakis strength nationally was seen, or at least a component of that was seen, because you raised a lot of money. Remember when you got up to $10 million, that was a big story. But didn't you strategically use money every step of the way?

Susan Estrich: There were no measurements. If you look at one of the differences between 1984 and 1988, you guys had straw polls. What did we have? We had two things, money and debates. We were perceived to win debates beginning the preceding July. Money became for us a very important measure. Whether Jack is right or not, that money is a measure of political viability, you can agree or disagree, but in 1987 it was treated that way. And we were able—whether we ultimately could make the final or not is an open question—to position ourselves as a candidate deserving of even more money in a way because we were able to say, "Look how successful we are. We are a national candidacy."

We did come from a [money] exporting state. We put together a strong team. Dukakis himself is a very strong fund-raiser. And we were able to make the finals as of October 1987 or November 1987 on the strength of our money. And when we took some bumps, as we did along the way, money provided at least something of a cushion to point to and say, "Look, we're still playing here."

Robert Beckel: Can I ask two or three specific questions? Is it a fair statement to say the person who was probably hurt most by money tactically and strategically was Gephardt—he lacked the money to compete on Super Tuesday. Fred, he would have been your toughest competitor on Super Tuesday had he had more money. Is that right?

Frederick Martin.   There was reason to believe that the message they were putting out in Iowa and in New Hampshire would have some resonance in the South. It's also true they had a base of political support in the South, with the congressmen especially. And my own view is that their being denied the funds to compete on television in the South was probably the best instance of a candidate being damaged for want of money. Do you think that's right, Bill?

William Carrick: I agree totally.

Robert Beckel: One last question, Sue, on the Hart money people. Who would you say of this group probably benefitted the most and who probably benefitted the least from Hart getting out.

Susan Casey: I think Dukakis benefitted the most. A lot of money people, as we all know, like to go with winners. That is why people were with Hart. When he pulled out they went with the next person they thought would be the winner. I think money was an important factor. As Jack has said, we all know money comes because people support you. You got all your money before Michael was really a candidate out there. There are a lot of reasons why he got the money. All of the candidates had a lot of support, but some people could not get that money.

I think that not only in the end but in the course of a campaign, the amount of energy that campaigns lacking money put into fund-raising and the amount of turmoil that goes on cannot be measured in terms of the ability to run a campaign. The Ailes and Atwaters can sit down and talk about strategies, but we also had these campaigns that didn't have five minutes a week to talk about strategy because they were worrying about how to get a plane ticket and an office open and things like that. So I think money in the early days plays an important part in making the campaign roll and in its legitimacy. The more you have the more you get.

You were the leaders. You had the money. If Biden had been in, he was going to have more money than others. That was where it was going to split. But I don't think that money went anyplace else besides Dukakis.

Robert Beckel: Money certainly begets money in this situation.

Let me ask you one question Fred, before we get out of the Democratic side here. At least in conventional wisdom, one of the reasons Al Gore got in was because he had the support of a Washington fat-cat group made up of a lot of fund-raisers called the Impac '88 Committee. Did that have a lot to do with Gore getting in? Second, looking back on it, how much money do you say Impac actually raised for Gore?

Frederick Martin: First, I can speak only from hearsay as to the first question because I was not hired by Gore until he had decided to run, so I was not part of his process of deciding whether to run. He himself has said it was a factor. Anyone who tries to run for President without considering where the money is coming from is a fool.

Second, it's wrong to believe that Impac endorsed Al Gore. It did not. Impac split all kinds of ways, and by the time Gore got into the race there were approximately 15 uncommitted individuals of a group that was about 50 to start with. Of those 15 or so, about 12 decided to go with Gore. Four or five of those 12, I would say, played a substantial role in our fund-raising and probably accounted for 10 to 15 percent of our fund-raising. They were an important factor.

William Carrick: One question to Fred on the money. How much of the $2 million media buy did you guys borrow?

Frederick Martin: We borrowed $1 million on March 2 or 3. Of that, approximately $600,000 or less went to media in the South.

Robert Beckel: How much of that was borrowed against your matching funds?

Frederick Martin: A substantial portion was borrowed with security pledged in the form of prospective matching funds.

Larry Eichel: In listening to the presentations earlier from the Republican campaigns, I was struck by one comment and one noncomment. The comment was from Ed Rollins that the worst thing a candidate can say to you is: "Money, that's no problem. I can raise that." The other thing was something that Lee Atwater didn't say. As far as I can remember, Lee was the only campaign manager who did not mention money in his presentation, and it was quite lengthy. I guess it's because it was no problem.

Edward Rogers: It wasn't ever a problem in the sense that our goals and what we were going to do with the money were set out very early. We met those goals. In its rawest form we knew how much we wanted to raise during 1987. By the way, we built a fire wall in the South with fund-raisers. We knew we had to raise our money and have it in the bank prior to the campaign getting started. Fund-raising was going to drive the schedule, and Lee dictated where the fund-raisers would be held.

Every fund-raiser—in Birmingham, Jackson, or Orlando—would have an organizational aspect to it. We usually had a meeting with a group this size, where George Bush would walk in with 50 county chairmen, county commissioners, party leaders, et cetera. He would walk out of that room with commits every single time. We had a good enough field operation to follow up on those people and give everybody something to do. That was how the fire wall was built while we were raising our money.

Our goal was to have $10 million in the bank, with virtually no liabilities, on January 1. We knew early on, it was common sense, that if we would lose one of the early primaries, money would dry up. Also, the $10 million figure wasn't necessarily arbitrary. It was to provide the money for what Lee called "the pig in the python," which was Super Tuesday, that fat portion of the primary season where a great many delegates and primaries took place on one day. That money, obviously, would have to be in the bank long before Iowa and long before New Hampshire.

Now it was thought that somebody was going to beat us and beat us early. But so many of the delegates were gone so early in the process that if we were going to win it, we would win it early. Certainly, we would be well on our way to winning, through the Illinois primary anyway.

We raised our $10 million. We had just over $10 million in the bank when the primary season started. We had a budget that called for us to be reactive in some ways. We had three very well financed opponents in the race, and they knew they had to beat us early. They knew how many delegates were going to be gone after Super Tuesday as well, so we were spending money on a par with them. They probably actually spent more than us prior to January 1, 1988.

Part of the discipline was, having put that money into the bank, not to spend it and not to nickel and dime county conventions and hospitality receptions at Republican events. It adds up. There was a lot of discipline not to spend that money.

Edward Rollins: To be totally accurate, to say the Bush campaign did not have money problems is not quite right. As Bob found out in 1984, there is not enough money to run a primary season today. It's absurd for us to sit around this table and not really discuss how screwed up the whole money process is. Even if you're an incumbent President or incumbent vice president and you go out and raise the limit, you will still flat run out of money.

Fortunately, you won it early, but you had to limp from mid-March all the way to the convention. You had to let people go on the RNC payroll and everything else. You weren't being challenged. Bob, in 1984 you raised all the money. When you were being challenged you limped, had to skirt around the law and the whole shooting match.

Robert Beckel: No!

Edward Rollins: My whole point in all this is that the whole process of matching funds, primary limits, the whole shooting match, is an absurd process. There are about seven campaigns sitting at this table that have no more business sitting at this table for several reasons. We were able to stay in and raise money because we were able to borrow against matching funds. In the final analysis, none of us were viable candidates to begin with. Jesse was an exception.

I think the whole process is so absurd today. Just as in the Kemp campaign, we raised $17 million, counting the matching funds, but we were doing things you would never do in a campaign. We were doing direct mail that cost $1.25 to raise $1.00. You would be out of business very quickly if the arguments coming back were, "Well, we're making 75 cents because we're getting a dollar of matching funds." So you were playing this funny game all the way through. It was keeping a lot of us in the game a lot longer. And maybe it's great we get to sit here at the table, but the truth is the process itself is absurd.

Robert Beckel: You make a good point. My question about Bush, Ed, is how much money had you spent total as of the night of the Iowa caucus? Was it $14 million or $15 million, something like that?

Edward Rogers: I don't think it was that high. It was more like $12 million, wasn't it?

Edward Rollins: Let's all be honest about Michigan. There were multi-millions spent by all of us out of foundations and congressional campaigns.

Roger Ailes: We spent $500,000 on media in the primaries. To win a New Jersey race, you have to spend $5 million on the air.

Robert Beckel: Isn't that really the point though? Given the situation you were in, you guys spent an awful lot of money in 1987, just like we did in 1984—about $10 million. You had money in the bank on January 1 because you had a big match. But if you had had a protracted battle against Bob Dole, you would not have been able to spend a dime in New Jersey, California, or any of the late states.

Edward Rogers: Bob Dole wouldn't either.

Robert Beckel: Bill, is that the same situation you were in?

William Lacy: At that point in time I will agree with him. We had a good enough financial operation. We were fortunate to be in a position where there was never a decision made prior to the New Hampshire primary based upon money. We could always make our decision based on what we believed was best for the campaign from a political point of view.

We really had a goal of trying to build a financial advantage over the Bush campaign during 1987, not in the sense of having more money but having more room on the limit to spend. So if we could get a quick start of out Iowa, even though we were going to be a little bit behind in terms of the cash that we had immediately available, we were going to be $2 million or $3 million ahead of where they were going to be all the way to the convention.

But we had a situation where there was always a debate within the Dole campaign about how to spend our money. And as all of you know, once you spend the dollar, the dollar is gone. You can't recoup it, you can't go out and raise another one, because once you hit the limit, that's it. So because the vice president had already locked in a very solid organization and the party establishment in the South—and because we were down, by our count, 20 points across the South—we made a fairly fundamental decision to limit organizational activities down there.

That decision was reversed in late 1987, and money was invested very heavily into organizational resources. That really didn't turn the trick.

Robert Beckel: How much money did you spend through New Hampshire?

William Lacy: I couldn't tell you.

Robert Beckel: About $12 or $13 million, I think.

Larry Eichel: You ended up in a situation where you had plenty of room under the limit?

Robert Beckel: The limit is $25 million, right? So basically you spent $13 million on three states, right? So you were in a situation where then you had to run in 47 states with about $12 million.

Edward Rollins: You run a year-long operation in New Hampshire and you can spend what you spend in an assembly race in California, $750,000. I mean, everybody may say everyone is a liar and cheat and violated the federal election law. And, if you did, you did your candidate a great service—by staying in New Hampshire and Iowa, I mean. You basically had to go 87 miles around the law, with people living in different states and commercials coming from different states. The whole shooting match—the whole process—is so absurd.

Larry Eichel: Pat Robertson didn't lack for money either. Money was part of the reason you were able to get it in. You had a fund-raising base, you knew it was there, and you knew how to work it. That was not your problem, was it?

Marc Nuttle: No. It was one of our assets going in. It was unique in a couple of ways. A lot of people who gave to the Robertson campaign were monthly $20 givers. The cost of raising those funds once you secured the contributors is the cost of the stamp to mail a bill to them each month for $20.

The other nice thing about having conditioned givers is it's kind of like running a business. You know what your projected cash flow is each month within a reasonable margin of error. By the end of the year we had a cash flow of $1 million a month. We didn't have to think about it, didn't have to anticipate it, didn't have to go out and prospect it. It was definitely going to come in through gift cards and pledges.

The only reason that the average contribution was $125 or whatever it was, with not quite 200,000 contributors, was because after 10 or 15 months they got over $100. It's as simple as that.

Robert Beckel: Mark, did you have an exploratory committee?

Marc Nuttle: Yes, we did. We formed an exploratory committee in July and August of 1986. As I said earlier, it had two basic purposes. One was to test our ability to get an organization off the ground. The other purpose was to test the number of potential voters. I think we were the only campaign for President to set the criteria and elements for what a testing-the-waters test is. If he didn't get three million names, he wouldn't run.

Robert Beckel: I know you were accused by some people of using the Christian Broadcasting Network list and all that. Did you take your fundraising list from your exploratory committee, which if I remember right, was not only very big but very successful in terms of the amount of money and numbers of contributors, and transfer that to or purchase that as the Robertson for President Committee.

Marc Nuttle: A testing-the-waters committee, when you become a candidate, becomes the main campaign committee. All Federal Election Commission filings must be complete retroactively to the first day of the exploratory committee. The exploratory testing-the-waters committee is bound by all of the fund-raising restrictions of the FEC. All assets are easily transferred.

Robert Beckel: Did anybody here not have an exploratory committee that they ate off and slept off until you announced?

Allan Hubbard: Du Pont didn't.

John Corrigan: Dukakis didn't.

Edward Rollins: We had a congressional committee that spent $2.6 million on congressional seats in 1986. We had a foundation that spent about $5 million to explore whatever mission we were doing. We didn't have an exploratory committee. (Laughter)

Robert Beckel: What about from the standpoint of Du Pont and also of Haig? I assume it must have been tough to find any financial base.

Daniel Mariaschin: It was a catch 22 all the way around. If you can't raise money, you can't hire staff, and you can't put people in the field. If you can't put people in the field, nobody is going to take you seriously when the press goes out and talks to the locals. It was a very serious problem. Whatever there might have been out there for us, coming in as late as we did, it had all dried up by the time our campaign was launched. There were a lot of disappointments out there. There were assumptions made that certain contributors would come forth, and they didn't. So it was just scratching around over the course of 11 months to do what we could.

Robert Beckel: Was that the same with Du Pont?

Allan Hubbard: Surprisingly, we did much better than we expected to do. Our goal was to raise $6 million by New Hampshire with matching, and we raised, I think, $7.8 million. I think the reason we were successful was twofold. Pete's candidacy touched a chord with a lot of people. Not in terms of great numbers of voters, but in terms of a reasonable number of donors. Second, he himself is a great fund-raiser. Consequently, we actually spent the limit in both Iowa and New Hampshire. We didn't skirt around anything. We were totally above board.

Edward Rollins: The family Christmas card list had a lot to do with it, too. (Laughter)

Allan Hubbard: Much smaller than you would imagine. I think we raised less than a half million dollars from the extended family.

Larry Eichel: I think we should shift to the fall. A lot of people thought we had exclusive public financing of presidential campaigns, $46 million dollars, and that was it. I think we found out that that wasn't quite the case this time. Ed Rollins had some comments before about the primary system. I wonder what his comments are about the system in general.

Then I would like to ask both Susan and Ed to talk about the soft money, independent expenditure kind of thing and how that worked. And then Susan made some comments earlier about the degree of coordination that there was or there wasn't.

Edward Rollins: I'm sure they had the same experience I had four years ago when I got a $46 million check from the federal government. I never saw so much money and never saw it go as quickly as it did. I think what happened this time was unprecedented in terms of the soft money operation that the Democrats came up with. We have always had an ability to raise tremendous amounts of money through our party apparatus. We also have a national party mechanism that raises unbelievable sums of money. But, I think, this particular time the Democrats—Mr. Farmer and others—went all-out and were helped by the fact that around the convention people believed they had a candidate who could win.

I would say there weren't any significant dollar advantages this time on our side, but my personal feeling is that the public money in the fall is important. I think the public money in the primary season is something that ought to be looked at in the sense of the cost of raising a dollar. When the law went into effect in 1974 a $1,000 contribution probably cost a third less to raise than it does today, and it went a heck of a lot further. So, obviously, there needs to be some reform there.

I also think there needs to be some reform relative to how parties themselves or contributions to parties are counted so that you don't end up doing all the things that we did this time or you did this time. I think we really ought to be very honest about it. You can't run a national campaign for $45 million or $50 million, not when you're spending $15 million to run a gubernatorial contest in one state.

Robert Beckel: Before we get into the two campaigns, I think it's important to understand how different this year may have been. Fund-raising is one area that I think always seems to get a back door treatment in all of this. But if you add up the federal money, what the two committees used in soft money, and a reasonably fair assessment of independent expenditures, including the labor unit and rest of it, there may have been as much as $350 million spent on this presidential campaign in about 12 or 14 weeks. It's not an insignificant amount of money.

How much money of your $46 million did you spend for media? Do you remember?

Edward Rogers: Almost 60 percent.

Susan Estrich: We spent around $28 million.

Robert Beckel: Susan, you used the soft money to do your field operations, right?

Susan Estrich: Right. I saw the figure kicking around that you guys raised $96 million. I don't know.

Frank Fahrenkopf: $96,686,000.

Edward Rollins: That's the party.

Susan Estrich: What strikes me about this is, in the first year which we think it was roughly equal, it was, in fact, two to one.

Frank Fahrenkopf: You're right.

Susan Estrich: That's a first step because, Bob, I don't think you had anything. We raised about $50 million in what is called soft money. We did so under certain rules established by Governor Dukakis, including the rule that we did not accept corporate contributions, PAC contributions, or contributions in excess of $100,000 from individuals. We did raise $50 million. Essentially, what that financed was our state organizations. So we were able to do what you folks [Republicans] had done in 1984 and what you [Beckel] couldn't do, which is use our public funds first and foremost for media and media production and, second, for a bare bones staff. Our lawyers advised us that we had to have, I think, our state campaign director and our senior communications person in each state with Dukakis/Bentsen. The remainder of the statewide organization was largely financed by the party.

And, I have to just second Ed on some of this. I happen to teach this stuff for a living. And my head spins by the middle of the campaign because you find yourself in the midst of archaic legal details about who is paid by whom and on what match. And there's soft money and there's the federal money and the qualified soft money. I think the system does badly need reform both in the primaries and general election.

Robert Beckel: You say there was $50 million raised by the DNC in soft money.

John Corrigan: Not in soft money. A total of $56 million was raised from January 1 to November 8 by DNC and joint fund-raising.

Robert Beckel: How much of the RNC in the same period of time?

Frank Fahrenkopf: About $96 million or $97 million. That includes the $8.3 million.

Susan Estrich: As does ours.

Terry Michael: Isn't that about $50 million more than your normal budget, Frank, and about $50 million more than the DNC's normal yearly budget?

Frank Fahrenkopf: I went into the campaign with the RNC's operating budget of about $50 million.

Terry Michael: So the two parties might be fairly equal?

John Corrigan: Paul Kirk did a great job. I worked for Bob in 1984. There was no money. The party had a debt. When we showed up and had the nomination, the party was in the black. They had spent a lot of money building up voter files for the state campaigns.

Robert Beckel: Of that $56 million, the lion's share was raised from July until November?

John Corrigan: I think somewhere around $36 million was raised from June to November.

Robert Beckel: In both of your cases, what percentage of your field people on the ground in each of these states were paid for by the respective committees as opposed to by the campaign?

John Corrigan: I would say—Charlie Baker may know better—70 percent.

Robert Beckel: Seventy percent were on the state payroll?

John Corrigan: The problem is, when you do that, you then incorporate into your program all of the legal restrictions on how that money can be spent. So they have to spend a fair amount of time doing ticket activities and not doing Dukakis-Bentsen stuff. We had lawyers in every state to make sure we complied with the law at every step. You can lose a substantial amount of control over money. We made a decision that we were going to help raise the money. But we also depended upon their good faith and willingness to help out the ticket while they were doing everything else that they legally were required to do.

Robert Beckel: That's one of the best answers I've ever heard anybody ever give. I was in states, watched every one of them, and their campaign [Republicans] controlled everything that went on at the state level. Your campaign [Democrats] controlled it as well, but that's okay because that is presumably legal in the broad sense of the word. But it is true that your state campaign managers basically controlled the flow of money out of the state. I mean, the state party chairmen had to get approval from the managers of these states to spend money.

John Corrigan: That's an exaggeration.

Susan Estrich: In some states, yes. In other states, no.

John Corrigan: I think as a general principle the Republican party has greater ideological and operational hegemony over their operations than we do. The Democratic party incorporates anarchy in almost everything it does.

Susan Estrich: We were doing it for the first time in the Democratic party. It may be a lousy system, but it's one that to a very large extent they [Republicans] have got down. It was one that this time Jack and Bob Farmer and others were creating because it didn't exist four years ago. There were a lot of state chairmen who didn't understand that money in their state party was not necessarily totally within their control.

Robert Beckel: Is that how the Republican state chairmen thought of it as well, or were they pretty conditioned to have the Bush campaign tell them where the money was going?

Edward Rogers: It varied state to state. They were virtually always part of the mix. Never were the state party chairmen a stranger to the Bush operation and a stranger to the leadership team. Never.

Frank Fahrenkopf: The other thing that is different—and it's hard to answer the question—we have ongoing, even in off-presidential years, an apparatus out there on voter ID and voter turnout. It's an ongoing thing year to year for us. So we are not just coming in and putting it in place in the presidential year where you can draw those clear lines. There are ongoing programs, so it makes it a little different.

Larry Eichel: If you had this money with no strings on it, is this what you would have done with it?

Susan Estrich: I would have given it to Jack.

Larry Eichel: Did you do with it what the law said you could do with it?

Susan Estrich: If there were no spending limits, I imagine we might well have put more of it on television. Obviously, you can debate all day how much you should spend on field in a presidential campaign. We used some of that money for generic TV and you guys did, too, but it was relatively less effective than our own.

Edward Rollins: Go back to 1972. The Nixon campaign spent $85 million on the record and at least another $100 million off the record, and that is not counting cash.

Robert Beckel: One last question on soft money. Dukakis
didn't want you to take corporate or union money. Correct? That
was part of his deal?

Susan Estrich: Yes.

Robert Beckel: Of that $56 million, how much was corporate/
union money?

John Corrigan: I have no idea. Basically, what Paul Kirk did
was to continue the existing programs through the DNC. We didn't
change any of the existing programs of the DNC.

Susan Estrich: The DNC depends on certain union money
for its maintenance and day-to-day operations. The governor was
not going to come in and tell Paul Kirk he couldn't take money from
labor unions to maintain the DNC during those five months that
we were the nominee. The stricture, Bob, was that Bob Farmer
and our entire fund-raising operation were not to solicit or accept
corporate or union money. Of course, unions spent money on their
own.

Robert Beckel: We haven't had a chance to hear from the
eminent Tim Ridley. Tim, you raised a lot of money in a very short
period of time. Would you do away with state limits?

Timothy Ridley: Had Senator Biden stayed in the race, we
would have been very competitive in terms of financing. Our financial resources would have been second only to those of Governor
Dukakis. We would have likely raised $8 million in 1987. We
hadn't anticipated borrowing against the match. Through New
Hampshire, with matching funds, we felt confident we could fund a
$13 million budget. That was the plan.

Given the eccentricities of FEC regulations—the travel exemp-
tion, the fund-raising exception, other off-line exceptions—you
could probably spend $2.1 million to $2.3 million in Iowa and easily
account for those expenditures within the limit. That level of spending is defensible from an accounting and regulatory standpoint. But
you're not going to win—at that level.

Ultimately, sometime 30 days out from the caucuses, a campaign
has to decide how aggressive it's going to be. If you're truly in the
hunt, most campaigns are likely to say "spend whatever it takes."
Yes, it's likely to mean a [FEC] fine, but what the FEC does 12
months after your campaign is over is not a very salient consideration in Iowa in January 1988. The Biden campaign obviously never
got to the point where it had to face any of those questions. Not
having actively faced them, I can be more candid.

New Hampshire is even crazier. The limit isn't $750,000. It's

$450,000. You can't run a credible campaign in New Hampshire for the last 10 days for $450,000.

If there is one reform I would like to see made in this process, it would be to eliminate the state spending limits. I'm pro-deregulation. Let the campaigns decide how they're going to allocate their resources. If somebody wants to go to Iowa and spend $8 million, let him do it.

Edward Rollins: They should reverse it—put a $450,000 limit on California and an $8 million limit on New Hampshire.

Timothy Ridley: Let that be part of the political and strategic decisions a campaign makes. Let them live or die by those spending decisions. Clearly, if someone could have legally gone to Iowa this time and spent $8 million, someone would have.

In hindsight, given Iowa's diminished place in the process, that $8 million decision would have been malpractice. So be it. Spending predicts strategy. Let the campaigns rise and fall on the strength of their strategies.

Robert Beckel: You didn't have to break the law or stretch the limits, the regulations of the FEC. Just to carry through on how absurd the laws are, Fred DuVal, isn't it true that the Babbitt campaign paid the salary of the New Hampshire state party executive director for a year before the New Hampshire primary?

Frederick DuVal: We donated her services to the New Hampshire state party.

Larry Eichel: Does the fact that you can qualify for the federal match on January 1, a year before the election, force the campaign to have begun by then? Is that really the starting line, and can that be changed? Would it have any impact on anything if it is changed?

Edward Rollins: George Bush started 10 years ago, 1978, putting his organization together. Anybody who doesn't start four years before the gun goes off is not going to be able to raise the money. Let's be perfectly honest about it. It takes two years, whether you can raise it by direct mail or what have you, to really get your list cranking up, to get your donors identified. It's a four-year process. Anybody who lets any other limit pass by and doesn't really begin until six or seven months is going to be the first one out.

Robert Beckel: Are any of you in favor of keeping the $1,000 limitation on contributors?

Frederick Martin: I am. I think the process has to be reformed. I'm not sure I would go along with all the reforms of my colleagues. I think the danger here is the role of private money in these campaigns. We used to have a property qualification for voters in the country. We now have a property qualification for candidates. If you're not able to raise $20 million, you won't be the nominee. It's that simple now. I think we need to reform this.

I think it's unfortunate that we all have to play with the state limits. We take cars from the wrong state and go into Iowa; we have our staff go in for four days and then sleep out of state to get around spending limits. Of course, that's absurd. But what is worse than being absurd is being corrupt. I think that the role of money has a corrupting influence on our democracy.

Edward Rollins: The law was passed in 1974. A thousand dollars was worth significantly more in 1974 than in 1988 and in 1992. An inflation factor would bring it up to at least $2,000. I think the absurdity of it is this: If you can send a candidate to Chicago for a fund-raising lunch and the limit's, say, $5,000 and you put 20 people together, you walk away with a $100,000. That's worth a day's investment. But if you fly someone to Chicago and he walks away with $40,000, he has lost an entire day or has to do two or three of those in a row.

As Gephardt said, instead of spending 100 days in Iowa next time, he would spend 100 days fund-raising and 10 days in Iowa. The whole democratic process gets screwed up by this inability of campaigns to raise money.

Sure, an incumbent vice president can get 17,000 $1,000 contributions. He can do it easily. A former incumbent vice president can go out and raise it easily. An incumbent President can raise it right there. All I did was to borrow the list from the RNC. The Senate campaign committee mailed them three times and I got all the money I needed. But to a candidate who's coming out of the blue, these limits put him at a serious disadvantage.

Edward Rogers: While we are on the subject of reform, it's tough to envision it as a practical matter unless you look at more than just the money aspect. For instance, if there were no state limits and if Du Pont were going to spend $8 million in Iowa, we would have probably had to spend more in Iowa as would Dole and Kemp. Now you're down to a much more important and more critical Iowa. But if Iowa were the same day as Arizona, then it would be a very different equation, a very different mix, in how money would be spent and what the campaigns did, and someone's surviving the one-shot Iowa would be much more likely.

William Carrick: In terms of Fred's comment, I don't think there is anything more noble in getting your money from people who have the capacity to run around and collect $1,000 checks from other people than there is taking a big check from Walter Annenberg or whoever was giving Nixon money. The nobility of the process is not enhanced by the $1,000 limit in any way, shape, or form. I think it would make a lot more sense to raise the limit, as a simple reform that we might get bipartisan agreement on, to $5,000 or $10,000, and the candidate could spend a lot less time raising money. You know, the Impac group's impact on politics is just as potentially corrupting as corporate or political action money.

Frank Fahrenkopf: I have got to close. The parties on a number of occasions, with [Chuck] Manatt and with Paul Kirk fundamentally came to agreement. I wanted it to go to $5,000. There was fundamental agreement in the Bob Strauss/Mel Laird commission after the 1984 campaign to go to $2,500.

But let me just close with this. You can't just say that money is bad, that money is evil and corrupts the system. We started that Strauss/Laird study with a lot of people saying presidential races cost too much money, until someone testified before that commission that in 1984, if you combined all the money that Mondale and Reagan spent, the federal money was a total of just under $100 million. One soap company had spent more advertising one brand of its soap that year than the two candidates for the highest office in the world had spent.

So the question is, Where does the money go? As Ed said, 60 percent of Bush's money went to television. So the cost of communicating—and politics is communication—goes to get on the airwaves, whether it's radio or television, to produce spots and to buy newspaper ads—that's what drives it. It's the cost of getting the message out.

Chapter 6

ELECTION CAMPAIGN STRATEGY: CONVENTIONS, VP CHOICES, AND DEBATES

Introduction by David Gergen and E. J. Dionne

America has suffered through nasty presidential campaigns in the past; it has endured more than its share of shallow campaigns; it has frequently watched with some embarrassment as one candidate has pummeled another against the ropes and there has been no referee to leap in and stop the fight. But rarely have all of those elements come together in the same campaign, as they did in 1988.

The 1988 race did have uplifting moments—the acceptance speeches by George Bush and Michael Dukakis were the finest performances of their careers—but, in the end, the campaign left an uneasy impression that there must be a better way to elect the nation's president. The voters certainly registered that view, as only 50 percent bothered to vote—the second lowest turnout of the century. The candidates and the press often expressed frustration, too. And when the campaign managers came together at the John F. Kennedy School in December for their quadrennial review, the air was thick with cynicism and unhappiness with the system. As the Kennedy School conference drew to an end, Fred Martin, campaign manager for Senator Al Gore, observed acidly, "I have never seen more whining by grown-ups over 24 hours. The Democrats whine about the mean attacks on them by the Republicans. The Republicans whine about poor Marty Plissner and CBS [Plissner is the CBS political director]. And others whine about [Jesse]

Jackson." Another participant quickly accused Martin of whining about whining.

The final morning session of the conference focused on the general campaign, and as the following transcript shows, a consensus emerged that Dukakis never had much of a chance to win the White House—and blew what small opportunity he had. The participants gave Bush credit for being a much stronger, more appealing candidate than had been expected, and they thought he ran a smarter, if more negative, campaign. Ronald Reagan also gave Bush a major boost: over the course of 1988, as consumer confidence grew and Reagan engaged in high-profile diplomacy with Mikhail Gorbachev, his approval ratings rose steadily and helped to elevate Bush as well. Representatives of the Dukakis campaign complained that Reagan's mantle protected Bush against every line of Democratic attack except the selection of Senator Dan Quayle as a running mate. They also argued that Reagan's remark calling Dukakis a mental "invalid," which reversed the momentum of the campaign at a key moment in August, was an intentional slur, a charge hotly denied by the Republicans. Even so, in the opinions of most participants, Dukakis had an outside chance of winning and threw it away. GOP manager Ed Rollins, summarizing the general view, argued that during the summer, when Bush was on the defensive and Dukakis had amassed a huge lead, Dukakis let Bush "get off the mat" without a fight and then stood passively as the Republican camp unleashed a series of attacks that drove negative ratings up for Dukakis and positive ratings up for Bush. The campaign was over by late September, said Rollins. Democrat Bob Beckel, campaign manager for Walter Mondale in 1984, agreed that the campaign turned on the inability of the Dukakis team to respond well to attacks. The Dukakis representatives refused to criticize their candidate and emphasized his belief that he had to lay out a positive foundation for his campaign during the critical months of August and September. Had he turned harshly negative during those weeks, he felt, he would have undermined the entire rationale of his candidacy.

Running through this discussion are three subthemes which provoked disagreement and will continue to shape American politics:

1. *Selecting a Vice President—Without Sound and Fury.* For reasons that no one can entirely fathom, a succession of presidential nominees have taken a bad stumble in choosing a running mate. Recall the fuss over Tom Eagleton, the resignation of Spiro Agnew, the eleventh-hour debate over Reagan dividing up the presidency with Gerald Ford, and the debilitating investigations of Geraldine Ferraro's husband. The 1988 race provided fresh examples in both

parties, as the selection of Lloyd Bentsen was at first overshadowed by a missed phone connection between Dukakis and Jackson, while the announcement of Quayle set off a firestorm among the 2,000 reporters covering the GOP convention. Neither controversy seemed to affect the outcome of the election, but each stirred new questions about the process. (It should be noted that at the Harvard conference, the campaign manager for Pat Robertson, Marc Nuttle, said he had polls which showed that Quayle actually added two percentage points to the Bush ticket, but others disputed that assertion.)

There is no perfect way to choose a vice president, but incorporating the 1988 experience, some rules seem to work better than others. A winning presidential campaign ought to quietly begin its homework early and complete the selection in a systematic, deliberative fashion. In 1984 Walter Mondale started early, but the process was so hurried in the end that his campaign did not fully understand the problems that lay ahead in the Ferraro selection. While Dukakis benefitted from a more thoughtful process in selecting Bentsen, his campaign let one vital detail slip: His campaign chairman, Paul Brountas, forgot to give campaign manager Susan Estrich the telephone number where Jackson could be reached. The ensuing flap not only undercut the positive impact of the Bentsen choice but gave Jackson enormous political leverage against Dukakis as the convention approached. In checking out prospective running mates, a candidate ought to employ someone with keen political as well as legal judgments. The selection of Quayle is still shrouded in mystery, but many Republican strategists believe the process was flawed because the Bush campaign posed a series of legal questions to him in advance and did not ask politically sensitive questions that would have revealed potential landmines. When the press dove into the story of his past military record, Bush campaign operatives did not have full answers and stayed up all night searching for them, prompting speculation that he might even be dropped from the ticket. The Quayle experience pointed up yet another rule: It is generally better for a candidate to announce his running mate in advance of the convention. Bush withheld the Quayle announcement in order to build suspense (a.k.a. a big television audience) for the GOP convention. As Roger Ailes said at Harvard, announcing a vice president at a convention can be like throwing a hotdog into the middle of a thousand piranhas. Reporters naturally focus on anything amiss with a running mate, and a convention also allows them ready access to the unhappy politicians who were passed over. Of course, it is always best for a candidate to go for quality and potential help in the electoral college, but he can never count on a running mate delivering many votes. In the 1988 race, many voters concluded that Bentsen was one of the best qualified vice presidential candidates in a long while, but he failed to bring a single state to the Democrats. Lee Atwater, the Bush campaign manager, argues that in retrospect John Glenn of Ohio might have been a better choice electorally. That view underscores a final rule, passed down from Richard Nixon: Recognizing that even the best running mate may not be much help, always ensure that he won't hurt the ticket. There speaks the voice of experience.

2. *Giving Jesse Jackson His Due*.   While reserved in their comments at the Harvard conference, Democratic managers in the Dukakis and Jackson camps were clearly preoccupied from the late primaries through the convention with achieving a happy partnership between their candidates. Jackson campaign manager Ron Brown, now chairman of the party, pointed out that after their man won seven million votes, many Jackson supporters believed he had earned the right to be named vice president. Jackson soon came to agree, but among Dukakis advisers there was little support, if any. After the Bentsen selection and the snafu over the missed phone call to Jackson, pressure began building among Jackson supporters to ensure he be given great recognition at the convention. Emotions reached such a high point by Atlanta, according to Brown, "My honest view is that our convention was hanging by a thread and that it took some extraordinary good luck for it. . . . not to come apart. We were really in the posture for quite a while of trying to convince our own people about how much we had accomplished during the 1988 cycle and what tremendous historic impact there was and what this meant to the political future of America. We had a tough selling job to do because there were extraordinary pressures."

What started as a quest for recognition struck the Dukakis team, however, as an aggressive upstaging of their man, and they still harbor resentments. Jack Corrigan, the Dukakis political director, put it this way, "I don't think you can ignore the fact that before the convention, the news coverage was dominated by Jesse Jackson and that there were plenty of other options and other ways to get to Atlanta than by bus with the traveling press corps. . . . We used to do a little analysis of network news coverage. And George Bush got 43 minutes essentially of biographical profile the week before the Republican convention. Jesse Jackson got twice as much coverage a week before the Democratic convention as Michael Dukakis did. While we emerged from the convention with a lead, I don't think that there was much information underneath it that gave people reasons and verifiable facts to carry around in their heads about Mike Dukakis. . . . [At the convention itself] Our 15 minutes of being famous was being consumed by somebody else. And that inevitably does its damage." Campaign manager Susan Estrich, echoing some of Corrigan's sentiments, pointed out that, from the end of the primaries through the convention, "Jesse Jackson was not going to go away." She says the Dukakis team worked hard during June to defuse potential conflicts with Jackson. But, in focusing so intently on him rather than on Bush, they saw their lead over Bush begin to slip away. The missed phone call then gave Jackson supporters a rallying cry. Eventually, of course, the two men patched up their relationship in Atlanta, but in the view of the Dukakis camp, the Democratic candidate had already suffered significant damage. Jackson did campaign extensively during the fall, but black turnout in November sank to 51.5 percent, down from 55.8 percent in 1984.

The story might be tucked away in history books did Democrats not face a looming possibility that Jesse Jackson could be even more powerful in 1992. In trying to accommodate Jackson, Dukakis agreed to rules changes for the next race that did not receive much notice at the time but could greatly enhance Jackson's delegate strength and his influence. The deal struck with Dukakis calls for proportional representation at virtually all levels. It reduces the number of "automatic" delegates—party officials who, it is presumed, put a premium on nominating the most electable candidates—and, by eliminating systems in such states as Pennsylvania and Illinois where winning candidates got almost all the delegates, the new rules could make it impossible for any candidate to assemble a delegate majority before the convention. This could make the convention the scene of much wheeling and dealing—something at which Jackson excels. To head off that kind of challenge next time, some moderate Democrats are calling for a scrapping of the new rules and argue that the potential rules fight will be the first significant challenge of Ron Brown's neutrality as chairman of the party. Beyond changing the rules again, Democrats in other camps seem no more certain about how to handle Jackson as a candidate in 1992 than in the past two campaigns. Some moderates such as Senator Chuck Robb (Va.) have indicated that white candidates ought to forget that he is black and be willing to disagree with him openly as they would with any other white candidate. Some Democrats also hope that other black candidates will soon emerge who will be more pro-establishment than Jackson. But if Jackson runs in 1992, he will probably continue to be a unique force in American politics and he could well be stronger at the next convention.

3. *Role of the Handlers.* Campaign managers have become increasingly visible in recent years, and in 1988 they nearly captured center stage, being frequently featured on television and in print. Ed Rollins, manager of Reagan's 1984 campaign, told the Harvard conference that the importance of handlers has been inflated and that they rarely make a difference of more than a point or two in the outcome. Yet there was a broad consensus at the conference that Bush enjoyed a major advantage in 1988 because he surrounded himself with far more campaign veterans than Dukakis and, unlike the Democrat, was willing to take their advice. According to Atwater, nearly two dozen members of the Bush team had held senior positions in previous presidential campaigns, and many had also spent several years in regional politics across the country. By contrast, Dukakis had only a handful of veterans, and most of them had previously concentrated on Northeastern races.

The problem for Democrats, argued Susan Estrich, is that the party's national campaign committees provide few year-round jobs for its managers, so that most take on legal or business jobs after campaigns end. She said that, as a result, several veterans of the past were unavailable to Dukakis. She also acknowledged that the governor preferred to hire people he already knew and that he was not acquainted with a number of Democratic professionals. Many Democrats in Congress have criticized Dukakis since the campaign for his failure to bring in more veterans and have insisted that the party train a cadre of managers for future campaigns.

Even if more Democrats are trained, however, there are major differences between the parties that may continue to give the GOP a competitive edge. Republican candidates tend to come from a narrower band of the ideological spectrum than Democrats, so that it is easier for managers from different campaigns to coalesce behind the winner of the primaries. The winner-take-all rules of the GOP primaries also bring their races to an end earlier than the Democrats. By the time of the final primary in June, the Republican candidate has usually established a decisive lead and can begin assembling his fall campaign team, while the Democrats take their nomination struggles all the way to the convention, making it harder to build a fall team. Democrats also have a history of turning to outsiders as nominees (e.g., Carter and Dukakis) who are more reluctant to bring in veterans of other years, while Republicans often follow a principle of primogeniture that helps establishment figures win their nominations and encourages establishment managers to join them. To catch up with the professionalism of the GOP at the presidential level, the Democrats will probably have to make more sweeping changes than now contemplated.

*   *   *

If there was a frustration at the Harvard conference, it was the inability of the participants to give as much attention as they wanted to the overriding political question that came out of 1988: How can future campaigns be conducted on a more substantive and constructive plane? Voters were clearly turned off. Not only did an extraordinary number not vote, but two-thirds said they wished they had choices other than Bush or Dukakis. Campaign managers apparently share that discomfort, but they are not fully certain what can be done to improve the process and feel powerless to change it alone.

In the eyes of the managers, several forces exist that encourage candidates to minimize serious policy dialogues and engage in negative, often personal attacks. Bush media adviser Roger Ailes put it most succinctly, "When I get hired by a candidate, my job is to help him get elected. I would like to change the system. I would like to spend all of my time on deep issues and talk about the homeless problem and figure out how to solve it, but it's damn hard to do it in a 10-week campaign when you are getting banged around by the opponent and the press is interested in pictures, mistakes, and attacks." While others accused Ailes of being too cynical, there is no doubt that his view is privately shared by many political managers.

The press is the target of most complaints. Bush campaign chairman James Baker pointed out during the campaign that when the vice president delivered a highly substantive speech on international trade, the networks ignored him, but when he attacked Dukakis he made the news. Dukakis political director Jack Corrigan bitterly argued at the Harvard conference that, in effect, the press aided and abetted Republican attacks by letting Reagan get away with a suggestion that Dukakis suffered from mental instability and by letting the GOP make other charges in advertisements and speeches that were rarely challenged for their veracity. Eventually (too late, say many), Dukakis returned fire. In the view of another Democrat, Sue Casey of the Hart campaign, "The fundamental thing that I think changed this time was the role of the press. Increasingly over time it has become more and more of a participant. . . . Jack [Corrigan] was making that point about the lies. I don't think that what he was saying was so much that they affected him, but that the press determined whether there was a political price that the Republicans would have to pay . . . [and] how they covered those lies or distortions, as they did with the Sasso thing, as they did with the Biden thing, as they did with the Hart thing, and as they did with Jackson. . . . We [the Democrats] have to accept the notion, which the Republicans did better than us, that the press is now a major participant in the process, and then, understanding that, go where they are going."

The campaign managers also seem to have convinced themselves that, even if the press were willing to pay more attention to issues, the public would not. "In America," said Ed Rollins, manager of the 1984 Reagan campaign and the 1988 Kemp campaign, "we don't stand out there and have great debates on great issues. And every time you start talking about issues, you lose some of the 18 points that swing back and forth. It's unfortunate, but that's the reality of the game." (Rollins believes that in almost every presidential race, roughly 18 percent of the electorate is up for grabs at the opening bell.) Echoing Rollins, Mondale's 1984 campaign manager Bob Beckel said, "The American people do not demand a hell of a lot. . . . I think they got what they asked for [in 1988], which was not much. I think this [is] a transition period going on, and we had two transitional candidates. . . ."

The Discussion

E. J. Dionne: In looking back and reflecting on what happened, everything ends up seeming much more rational than a campaign usually is. The notion of even the phrase, "a decision was made," is often in and of itself misleading. We have two or three subjects we would like to get to before the end of this session.

David Gergen: Our deliberations would not be complete without some discussion of what many in this country regard as a shallow campaign, a campaign which left the public highly dissatisfied and in which turnout was extraordinarily low. We should discuss how campaigns are conducted and what role and responsibility campaign managers had, not only in helping to elect somebody, but in worrying about what happens after an election and how well positioned the winner is to govern the country.

E. J. Dionne: One of the things we want to talk about is what responsibility there is for candidates who take public money. Is there any responsibility for the candidates to do particular things? And is there any way candidates can be held accountable for that money they take?

David Gergen: We're going to start with the Bush campaign and march through that as much as we can. After Roger leaves, we're going to look to Frank Fahrenkopf, Ed Rollins, and other Republicans who are here to help discuss some elements of that.

Easy first question, Roger: I think one of the great surprises in this campaign was the personal transformation of George Bush. Can you explain that? How did you manage it? What was behind it?

Roger Ailes: Well, as everybody knows, I did talk with him somewhat about his performance and so on, but it was much less than people think. I think George Bush was dramatically under-sold. By the time he got to the convention, he had been described as a wimp, a man who couldn't make a speech, and a man who would cave under pressure of the campaign. I think the public saw him at the convention do a good job and give a good speech. And they said once again the media have hoodwinked us; this guy is not as bad as everybody keeps telling us he is. And so I think that played into it as much as anything else.

Other than that, it's well known that I slowed him down a little bit. But beyond that, I think it was psychological on his part. He was vice president of the United States; he understood that role. In his own mind, he decided that at the convention he would step out. He didn't want to do it before then even though there was pressure from the campaign management team to get him to separate himself from Reagan a little bit on issues and speak out more forcefully and so on. His timetable called for the convention, and at the convention he made his move. From then on he was free. Once he said goodbye to Reagan on that tarmac in New Orleans, he changed and he became in his own mind what he wanted to project, which was a presidential candidate.

David Gergen: You had arranged for him to be with Reagan about two weeks after the convention for another campaign event in which he was terrible. Did Bush simply revert to being vice president? Was that the psychology? Was Reagan almost a father figure to him?

Roger Ailes: Pop-psychology says that he was somewhat of a father figure to him. I know he respected the President. The President was older. The President would, as George often said, give him tips about campaigning and about speaking and things like that. So I guess in a pop-psychology sense you can say that they had somewhat of a father-son relationship, but I think that's stretching it.

E. J. Dionne: Did you and Bob Teeter give the country Dan Quayle?

Roger Ailes: Well, Teeter takes no responsibility for that. No, I don't think so. The senior management team was asked to turn in a memorandum on vice presidential possibilities. As far as I know we all did that. I certainly did. I'm sure that, knowing the vice president, he had a network of other people he consulted—Frank and others—who submitted names. I think that group of names was probably immediately narrowed to 10 or 15 people.

There was a whole separate set of people who were responsible for checking out those people. Once we submitted the names, we had very little to do with it. We did have one final session in which there were probably seven or eight real people still being considered.

E. J. Dionne: Who were they at that point?

Roger Ailes: I don't want to get into that. I don't think that it's appropriate for me to talk about it. We were asked to do it on a confidential basis, and I will continue to do that. I think that most reporters, by process of elimination, figured out who was on that list. But we were asked to do it confidentially and not to comment on it.

But Quayle was on that list. And I think that if there are any reasons other than the public reasons that the vice president has already given for Dan Quayle, we may never know what they are. He alone made the decision, and if he writes a book some day when he retires, maybe he'll tell us more. But for the moment he has told us why he selected him, and I have no reason to disbelieve him.

David Gergen: Was one of the major criteria in your sessions to find someone who would appeal to the right?

Roger Ailes: Well, we knew that conventions are controlled by the left for the Democrats and by the right for the Republicans, and we weren't going to fly in the face of the conservatives. But there were people on the lists who were considered moderates or conservatives. There was not an excessive amount of discussion of that.

David Gergen: Was Atwater pushing the theory that you needed someone from the baby boom generation?

Roger Ailes: No, he was not.

E. J. Dionne: Was anybody pushing Quayle?

Roger Ailes: Well, I probably spoke out because I knew him better than most. When it got to each person in the meeting, whoever knew the person best spoke. I knew him because I had done his reelection campaign in Indiana, although I didn't know him well. I probably have been in his home once filming, probably once in Indiana, and a couple of meetings in his office. But I knew a little bit about his legislative work on the Job Training Partnership Act and on defense. I knew that whenever MacNeil-Lehrer wanted some expert on defense procurement or that sort of thing, he was considered an expert and a good guest.

David Gergen: Did you consider him qualified to be vice president?

Roger Ailes: Yes.

David Gergen: Do you still consider him so?

Roger Ailes: Yes.

E. J. Dionne: What kind of process did the Bush campaign go through in trying to vet these people? How much investigating was done? Were questionnaires given to them? What did you know about any of these guys?

Roger Ailes: I knew nothing about that side of it. As I say, I was part of a team that just said, "Here are some fellows. This is what I know; go to work."

E. J. Dionne: Was everybody taken by surprise, as it seemed?

Roger Ailes: Quayle certainly was.

E. J. Dionne: When the doubts about Quayle emerged, when all the stories about this or that started coming out, was that all a surprise?

Roger Ailes: The vice president reacts to that kind of crisis much more calmly than the staff does. I never saw him get particularly upset. He was a little upset that the guy was getting pounded for things that did not seem to have any basis.

You've got to remember there were 15,000 people from the media in New Orleans, and it was like dropping a hot dog in a tank of 15,000 bluefish, if you will. I was going to say sharks. That hot dog goes quick, you know what I mean? And it started really bumping in that tank. Because it was basically a hot dog in terms of the charges, and 15,000 bluefish can eat a hot dog pretty quickly.

E. J. Dionne: Did this give you doubts about the idea of naming him at the convention? Can you talk about the discussion of waiting until then? Who was for what?

Roger Ailes: I think the vice president decided that he wanted to wait until the convention. And, of course, as you know, in staging conventions you try to make them as interesting as possible because basically they are boring as hell.

Frank, you want to comment on that?

Frank Fahrenkopf: I was going nuclear because the rumor was that the announcement was going to be made at the Texas breakfast caucus on Thursday morning. I was very upset about that because I thought if the announcement was made then, the Friday morning news would be the selection of the vice president rather than the acceptance speech.

I was opting for what we did with Reagan in 1980 in Detroit: naming the vice presidential candidate after the roll call on Wednesday night. In fact, I could envision the glass elevator in the Marriott and Bush coming down, going over to the Superdome, and saying, "thank you for having confidence in me, and please nominate whoever tomorrow." That's what I was arguing for. I didn't find out the announcement was going to be made Tuesday until I greeted the boat in New Orleans on Tuesday.

E.J. Dionne: Why did he speed it up?

Roger Ailes: Well, on the plane down we didn't know who it was going to be. At that point the vice president was up in the cabin, when Baker went up. I think he probably told Baker at that point. When he landed on the tarmac of the naval air station, I think he informed the President—just before the President left.

We went to the commander's house on the base, and we were in a bedroom there with Bush—Atwater, Baker, Teeter, myself, Fuller. And the vice president said it was Quayle. Well, on the plane there was some discussion of whether we should hold this announcement. There was feeling that the media was starting—the media tends to want to set their own timetable for political events. They didn't have any news and needed something badly. We were starting to worry about getting stories that we were teasing—that we were fooling around with them, that we knew who it was and we weren't going to tell them—and so might create some negative press.

And so there was sort of a press stampede—to now that the decision was made, let's go with it. Let's just get it out, change the chemistry a little bit, make the convention a little more exciting. And I think that's why, at that moment, that Bush said in that room that it was Quayle and I said that I thought we should announce it as soon as we got into town.

E.J. Dionne: And what was said in the room?

Roger Ailes: About that?

E.J. Dionne: Yes.

Roger Ailes: Nothing. Everybody just started moving to get the thing set up.

David Gergen: How well did George Bush know Dan Quayle?

Roger Ailes: I have no idea other than the fact that he campaigned for him. He knew him from working on the Hill with him as president of the Senate, but I have no idea what their personal relationship is.

David Gergen: There was a leak to *The New York Times* on Saturday. There was some interpretation that the story was planted by someone in the campaign in order to torpedo Quayle.

Roger Ailes: I heard about that. Nothing surprises me, but I didn't have any first-hand knowledge of it. There were a lot of attempts to sabotage a lot of people.

David Gergen: Right.

Roger Ailes: If we went on that, we wouldn't have a vice president.

David Gergen: In what respect do you think that the process of background checks should have been more thorough?

Roger Ailes: I have no idea of what was done, so I can't comment on whether it was thorough enough. But here he is today vice-president-elect of the United States, having been investigated presumably by some of the best in the world with all the resources in the world, and I still don't know what he was guilty of. So the answer is I guess not.

E. J. Dionne: As all of this stuff on Quayle was unfolding you or someone in the campaign looked at the rules of the convention on how to nominate someone else. How close did you ever come to taking him off the ticket? What was the discussion like; what were the arguments for and against?

Roger Ailes: It was a very brief discussion. Somebody raised it; somebody said that's nuts. And we went on and proceeded with . . .

David Gergen: Was that at the overnight?

Roger Ailes: The overnight session. When it gets to this . . .

E. J. Dionne: What's "this"?

Roger Ailes: Well, there were accusations, but there was no evidence of anything. I think the vice president personally shut down any discussion of taking him off the ticket. Baker left the room, and when he came back in the room there was no more discussion about it. And when I saw the vice president—I'm not sure where in that period—for a few minutes to discuss the speech, it was very clear he was going forward. He saw absolutely not one ounce of reason or evidence or anything else to take him off the ticket. He was angry that the media was eating the kid alive, as he said. He said they were eating this guy alive and it was basically baloney.

David Gergen: Is it fair to say that there was a feeling within the campaign staff during that long session that you were not in possession of all the facts in the way you should have been?

Roger Ailes: Well, I don't know that we felt we weren't in possession of the facts, but there was certainly an attempt made—I think Kimmitt and Darman went over and spent some time with Quayle to review all the facts. And basically they came back and said we had all the facts.

E. J. Dionne: Ed, what was the reaction among other Republicans, notably Kemp, when they heard the words Dan Quayle?

Edward Rollins: I think most Republicans were somewhat surprised by it. Jack is the ultimate optimist. A lot of people, including myself, had tried to dissuade Jack from the fact that he was really a serious candidate. I just didn't think that Bush would ever pick Kemp. I thought in the final analysis the real decision was whether he would take Dole or someone else. Somewhere along the line, whether it was three weeks out or one night before, he made the decision that he didn't want Dole as a running mate and that he wanted Quayle. But I think people were somewhat stunned by it.

The environment in this convention was unique. I have been to several. Frank's been to a number. We were very concerned. I did commentary at the Democratic Convention. There was this tremendous enthusiasm, and everybody really thought they had a winner.

At our convention we had a pretty depressed group of delegates who certainly were very, very concerned about what was going to happen. Obviously they were overreacting to the polls and couldn't understand a lot of things that would happen. The Quayle thing was sort of thrown on that, like a match on gasoline. And the rush in judgment on him just sort of stirred that.

I think that just goes even more to the point that not only did everyone expect Bush to have to rise to the occasion and hit a home run on his speech, but by that day he had to rise and hit a grand slam home run. And obviously he did, which I think makes his performance that much greater.

I think people like Dole took it as an insult in the sense that Bush's choice was a peer and someone who obviously was his junior. But Kemp, I think, was relieved that the choice was a conservative. He obviously had known Quayle well and had respect for him.

David Gergen: Bill, how angry was Bob?

William Lacy: Frankly, I didn't talk to the senator about it. And I saw him once at the convention before he gave his speech and never really talked to him again. I think that he was a little bit concerned about the process of selection more than the final selection.

E. J. Dionne: What about it?

William Lacy: Again, I haven't discussed this with him in any depth, but he was in a position where he believed that he was the number two person in the race and that justifiably because of his experience and seniority should be treated in a very special way.

Edward Rollins: Going back to Kemp, Kemp resented it a little bit—and there were obviously rumors that Kemp wasn't going to get it. And any campaign doesn't control all the operatives. People were saying that Kemp wouldn't get it because he was a lightweight. So when he picked someone like Quayle, who was obviously not considered one of the pillars of strength in the Senate, that in itself added insult to injury. It made a few of the camps a little bit more resentful than they probably should have been.

In every cycle we screw up the vice presidential process very badly. Four years ago we sat here and talked about how Geraldine Ferraro was picked. I sat in sessions with others and talked about how Dole was picked and how Spiro Agnew was picked. It's probably the most important choice the presidential candidate has to make. And somehow we always try to make it a big show at a convention. It happens every cycle; someone who has very valid judgment in most things somehow ends up making bad judgments.

I think that the problem in this particular case obviously was that we wanted a suspenseful convention because Roone Arledge said he wasn't going to cover it, which was absurd. The Democrats, I think, showed great judgment in doing it the way they did this time, with someone who, obviously, if named on Wednesday of the convention, would have caused some problems.

Somehow we go through this process every four years and we try to keep it so confidential, I think, that one of the breakdowns here was that Bob Kimmitt, a very, very fine, decent guy who had been an Army officer when he was in the White House, a staff secretary, probably didn't ask all the political questions. He was not a political guy but obviously could ask the legal questions.

When I have a candidate, I always tell him, "I'm your priest; you confess all your sins to me and I'll tell you whether they are mortal or venial." And, I think if Roger or some others had been in the mix at the decision time, they could have raised a lot of political issues that might have at least prepared you for the onslaught that was coming.

David Gergen: How did you respond?

Roger Ailes: As I said, I don't know what information the vice president was given. I don't know how they arrived at that information exactly, so I can't comment on it. I assume that the vice president did talk to Baker or Teeter or somebody at some point for some political judgment. Maybe that's not true. I don't know.

E.J. Dionne: Was Baker against the choice? And how did Bush react to the fact that Baker somehow managed to get it out that he had been against the choice?

Roger Ailes: Baker never expressed displeasure with the choice that I know of.

E.J. Dionne: Before or after?

Roger Ailes: That's right.

David Gergen: Did you have pressure from outside the campaign to drop him?

Roger Ailes: Well, we were pretty insulated at that time. But when I'd go back to my room, there would be a few phone messages, so I certainly assume that there were a few phone messages from others around the country saying, "Gee, what's going on down there?" I didn't return them after I realized what they were about. I suppose others didn't either.

You're insulated, you are on a very tight timetable, and you try to make very critical decisions while recognizing the seriousness of the situation. You're trying to deal with just facts and not the emotionalism of others. And it's getting those facts and then making a decision that has to be done quickly.

E.J. Dionne: What did you think as you were watching TV reports on this choice and what was coming across on television?

Roger Ailes: Well, everybody was first trying to figure out how it happened and to pin it on somebody. And I think they were surprised that I wasn't running from it and that I had made that recommendation—and, I didn't, wouldn't, won't run from it. So I didn't have any feeling about it whatsoever. Based on the information we had and based on Darman and Kimmitt's trip, I thought that there was excessive press behavior for lack of a story. We either would weather it or we wouldn't, but certainly we were going to keep him on the ticket.

Graham Allison: Just a footnote, Roger. You talked about the hot dog and 15,000 bluefish. Is that just retrospective, or had you thought about it ahead of time, would you have dropped this hot dog into the bluefish, and what did you think would happen?

Roger Ailes: I considered the hot dog to be the information they had about Quayle's background that would show him to be unqualified for vice president as opposed to him as a person.

Graham Allison: But there was going to be a surprise in that there were 15,000 bluefish in the tank.

Roger Ailes: Well, listen, if you had Bob Dole and he had said something off the wall about George Bush, as he is likely to do, that would have created additional bacchanal. Any choice had some doubts on it.

David Gergen: Who decided to put him on the networks?

Roger Ailes: Baker.

David Gergen: Baker did?

Roger Ailes: As far as I know, it was Baker.

David Gergen: With what point in mind?

Roger Ailes: Well, we felt that we had nothing to hide, and we didn't. I say Baker. I'm sure that press people were involved. Lake and others were there. They must have had a conversation. I wasn't privy to it, but I think the feeling was that he wasn't guilty of anything. And I don't think they correctly assessed the trauma to him at that moment in putting him into this network interview situation that night. But the feeling was there nothing to hide; therefore, the more exposure, the better.

David Gergen: In future campaigns, how would you recommend that a vice presidential choice be made?

E. J. Dionne: And when?

Roger Ailes: There are too many variables pressing on the decision. I think that it's a legitimate question. First of all, you are never going to be able to influence him because the candidate, if he is half a candidate, is going to have the major say. He's the 800-pound gorilla. And he may have decisions about how that should be done.

We thought that the procedure of trotting John Glenn out and raising his hand like a supermarket sweepstakes winner was wrong. Perhaps the way we did it or the vice president did it without the meetings was wrong. I think we were all making mistakes.

I think that Ed's correct, that we should have more political input, but candidates get very concerned about leaks on these kinds of things. They are concerned for several reasons. You have to tell many people they aren't going to get the job. In many cases you have personal relationships with these people. You can't reach them. There are a lot of problems involved in that process. And the time frame escalates quickly.

But how would I improve it? I was there when they picked Agnew in 1968. I saw that process. And I was a young kid; it was my first campaign.

David Gergen: That was the last time that you went up for vice president?

Roger Ailes: I wasn't, but I saw. If you think that this process was bad, I thought that process was worse. They had the Lindsey wing of the party and the Reagan wing of the party, and by process of elimination to avoid anybody walking out, they narrowed the field to somebody.

E.J. Dionne: To what extent was this a process of elimination?

Roger Ailes: I have no idea. I wasn't in it. As I say, I sent a memorandum giving pros and cons on 10 or 12 people. When it narrowed down to 6 or 7, I was asked again. Originally I thought that George Deukmejian would be a good choice and that was the first thing that I probably said or the first position I took. Deukmejian took himself out of the race for political reasons, and we moved on.

David Gergen: Deukmejian took himself out several weeks before the process started.

Roger Ailes: The first memorandum was, I believe, in July sometime.

E.J. Dionne: Did you set up Huntington, Indiana?

Roger Ailes: No.

David Gergen: Did Darman set up Huntington, Indiana?

Roger Ailes: I don't know. Somebody might want to comment on that. I don't honestly know. I wasn't there.

I knew we felt that Quayle wasn't guilty of anything and the more exposure to the press, the better. The press was getting angrier and angrier because they didn't have anything, and they had been pounding on it for a long time. They just got a little too aggressive.

E. J. Dionne: Did you think that would happen? Did anybody in the campaign think that through?

Roger Ailes: You have to understand guys like me see the press that way most of the time. So I didn't see anything unusual in their behavior. Maybe the American people did.

David Gergen: Was Huntington, though, a trap?

Roger Ailes: No, no. I think everybody was surprised by the audience reaction.

E. J. Dionne: Meanwhile up in Boston what was the reaction to this choice? And what is your view of the theory that, in fact, Dan Quayle, far from being a disaster for Bush, ended up drowning you out?

Susan Estrich: Our first reaction when we heard Dan Quayle was chosen was pleasant surprise. In terms of his voting record and his experience, in terms of the reaction we saw coming out of the Republicans, in terms of the impact it was having on the Republicans' ability to communicate their anti-Dukakis message at their own convention—all of these were obviously positives from our point of view. And, in particular, such issues—and Roger and I have talked about this—as plant closings, which we thought was a very strong issue for us, and Dan Quayle having led the fight against Lloyd Bentsen, provided a really sharp contrast on an issue that worked for us.

And, again, it was at the point that we were expecting four days of Dukakis-bashing. And if you watched the evening news, what you were getting instead were questions about Quayle. But what started out as something that we thought could be used very effectively to our advantage quickly turned in the other direction, culminating with the Huntington, Indiana, press conference.

I think there was a sense—and this goes back to something that we talked about earlier—that these politicians were out there somehow being destroyed by this intensive press scrutiny. And I think two things happened by the time of Huntington, Indiana. First, I thought that George Bush's defense of Dan Quayle helped George Bush in terms of his own character problems coming into the convention of weakness and of not being a stand-up guy. Standing up and defending Dan Quayle was something that he did with strength and conviction. His going out very strongly to defend his choice helped him, in fact, deal with the character problem that he faced coming into the convention.

Second, I think that Huntington, Indiana, press conference, at least when I saw it on television, was one in which the press came out looking so bad that Dan Quayle began looking beleaguered by the press, not by his own misdeeds or alleged misdeeds.

Then it was followed by the incident when he was taking out his trash and was asked about that whole Paula Parkinson case and the like. My sense was—and I think, Tubby, we started to see it as well in our polling—that far from dragging the ticket at that point,

George Bush's own favorables were coming up. The reaction was that the press had gone too far. What's been called the invisible hand pulled in very strongly right then. This year of press attacks on character or perceived press attacks on character ended to George Bush's great credit.

Now much later, questions were raised about Quayle, and Quayle was one of the few judgments George Bush made that Ronald Reagan provided him no protection on. Many of his other vulnerabilities, our Bush vulnerabilities, were things where Ronald Reagan gave George Bush a lot of protection. This wasn't one. And later on we tried to use the Quayle issue on offense to some effect.

But in August I think that George Bush's strength in defending him and the view of the press which emerged in Huntington and at the end of his street, Quayle helped.

E. J. Dionne: The irony—and I want to ask Roger about this—is that in the end the press came out unpopular, but the attacks on Dan Quayle really pulled him down in the long run. By the end of the campaign somehow that whole thing sank in and Quayle became very unpopular.

Roger Ailes: I don't know. What was the victory, 54 to 46? What would it have been without Quayle, 58 to 42?

E. J. Dionne: What do you think?

Roger Ailes: I'm not sure. My guess is that there was no movement. I think we may have hit our ceiling in that situation. I'm not sure that Quayle had any net effect. Paul, do you have a different feeling?

Paul Brountas: I'm not sure it had any net effect. I think that what we tried to do later on after August was to show the contrast. I think Ed Rollins said it best: that this is the first presidential decision that the presidential candidate makes.

We went through a very careful process. We didn't parade people around. We tried to avoid the Mondale problem of parading people. And, in fact, Lloyd Bentsen told me, "I don't want to be involved if I'm going to be embarrassed."

So what we were trying to focus on was how presidential candidates make their decisions. With whom did each consult? Did he consult with other people? George Bush criticized our process and said that he was going to keep the process ladened with suspense until the end and that only he and his associates would know.

We took a different approach. I spent several days in Washington talking with senators and congressmen. We were on the phone with governors and other political and nonpolitical leaders throughout the country. We did keep it very quiet. I mean, there was a committee of one. However, I consulted with Susan, and Susan solicited the key aides to the campaign. We believed we learned from the mistakes of the past.

So we thought we had an issue: that this was the first presidential decision. Who made the best decision in terms of the result, the person, is he qualified, is he a senior statesman, a knowledgeable and respected senator, or is he junior and inexperienced? The second issue was how we did it. Does the process give you indications as to how the candidate will make presidential decisions in the future?

So I believe we did use it effectively as the campaign went on, but there is no question about it—Susan's right—during August, Quayle dominated the news for 10 days.

Roger Ailes: Can I ask a question? It was clear to us that one of your major negative things was going to be judgment. And Quayle played into that. You were doing Noriega, you were doing Iran-Contra, you were doing Quayle. When did you arrive at that theme? We saw it in free media; we saw it in paid media; we saw it early; we saw it late. But it seemed sporadic. How was that used?

William Carrick: Huntington, Indiana, was a very important event in this campaign. It marks the turning point in the dynamic of the race. Judgment would have been a good argument up until the point where a larger issue, which was the role the press was playing in the campaign, became more important. It obscured questions about the candidates to a great extent. For a long period after that what we saw was the Bush campaign essentially being complimented on their ability to manipulate the media by the media. And that was very different from the dynamic of the race in 1987.

Questions came up in October about the conduct of the campaign. And there was a late return to a focus on character. But if you call 1987 the year of character issue, 1988, after the Republican convention, it's not an issue at all. There were basically no inquiries into truth or values or anything except tactics and the effectiveness of tactics. I think that that was a very clever move by the Bush campaign.

Edward Rollins: I think that's one very important issue. With a 10-week campaign, anytime you can lose a week in the campaign, you are way ahead of the game. As Roger said earlier, in America we don't stand out there and have great debates on great issues. And every time you start talking about issues, you lose some of the 18 points that swing back and forth. It's unfortunate, but that's the reality of the game.

So every campaign week lost to some other issue puts you way ahead of this business. And Roger had a plan; he had cycles; he had media programs and what have you. But with everybody focused on Quayle as they were, he became a terrible distraction to your campaign at a very crucial time. And I thought that he was a tar baby.

I agree with Roger. I think the damage that was done by the decision was done very quickly. Any Democrats who were thinking about going with Bush, went right back to you. Republicans always come home. I don't care where they go in the meantime; they always come home in the final analysis.

I heard bitching and moaning from many in this country, and from Republicans, but in the final analysis the choice between Quayle as the second choice or Mike Dukakis as President was a very easy choice for them to make. At least 3 weeks out of that 10 weeks, both national media and your campaign were focused on Quayle. Basically that gave us some significant advantages.

Susan Estrich: We disappeared for a number of reasons, one of which was we were not out there campaigning full time. But even when we were out there campaigning in August, we disappeared around Quayle.

In answer to your question, Roger, on judgment, there were five or six issues that Tubby isolated early on that could be packaged into judgment: Iran-Contra, Noriega, and terrorism. Quayle emerged as one. What we found was, and I get back to Reagan here, that on all of those issues except for Quayle and the quality of his campaign, they all related to action Bush had taken or not taken as vice president within the Reagan administration. And by and large, while they were not totally ineffective, the public had already decided that Reagan was responsible overall and they forgave Reagan.

So their impact and their saliency against George Bush was much diminished by something we didn't talk about yesterday but which I think ultimately is a lot more important than most of the tactical decisions we made one way or another. That's the impact of Ronald Reagan on this race and the popularity, the growing popularity of his presidency coupled with the peace and prosperity, which gave you your strongest theme.

David Gergen: Just a couple of questions. Were you bluffing the Dukakis people on the debates?

E. J. Dionne: When you put this man [Brountas] through such misery.

David Gergen: You knew that you were going to do debates.

Roger Ailes: We thought that we would certainly end up having to do debates, although we did think that there was some argument that we could get away with one if we had to. We certainly never intended to do more than two no matter what.

David Gergen: Did you intentionally play the role of the heavy in those debate negotiations?

Roger Ailes: No. It's my natural personality.

Paul Brountas: You do it very well.

Roger Ailes: Well, every time Baker said, "Listen, I've got to leave, I'm going to leave you two with Ailes," we got another concession.

David Gergen: Roger, I want to know about the conventional wisdom that says you can't attack when your negatives are high. Your campaign attacked and you brought your negatives down. Did you believe all along that Bush could safely go on the attack against Dukakis to drive those negatives up?

Roger Ailes: Well, there are two things that you have to do: You've got to get your negatives down and you have to get the other guy's up, but you also have to increase your positives. We had to do that. So I'm not sure we ever went into negatives 100 percent. We always kept positive on the air. We kept positive 60-second ads on cable throughout. We kept positive on the networks. We tactically used negative advertising.

E. J. Dionne: But it was Bush himself who did that.

Roger Ailes: Well, our feeling was you do both, you go out and do major issue speeches and you know that you are not going to get an ounce of coverage. But you have to do those. Otherwise, they'll say that you are just doing negatives. So you do your ethics speech and you do your program speech and you do all the things that the news media is not interested in. And then once every two weeks you get a major attack on the other guy and you get massive coverage. So you just have to work back and forth all the way through the 10 weeks doing positive and negative.

And I'm sure they did the same thing. And we did the same thing, knowing full well that we would take a bad news hit when we had to do issues.

Judy Woodruff: Roger, I was traveling with Bush. He was criticizing Dukakis in literally every speech.

Roger Ailes: The mix became half good news and half bad news. It's paying heaven and paying hell. It's the old evangelist style that every candidate uses. I don't think that Dukakis had a much different formula for speaking than we did. He had major issue papers. Somebody said he put out more than we did. I don't know that. We ended up binding ours in a book so that we would know that we had them.

Susan Casey: Roger, I thought that doing the negatives in the attacks was the way you were building your positives, to get rid of that "wimp" thing. And I thought that was really clever. You could do the negatives to build your positives.

Roger Ailes: Well, somebody said the "wimp" thing was fairly well gone after he defended Quayle. After he had gotten through the Dan Rather thing, he became the nominee of the party, he gave a good speech at the convention, and he defended Dan Quayle. By then people were feeling that he was tough enough.

But, actually, the two candidates were very close together. In the beginning Michael Dukakis had stronger numbers—and Tubby probably knows this better—on the strength issue. By the end of the campaign Bush was seen as the stronger.

Irwin Harrison: Bush never had that high wimp factor. I don't know where that came from.

Roger Ailes: That was way back. That was right after the *Newsweek* coverage. That changed fairly quickly after that.

David Gergen: If you had been the third man in the Dukakis campaign, what would you have done differently in their campaign?

Roger Ailes: I would have done the same thing I did in my campaign. I wrote in the contract what my turf was and made sure that I held it and that I could make the decisions I had to make quickly.

E. J. Dionne: What would you have attacked Bush on?

Roger Ailes: I would have stayed on the air with plant closings even after the bill was signed. I think they had some very good positive ads early—those that had the graphics at the bottom. They group-focused well. They group-focused by our side well. I got very nervous about it. I was so happy the day they took those off the air. And I don't know why you did it; God must be on our side.

Susan Estrich: Well, it wasn't exactly God. (Laughter).

David Gergen: How would you have handled a negative campaigning for Dukakis?

Roger Ailes: I think they made a mistake by changing tactics. Our impression was Michael Dukakis was a liberal governor and he was trying to pretend he was a moderate or conservative. He was running on our issues. He was running on crime, which is a Republican issue, saying that he lowered the crime rate and so on. And he was constantly getting forced over to our issues. He had us on plant closings.

So we took an air strike into his base on the environment. He immediately reacted, immediately defending environment and attacking us on environment. Frankly, that was an issue we could afford to lose because liberals always get the environment in the end. It didn't matter. We felt as long as the argument was on issues that were good for us—crime, national defense, and what have you—that if we controlled the agenda and stayed on our issues, by the end we would do all right.

David Gergen: But your argument is if you had been in his shoes, you would have changed the agenda?

Roger Ailes: I would have changed the agenda, that's correct.

E. J. Dionne: When did you win the election? Do you think that it was won before or after the second debate? I mean, was it still open before the second debate in your view?

Roger Ailes: Oh, yes. I still felt there was a chance. I felt that there was a chance to flip it in the last 15 days after the second debate. They had to get through the eye of the needle. I thought it would be awfully tough to do. But they were getting some help by that time by the free media because the media have an investment in the horse race. They don't want low ratings on election night; they've already sold their spots for X number of dollars. But I think at that point there was still an opportunity to flip it but not a big one. We would have had to make a mistake at that point and they would have had to capitalize on it.

Clearly, they could have done it had Dukakis done a better performance in the second debate. I think that hurt him because while it ignited this sort of Harry Truman finish, it also demoralized their own troops. I have to believe that kind of thing demoralizes the troops because presidential candidates at that point are looked at very closely and people say—they said to George Bush—you have to hit a triple homer, you have to hit a home run at the convention on your speech. And he did. And they said to Michael Dukakis, you have to hit a home run in this debate, and he didn't. And people after all reduce it down to fairly simplistic language: I want a President who can hit a home run.

E. J. Dionne: Now, let's go all the way back and take up the Democratic side from the vice presidential choice on. The one vice presidential choice who by every objective measure was a failure was Lloyd Bentsen. He didn't carry Texas. He didn't carry the South. What happened? Can you describe, Susan, Paul, Jack, the process you went through in selecting him, leading up to the kitchen table in Brookline?

Paul Brountas: I should say, first, that when the governor spoke to me about taking on the assignment, I wanted to prepare something fairly quickly so we would be ready. He resisted and said, "We don't want to discuss it now; I don't want any memos until June 7, until California is won."

On the morning of June 8 I gave him a memorandum; I showed it to Susan and nobody else. He read it at breakfast and we talked about it on the plane for a couple hours coming back. And he said, "Okay, go to work." So we had an agreed-upon agenda and a process that we were going to follow, and we followed it. It essentially involved reaching out and talking to literally hundreds of people and getting their ideas and suggestions.

Then I went to Washington and started interviewing prospective candidates as well as other people for suggestions and comments. I handed him a list of about 25 or 30 prospects initially. It quickly narrowed down to about 10 or 12. Sam Nunn and Bill Bradley took themselves out of the competition fairly quickly. Sam Nunn did agree to wait until Dukakis had a chance to talk to him personally.

Then we went to work together and set up a team to do the background work. Vicky Radd headed up that team with some lawyers and others. It was a very, very thorough and careful process. I personally interviewed each of the candidates and each of the candidates' wives and asked them some difficult questions. I think that the wives found them more difficult than the husbands.

Graham Allison: Can I interrupt for just a second to ask you a question? Did you not at some point, even early before this process, sit down and say, "We've got to get the 270 electoral votes? No Democrat has been elected without Texas. Bush is from Texas. There is a problem. How are we going to get to 270? And Texas is going to be critical in all of this." Therefore, there was no choice; Bentsen had to be there. I mean, while you went through the process and talked about other people, in the back of your strategy planning if he fit and there weren't any problems, you had to go there.

Paul Brountas: Well, there was input from key political advisers, Jack Corrigan and other senior staffers, who had analyzed the electoral college countless times. Others also had input. But insofar as where we were heading and how we would narrow the list, we were looking for the best qualified candidates.

And then we finally narrowed the list down to a few candidates. I had breakfast with Governor Dukakis to review the final list two days prior to the day the announcement was made. I spent two or three hours with the governor that morning, flew to Washington, and met with Jesse Jackson to complete his interview. In the afternoon the governor met with Susan Estrich, Jack Corrigan, and Kirk O'Donnell. During the course of the day he also called several other people for their thoughts and reactions.

E. J. Dionne: Like who?

Paul Brountas: I don't know. He had a list of people he was going to call.

Due to a storm in Washington. I couldn't get back to Boston. At about 7 p.m. I was on the phone at the airport. I remember the embarrassing article that appeared in *The Boston Globe*. There were several reporters around. I called Susan and the governor several times and reported on my meeting with Reverend Jackson. At about 8 p.m., I tried to reach the governor again and Kitty answered the phone. Michael was outside. She said she thought that he was going to decide the vice presidential nominee later that night.

A young lady whom I had never seen before and apparently was an intern from *The Boston Globe* was talking in the phone next to me. But she was also listening to me. The next morning a story in *The Globe* reported that I asked Kitty to put Michael on the phone, indicating that this was the most important decision that he will make in the campaign and he should not make the decision without one more go-round with his advisers.

The governor came to the phone and we made arrangements to meet, if I could get back, with Susan and Jack at his home at about 10:15, and we did. At that meeting, we went over the list one more time. Also, since he had been talking to several people individually during the day, I wanted to hear what he had heard. I also wanted Susan and Jack to make any additional suggestions.

At about 11:30 that night we went around the table. There was unanimity for Senator Bentsen. Governor Dukakis then said, "Well, let's call Bentsen now," which would have been a good idea because we would have been able to act quickly the next morning. Unfortunately, Senator Bentsen had turned off his phone because he was getting a lot of disturbing calls from the press. We were not able to reach him until early the next morning.

E. J. Dionne: What happened between you and Jesse Jackson? What was said back and forth at that meeting? And why did you wait until the end? If Jackson was under such serious consideration, why put him at the very tail end of the list just before you announce?

Paul Brountas: Because we were not able to get all of the information that we needed from Jackson. Everybody else got the information to us before he did. We had talked about meeting in Texas the Friday before, but we didn't have the responses to our questions. His lawyers were sending us additional documents, but they hadn't arrived. When they did, we needed more time to review them.

E.J. Dionne: What did you say to each other at that meeting?

Paul Brountas: I talked about the process—what we were doing, why we were doing it that way, what we were looking for, and how the vice presidential candidate could help the ticket or not help the ticket.

E.J. Dionne: What did you tell him about how he might not help the ticket?

Paul Brountas: I'm not going to get into that conversation. We didn't focus on why he might not help the ticket. Instead we talked about how he could help the ticket, and he told me why he should be the vice president.

David Gergen: Was there anybody in your campaign who thought that he should be on the ticket?

Paul Brountas: I don't think anybody said he ought to be on the ticket or not be on the ticket. It was assumed he was going to be one of the finalists, that was clear. He had earned the right to be on the ticket by getting seven million votes and he was considered for the ticket.

Robert Beckel: Did you know, Paul, that early in June after the California primary there was enormous pressure building on Jackson. At a meeting that took place in Chicago, his own people put a lot of pressure on him to run for vice president. Even though you all wanted to be fair and open on this, did you understand the intensity of the campaign, particularly in the black community? Did you think that it may have made sense to cut the Jackson deal off because you had nobody telling you politically it made any sense? In fact, I know a number of people said that it would be devastating to have him.

Paul Brountas: No. We thought of that. Our response, at least the majority response, was that there were seven or eight candidates, one of whom was black. How do you go in advance to the one candidate who is black and tell him, "You're out of the race," before you have considered or talked to all of the candidates, before you make your final judgment, particularly when he came in second? In our view, it would have been unfair and a terrible mistake.

E.J. Dionne: Did Jesse change his mind on this in the course of time between California and as it got closer to the choice?

Ronald Brown: Change his mind in what way?

E.J. Dionne: Did he move toward wanting it more? Was he influenced by this movement that was going on?

Ronald Brown: This was an evolutionary process that started, as far as my personal knowledge, the day after the California primary. It really started, as many things do in this business, with a press question. In a 24-hour period it went from "I deserve serious consideration" almost to "I ought to be on the ticket." And there was a lot of discussion about how far to go with this, how far to take it so as not to look like you were pleading for it.

There was a lot of concern about the appearance of it. And, obviously, this concern was highlighted because some of us thought that it wasn't going to happen under any circumstances and, frankly, didn't want to see him in a position of appearing to be asking for something that was not in the cards.

But only he can answer this. My own observation was that at first it was something that you expected to be asked, and then you were somewhat titillated by it, and then you began to think that it made a lot of sense, and then you began to think why not me as compared with the others.

So, yes, there was an evolution, and it happened pretty fast. I would say by the time we left California he thought he ought to be on the ticket, he thought that he deserved it, and he thought he had earned it and that there had better be a reason other than his race for not putting him on the ticket.

E.J. Dionne: What if the Dukakis people had cut it off either before or right after California, saying they had polling numbers that showed Jackson pulled them down 10 to 15 points? If that had happened at that stage, what do you think would have happened?

Ronald Brown: I think the information that Bob Beckel gives is important. There was enormous pressure building. I'm not sure that it would have been easy for Jackson to accept that decision earlier. I think that there would have been tremendous pressure on him. He had run an extraordinarily constructive presidential campaign and wanted to be seen as a constructive force in the Democratic party. I think the Dukakis campaign was in a dilemma. It would have been very hard for them to cut it off early.

Paul Brountas: In fact, he did comment on that during our meeting. And he said, "You know, I'm hearing about polls that indicate I would hurt the ticket, but I received seven million votes, and let me tell you how many black voters I can turn out if I'm on the ticket." He had assembled convincing facts and figures.

Ronald Brown: He was, in fact, prepared to clearly articulate the reasons for selecting him and was beginning to do that. I sat in the first meeting with him and Paul and we talked about how the VP selection process was going to work and pretty much were assured that he was going to be in the process throughout and was going to be kept informed of the process throughout. That was the commitment among the three of us.

David Gergen: Ron, was it your view at the time that he would help the ticket?

Ronald Brown: Compared to what? Compared to what happened? Compared to what our expectations were then? I don't know. Whether Michael Dukakis would have won with Jesse Jackson, I don't know. The way things came out, I rather doubt it. Whether Jesse Jackson on the ticket would have been better than the way it turned out—I think it's possible.

Robert Beckel: Ron, let me follow up on that question. You had a situation developing which I thought was one of the best and least reported political moves on your part in your service to Jackson. You almost had a run-away organization on your hands, as you know.

In early July there were rump meetings going on all over the country. The amazing thing to me is this press corps, which had a lot of nothing to say in July, missed it all. You almost had a run-away situation. You had a couple of blow-out meetings in California. Jackson couldn't keep his hands on the edge. You had Chicago meetings, meetings in the South, grass roots, Jackson roots from 1984; Mississippi, Alabama, and Georgia were threatening to march on the convention. Lots of stuff was going on. Did you not think at a certain point that it was going to get out of hand, and you may have a situation at the convention where you couldn't control your delegates?

Ronald Brown: My honest view is that our convention was hanging by a thread and that it took some extraordinary good luck for it not to come apart. We were really in the posture for quite a while of trying to demonstrate to our own people how much we had accomplished during the 1988 cycle, what tremendous historic impact there had been and what this meant to the political future of

America. We had a tough selling job to do because there were extraordinary pressures.

I had just come into the campaign in May. At that time I was suspect for being an insider and too much of a party person and all that, which is quite the opposite of what I am going through now with regard to the chairmanship of the Democratic National Committee. But it was a difficult situation.

I think that I was never sure, because of what you pointed out, Bob, that was clearly understood by the Dukakis people or by the press. It was often portrayed as if we were trying to stick up the convention and doing awful things to create disorder and whipping up this fervor. As a matter of fact, what we were trying to do is keep a lid on it and come through the process in some kind of rational way.

There were some very difficult times during the summer right before the convention, which Paul mentioned earlier, such as the caravan coming down from Chicago. I was in Atlanta then getting ready to go into negotiations with Paul and trying to figure out what the agenda was. I flew up to Nashville to meet the caravan the morning before I met with Paul for the first time. There was a lot of fervor in the room, I mean a lot of strong feelings about what ought to happen. This, of course, was after the missed phone call. There were a lot of things that had fanned the fires. So we were in a very hairy predicament.

William Carrick: I know how Ron Brown behaved in all this. I know that he was extremely responsible and performed a great service to the Democratic party.

I think the real question is where Reverend Jackson was. You had these competing forces of pragmatists who did not think he was going to get the nomination under any circumstances versus this sort of grass-roots fervor that almost felt that he should demand the place on the ticket. Where was Jesse Jackson?

Ronald Brown: You know, in all honesty, we were on the same page throughout. I wouldn't have been there if we weren't on the same page. It wasn't a question of Ron Brown trying to contain or hold down or make Jesse Jackson rational. I think the fact that he asked me to play the kind of role that I played shows where he was.

You know, we talked five times a day and two times a night. He knew exactly where he was and where I was. Jesse Jackson during 1988 went through a personal evolution too. I mean he was very intent on expanding his base and being a constructive force and playing a significant role in the party. He knew what that meant.

There were a lot of things in the balance, though, such as the question of whether he wanted to be the vice-presidential nominee. Was he upset about not being selected? I think the answer is probably yes. But did he want a future in the Democratic party, and did he want the Democratic nominee to win? Did he want to help in that process? The answer is yes.

So I think that we were really in the same place. Clearly, he wanted to maximize his impact at the convention. We had some specific goals. We wanted to have a real impact on the convention; we wanted to have an impact on the platform; we wanted to have an impact on the fall campaign; and should Governor Dukakis be elected, we wanted to have an impact on the transition and in the new Dukakis administration.

So there were specific goals that were clearly spelled out. Paul and I talked about them in detail several times during that intense 42 hours and finally came away with, as Ed Rollins has described it, a really upbeat, super-enthusiastic convention united behind the candidate.

Judy Woodruff: In connection with that, Ron, you said a minute ago you were trying to tamp down the fervor of all of Jackson's supporters, but to what extent was Jackson himself contributing to raising their hopes?

William Carrick: For example, the speech he gave when he arrived in Atlanta at Piedmont Park was not a conciliatory speech, saying "We're going to all unite and come out of Atlanta and beat the Republicans." It was, "We've got an agenda, we're here, we're going to accomplish specific goals and if they don't listen to us . . ."

Robert Beckel: What did you expect him to say, Bill, "We love these guys"?

William Carrick: No, I'm not saying I expected that. I'm not editorializing about the speech.

Ronald Brown: In honesty, when you're in the eye of a hurricane there's got to be a lot of mutual confidence and trust. And I think during that process I had built with Jackson a relationship of mutual confidence and trust. He knew everything I was talking to Paul and Susan and others about. We knew what dynamics were taking place. We knew where we wanted to get. We knew it was going to be tough getting there. And we had a very tough balancing act.

He had taken everything to the brink. I don't mean deliberate brinkmanship, but after all he had done real well in this campaign. He had excited a lot of people, generated a lot of enthusiasm and broadened his base. He had done just about everything he set out to do except get the nomination. And he had a real responsibility to a lot of folks who believed deeply in him. So I think he was feeling that. And there was a very delicate balance.

One of the things that was missed is that we had a real outside-the-convention problem at one point. It was one problem dealing with the people in the hall. There was another problem dealing with people with different expectations and a different agenda who were outside, who really were our responsibility because we were going to be, fairly or unfairly, saddled with that responsibility. So there was a real difficult, touchy problem for us. And I think he was addressing that in the speech he gave.

E. J. Dionne: I want to go to Jack for a second and then to Susan and Paul. Jack, you were a hawk in the campaign in this issue. And at some point you were quoted publicly as being very angry about the way the Jackson people and Mr. Jackson himself were dealing with the Dukakis campaign. Can you talk about your reaction at that time and what you were going through.

John Corrigan: I don't think that I was quoted as being angry. I made one comment which became controversial, obviously, because Reverend Jackson didn't like it. The comment was that we were going to treat him the same way as any second-place finisher. That was unfortunate—it came out a little different than I intended it to. I was quoted accurately, but what I was trying to say was that most of the issues that a challenger faces coming into a convention against the front-runner and apparent nominee are fairness issues: Are you going to get enough seats? Are you going to get enough credentials? What is the platform going to reflect? What are the rules going to be like? What kind of place is going to be accorded to this second-place finisher at the convention?

I had worked for Kennedy in 1980, and we had very strong feelings. We were not treated fairly with respect to the number of votes we got. What I was trying to say was that in 1988, Jesse Jackson was going to get every consideration that he was entitled to based on the number of votes he got. In retrospect, it would have been a much better idea if I had said that.

But I don't think you can ignore the fact that before the convention, the news coverage was dominated by Jesse Jackson. There were plenty of other options and other ways to get to Atlanta than by bus with a traveling press corps. That attention was pointed out earlier. I think that anytime you win the nomination early and can consolidate the party, you can move on to the general election. If you face a challenge through the convention, then that forces you to do internal politics rather than external politics and it keeps the focus off consolidating within the party. It's a very quantifiable fact.

We did an analysis of network news coverage for both conventions. George Bush got 43 minutes, essentially of biographical profile, the week before the Republican convention. Jesse Jackson got twice as much coverage a week before the Democratic convention as Michael Dukakis did. While we emerged from the convention with a lead, I don't think that there was much information underneath it that gave people reasons and verifiable facts to carry around in their heads about Mike Dukakis.

David Gergen: At the convention itself, as it was on TV, Jesse Jackson dominated the first days of that convention. It was known as the Jesse Jackson convention. Did you during that period of time also feel that this would hurt in terms of the general election position?

John Corrigan: I definitely felt that it hurt us because it took up time. There are only so many minutes that you are going to get coverage, and basically what we're in here is a communications process. You are trying to teach people as much as you can about Mike Dukakis and who he is and what his values are. Our 15 minutes of being famous was being consumed by somebody else. And that inevitably did its damage.

David Gergen: Did you also feel after the convention that the degree to which this troika idea arose and the association with Jackson was a drag on you, particularly in the South?

John Corrigan: I think that's a judgment call. We needed Jackson's support; we definitely needed the support of his basic constituency. We needed it to turn out in significant numbers; we needed the normal percentage for the Democratic candidate. We were always very clear about that. We were trying to unify the party and bring these people in organizationally, particularly around the country. And we did a fair amount of that.

Anybody who ignores the last 20 years of American politics and the impact that race has on it is either blind or willfully blind. It definitely exacerbates not only the fundamental tension in American politics but in the country itself. So highlighting racial tension is never a good idea.

David Gergen: But in effect, were you in a position where you had to let him dominate the media in order to keep the convention together?

John Corrigan: We were in a position where we couldn't control the media coverage because Jackson is much better at it. It's a natural drama that he was playing into. What we were trying to do and what I was trying to do in my interview with Robin Toner was say in advance what we were prepared to do, the basis on which we were prepared to accommodate Jackson and deal with Jackson, which was that we would agree where we could agree and we would disagree where we couldn't agree.

We agreed to much of what Jesse Jackson and Mike Dukakis agreed on in principle in terms of the party platform. The party platform is a very progressive document, and it reflects the common ground in the Democratic party. We agreed to the most sweeping rules changes in 20 years. It was a one-day story on a matter that's dominated the Democratic party for 20 years. Essentially what we now have is the most pure form of democracy in the world. There is nothing but proportional representation. That ended 20 years of internal conflict within the party, and it was a one-day story. We essentially got no public political credit for it; basically, the coverage just kept going to the higher level of conflict. And that was the problem.

Susan Estrich: A lot of people would ask me why Jesse wouldn't just go away the way the Republican opponents did so that we could be in the position of being able to go into a convention running our own show. And I think the reality here for us from June 8 on was Jesse Jackson was not going to go away. He was not going to disappear into the sunset. He was going to be a factor right through the convention, and the only issue was whether it ultimately would be a unified convention or an ununified one.

I think most people assumed that by Thursday night Jackson would be on board. But how bad would it be? Ron and I were both legitimately concerned that it could be quite bad in getting there. You asked if Jackson dominated the coverage. Yes. He got an awful lot of coverage. I'm not sure there was any way around that. He was going to stay a factor.

I think the missed phone call was unfortunate. There was no malevolence on anyone's part. We had tried in the platform rules and credentials process. Jack and Tad Devine and others worked very hard on this to avoid one of the mistakes of 1980, which was giving Kennedy a real issue to come into the convention with. Kennedy was going to be at the convention too in 1980; the only question was whether he would come in with real issues to rally people around or whether he would come in just with himself. You are always stronger when you have issues.

We worked very hard at this in June. And our lead kept bouncing down as we worked toward it because this was not exactly communicating our Bush message. But we worked very hard in June to deal with what we thought were the substantive issues that

Jackson could have used as a rallying point at the convention. We wanted to get those resolved quietly in June. Unfortunately and unwittingly and unintentionally, we then gave Jackson an issue: not did he get called first or second, but the whole issue of respect, which had been the starting point.

E. J. Dionne: Let me ask this question and go to Ron. If you realized you had a kind of tinderbox in your hand, why didn't you pay more attention to this phone call when you knew that almost anything in this very tense situation could ignite that tinderbox?

Paul Brountas: May I comment? I think the real problem was not the late phone call to tell Jackson that he was not going to be nominated—and Ron can either confirm this or deny it or wish to say nothing—but rather the fact that Reverend Jackson wanted to be consulted before the choice was made, and was not consulted. He wanted to be advised who would be selected before Governor Dukakis notified the nominee of his selection. And I told him during our meeting that would not happen.

E. J. Dionne: How did he respond?

Paul Brountas: That was his major concern. Reverend Jackson felt that he had the right to be consulted, that he had come in second, and that his showing gave him the right to be consulted and to raise objections if he did not approve of the selection. But, he also added, "I'm not going to make the decision; it's Dukakis's decision."

David Gergen: He wanted you to come to him with the name of the person that you had selected and to talk it over with him first?

Paul Brountas: Right.

Milton Gwirtzman: That's not unusual. That's done very often by presidential candidates who are about to be nominated. I remember in 1968 during the Democratic Convention in Chicago, Vice President Humphrey called Senator Kennedy in Hyannis Port and asked him who his preference was between two possible nominees for vice president, Senator Muskie and Fred Harris. He also called others. It's not unusual in the Democrtic party for important leaders to be consulted on the vice presidential choice.

Paul Brountas: I told him that we weren't going to do that because if we consulted with him, we would also be obliged to consult with the others around a circle.

David Gergen: Under the circumstances it's still puzzling why, when you had a missed phone call, you didn't hold up the proceeding.

Paul Brountas: Let me tell you what happened. It was around 11:30 or 11:45 p.m. when we tried to reach Lloyd Bentsen. Earlier in the day, I had spoken with Reverend Jackson and said that the governor would probably be making up his mind within the next 48 hours and that I would like to know where he would be that night, the next day and the following day. He gave me his telephone numbers. The first night he would fly from Washington to Cincinnati and would be leaving the next morning around 8:00 to 8:30, something like that. So I had his number. But I failed to give it to Susan that night.

The next morning the governor called and said, "I just talked to Lloyd Bentsen and we're ready to go." We had a charter flight ready to go to Washington on a moment's notice. I took the charter to Washington to pick up Lloyd Bentsen and his wife. Susan went to the statehouse, where she was to meet with the governor and call the candidates to notify them of the Bentsen selection. She met the governor in the office about 8 a.m. and started calling. Susan didn't have Jackson's Cincinnati number. She called Reverend Jackson at his regular number.

Susan Estrich: We called the other number.

Paul Brountas: It might have been around 8:00 or 8:15. By the time they called, Reverend Jackson had left Cincinnati and was enroute to Washington. There was nothing intentional in the late call; it was a mistake. I told Reverend Jackson the next day it was a mistake and that I was sorry it happened.

David Gergen: Could you not get through on a Secret Service connection?

Susan Estrich: I've got to be honest; I don't know. By the time the damage was done, he had already left. I think by the time he landed he had word. The governor's secretary was under instructions to try everything. We realized that we missed him. She got very concerned and started calling different offices, Ron and the like and leaving messages. But it wasn't until later that Ron and I talked and we made the connection.

I think a good-faith effort was made, but the point was—and it was a legitimate point and we take responsibility for it—that they had given us the number and a time of departure. In the rush of doing this, it wasn't communicated. And neither the governor nor I, as we made the calls, knew that we had to get through to Jackson by 8 o'clock or we were going to miss him.

Ronald Brown: Let me just say a couple words about process, and then I have got a little different view of the impact. And I happen to think that the missed phone call was, as far as playing into the dynamics of what ultimately happened, one of the most important things during the process for different reasons than most expect.

I had a call about 10 o'clock in the morning, maybe shortly before, from Nick Mitropoulos, who is a friend from up here. And Nick was not calling me as a Dukakis person to a Jackson person, but it sounded to me like a buddy who wanted his friend to know before the world knew what had happened. And Nick said, "It's going to be Bentsen." And I said, "Oh?" I said, "Has the governor called Jesse?" And what I got back caused me to get a terrible pain in the pit of my stomach because it was kind of, "Well, I don't know, I'm not sure, I don't know what happened." I really didn't know how to read it. I knew that we were in trouble. I knew we were in serious trouble.

David Gergen: 10 o'clock in the morning?

Ronald Brown: In the morning, 10 o'clock in the morning.

Susan Estrich: I should add Nick was in the office with me at this point. And this was part of Nick's and my effort, realizing that we hadn't gotten through to Jackson, to try other channels and see what we could do.

Ronald Brown: I don't remember if I said this to Nick or Susan or who, but I said something like it seemed to me that that was the most important call that Governor Dukakis could make, more important than the Bentsen call because everybody knew what Bentsen was going to say. He was going to say yes. A lot of people might disagree with that, but that might have been a much more logical sequence of calling.

Anyway, I realized at that point we had a major problem. I knew Jackson was in the air. I tried to get him on the plane. Sometimes you can get through on the plane. I tried to do that and couldn't get through. I took something upon myself that Jackson ultimately was not happy about, and that is I called Susan. I said something to Susan like, "What in the world happened?" I think I said the governor ought to get on the damn phone and get Jesse right away, something to that effect.

Susan Estrich: Right.

Ronald Brown: And Susan proceeded to try to explain to me what had happened and indicated that she was sorry that it had happened.

David Gergen: But you couldn't reach him on the plane?

Susan Estrich: We couldn't and he couldn't.

Ronald Brown: At any rate, Jackson called me as soon as he landed. And I said, "Have you heard?" And he said, "I just heard from a journalist. Meet me over at the Grand Hotel in 15 minutes." That day was spent trying to piece things together and figure out how to function in this new environment.

More important than how or why or whose mistake is really how it affected the dynamics from then on. My own view is that as bad as it seemed to be, it probably helped in several ways. First, it gave the Jackson forces significantly more leverage at the convention. It allowed us to be significantly bigger, real players at the convention, and I honestly believe it ultimately allowed the Jackson forces to leave with dignity—to leave with the view that we had really played a significant role, that we had been listened to, that we had participated and had accomplished a lot and that it was worthwhile. In other words, I think it ultimately played toward allowing us Democrats to come out of it in a unified way without bitterness and without rancor. Now, they would be calling us all the most brilliant strategists ever if we had planned it that way. A series of events occurred without which maybe we wouldn't have been as successful.

The second way in which it helped is that it took almost all focus off the Bentsen selection. All the focus was on the missed phone call. And all those within the Democratic party, principally supporters of Jesse Jackson, who would have been furious about the Bentsen selection were focused on the missed phone call. So the Bentsen selection got a free ride for three, four, or five days.

David Gergen: Do you think that helped the ticket to dominate the news at a time when they wanted to introduce Lloyd Bentsen?

Ronald Brown: I think it did because ultimately Lloyd Bentsen himself overcame any . . .

E. J. Dionne: Let the record show that when asked if it helped the ticket, Susan Estrich nodded her head vigorously no.

Ronald Brown: We can differ on that. My own view is that it helped to create the situation that we came out of Atlanta with, which by any analysis was an extremely positive, upbeat, feel good kind of convention.

E. J. Dionne: Can I interrupt for one second? Marc Nuttle needs to catch a plane to Oklahoma City and wanted to make a comment on the Quayle selection. And then we can get right back to this discussion.

Marc Nuttle: While the Democrats were addressing the Jackson situation, there was an undercurrent building in the Republican party with regard to the selection of George Bush's running mate. This undercurrent was not nearly as detectable by the press and public as the Jesse Jackson situation was.

There were conservative elements in the Republican party structure that were fearful that Michael Dukakis's move would be perceived to be toward the middle. If this occurred, George Bush would also make the strategic decision to position himself as a moderate. At the Republican convention there were six states controlled by neo-conservatives and Robertson activists, which just happens to be the number of states required to sign and submit a petition to the convention floor to add nominees for vice president.

It was part of my job to prevent open warfare between party factions, to keep the boiling undercurrent from perculating to the top. A part of the 1988 story is that the GOP became the better manager of diverse groups. And I give great credit to Frank Fahrenkopf and other party leaders for, from day one, keeping a good handle on internal politics.

What happened is this. Dan Quayle was a threshold conservative. He was right on five key issues that brought all factions in line at once: SDI, balanced budget constitutional amendment, line-item veto, freedom fighters, and abortion. Of course, the establishment branch of the party would back whomever Mr. Bush picked. Therefore, virtually the entire GOP base was satisfied and cemented. Also, it made every senior adviser's job a lot easier in the general election because Quayle as a threshold conservative mollified conservative activists. When Quayle was openly attacked, he became a cause célèbre. Nothing activates people on the right quicker than for one of their own to be attacked, particularly by the press.

I have a poll that indicates that Dan Quayle actually gave a 2-point overall bump to George Bush because of the activist intensity that resulted from his selection and ensuing crisis. By late October, an additional 12 percent of the new right conservatives who had indicated they were not going to vote at all changed their minds to vote for Bush. Quayle was the reason given. This is about 2 percent of the general population. Further, conservatives were galvanized to work as volunteers in the trench warfare—manning of the phone banks, precinct work, and so on.

There was another important point that Jack Corrigan made. He said that there was a turn of events at Huntington, Indiana. It was a turn of events, but it was the second turn of conditions that helped bring undecided conservatives into the Bush-Quayle column. Many organizations, such as certain business political action committees, were speaking to their members all over the country, explaining that Dan Quayle was a good vice presidential selection and that he was being persecuted. Middle American nonactivists were responding, "Well, I don't know, I don't know if I buy that or not." But the premise was out there cooking. Then Huntington came along as the second element and they started believing the proposition. Therefore, you had the organizations saying it and now the people were believing it. After Huntington, Quayle ceased to be a major problem. The Republican party for the first time since 1980 brought together new diverse groups and melded them together in an organization that was absolutely one coordinated effort—a team that everybody was comfortable with.

David Gergen: Does the 2-point bump you're saying was nationwide at the end accord with everyone else's interpretation?

E.J. Dionne: The data that I've seen suggested a 2-point drop.

Irwin Harrison: I didn't think that there was a 2-point bump, but Quayle didn't move it very much in the end.

David Gergen: Marc, did Quayle help to cement the South or was the South going into the Bush column by Labor Day anyway?

Marc Nuttle: The South was moving into the Bush column after the Republican convention. Quayle helped to cement and intensify those conservative groups that I was coordinating. Let me reemphasize that when I say a 2-point bump in the final vote outcome, I mean that by increasing the turnout among conservatives, without causing any other voters to change their minds, the resulting net effect was a 2-point bump. There was a group of voters who responded to increased turnout programs in certain key states that we focused on.

David Gergen: Are you essentially talking about the evangelicals?

Marc Nuttle: Well, that's part of the category, but new-right conservatives and many ideological social conservatives.

E.J. Dionne: Would they have gone to Dukakis under any circumstances?

Marc Nuttle: Yes. But that's another discussion about different issues and circumstances. The point here is that cause- and issue-driven groups were apathetic and unenthused, both liberal and conservative; they would have stayed at home. There truly was a perception in this presidential campaign that neither one of these candidates had a zealous following that could be difference-makers. Dan Quayle helped solve that problem for George Bush.

David Gergen: And how large a factor was the evangelical vote in the end?

Marc Nuttle: Well, it can be measured two ways. Consistently for the last two years about 33 percent of the general population of the United States has self-defined as evangelical and born-again. Evangelical and born-again may be a broad term, but one doesn't self-define that way by mistake. The point is it means something specific to anyone self-defining in this manner. Of that group it broke by, in my opinion, 60/40 for Bush, which based on turnout factors in 1988, is a net result of about 6 points or so to the bottom line vote in a general election.

The Robertson support nationwide was somewhere around 8 to 10 percent hard. Upwards of 80 percent of the Robertson base voted for George Bush. This base is part and parcel of the aforementioned 33 percent evangelical demographic subgroup.

David Gergen: Eight to ten percent of the general population?

Marc Nuttle: Eight to ten percent of the general population was a core vote for Pat Robertson.

Paul Taylor: I wanted to bring a perspective to the Jesse Jackson conversation for that seven-week period between the end of the primaries and the convention. My perspective is different from the drift of this conversation and the drift of the coverage which was to portray him as an aggrieved party, especially after the missed phone call.

My sense was that the day after the primaries ended, Jackson made a decision to put the vice presidency on the table. And he knew then that he was going to set off a seven-week period of public lobbying for the vice presidency, something that basically isn't done in American politics. It's only done by someone like Jesse Jackson, whose roots were as a kind of movement politician who understands marching on city hall and understands manipulating the media. He knew that he would get seven weeks of being able to dominate the media coverage. That was the first important decision he made.

And the other important decision was always knowing that on the final night of the convention he was going to be part of the team. Everything else, it seemed to me, flowed from that. If it wasn't a missed phone call, it would have been something else. He needed to stay in the story because his leverage is coverage. He needed to create drama to create leverage. The thing that he also needed to do was end his candidacy. He had had a very historic year. He needed to bring it to a close. He needed to stay on stage through that seven-week period.

I always felt that the Dukakis people somewhat got a bad rap. Jesse Jackson is not an easy man to deal with in this circumstance because he plays by a different set of rules. He plays very effectively by that set of rules. From his point of view, more power to him. That's a self-interested calculation that he's entitled to make. I think that there was no successful way for a conventional politician to deal with him. Under the circumstances, I think they did pretty well.

Paul Brountas: I agree. I think that that's a very accurate assessment. It was apparent to me in my first meeting with Ron, when he said, "Look, these are our concerns," that we ought to get together privately and find out what the real problems were. It become apparent that we could solve those problems if we acted in good faith. There would be some give and take, and some people were not going to get what they wanted, but we believed we could solve the problems and come out of the convention unified.

It also became apparent to me that the missed phone call wasn't the issue. The issue was defining the relationship for the future. I pointed out to Ron our concerns over Jackson's attack on Dukakis for several weeks prior to the convention and also reminded Ron of what happened in Prospect Park in Atlanta when Reverend Jackson arrived for the convention and spoke for over an hour and used the word "partnership" more than a dozen times and also talked frequently of "shared power" and "shared responsibility." I indicated that we were troubled by the use of those words and the meanings they conveyed. After Ron and I met with Governor Dukakis and Reverend Jackson, those words were never used again.

John Corrigan: One thing that I would like to put on the record here is—I don't disagree with Paul in terms of the seven weeks of news coverage—we had made some decisions early on that we were going to use the process of unifying the party as a means of practicing inclusionary politics. And that meant that on the platform we would agree where there was substantial agreement between the two campaigns and we would only disagree where basically it was a matter of principle that Michael Dukakis could not compromise on. We could not agree, for example, on a Palestinian state; therefore, we were not going to compromise on that.

Ronald Brown: But nobody asked for that either, Jack.

John Corrigan: We can debate. The Palestinian homeland issue is quite complicated, and there were a variety of proposals offered in terms of platform language. With the rules process we would agree in terms of our commitment to proportional representation and essentially letting the people decide who the nominee was going to be.

We would use the convention as a means of bringing people into the campaign. While we were frustrated to some extent about the time we lost on the network news every night, in terms of actual result and actual decisions made, by inclusion in the Democratic National Committee and inclusion in the platform language and agreement on the rules process and every other sort of internal party process issue, we had a commitment to fundamental fairness and inclusion that we followed through on.

E. J. Dionne: Bob Beckel. And I want to ask Ed Rollins a question and then close it down with a question to Ron Brown so that we can move on.

Robert Beckel: Just two quick points. One, I think that you also ought to take note of the fact that Dukakis made a very smart decision dealing with Jackson early on, deciding to meet regularly with Jackson through the year. That probably saved this thing through the end as much as anything else because he established a relationship. It was a mistake that Mondale made consistently over and over and over again.

And I have one response to you, Paul [Taylor], because I got involved in that thing. My only point in not blaming the Dukakis campaign for this thing was that anybody should have assumed he was going to stir it up—we know Jesse, that was a given, that was going to happen. The point was not a question of whether he would take advantage of seven weeks. He would take advantage of seven weeks whenever he could. But the point was, knowing that full well, you had to make a fundamental decision early on to say, "Okay, we're going to have the seven weeks."

E. J. Dionne: Ed Rollins, other than joy, what is the reaction of a Republican listening to all this talk about what the Democrats had to go through?

Edward Rollins: First of all, however it came out, he came out very, very well due to the efforts of the people here. He did come out with a unified convention. And I sat there for four days, and I'm sure Republicans did all over the country, expecting this baby to blow apart. In that small hall, I had concerns for my physical well-being as well as the other people who were there. I think that if it hadn't been managed well, it could have been a disaster.

But let me just say this. Republicans from day one always felt the Jackson factor was going to work to our benefit. My personal feeling is that there were missed opportunities on the part of the Bush campaign after the two Super Tuesdays to wrap Jackson and Dukakis together on foreign policy and really basically drive some wedges between the two, to bump them together or force one of them to move one way or the other. They didn't do that. And part of the reason that they didn't do that is that they had run out of money after Super Tuesday and went into cruise control.

I can honestly say that I don't think that Jesse Jackson was anything but a positive factor in this entire campaign. I don't think that we picked up votes anywhere. And people may argue that the South and what have you came about because of the Jackson high profile on the Democratic party, but I don't believe that. I think that Jesse Jackson throughout this campaign process was a very positive force. We expected him to be a very significant factor in helping our ticket. But you had momentum moving forward and coming out of your convention.

David Gergen: Let's go back to Ron Brown just briefly. You said this convention was hanging by a thread. Were there developments other than those that were in the press, particularly the meeting that took place between the governor and Jesse Jackson, that turned that convention around or held it together?

Ronald Brown: In order to answer that I really have to go back to Paul Taylor's scenario. It sounds logical, but it just was so much more complicated than that. There really was no Jesse Jackson decision on the vice presidency. As I said at the beginning, it was a situation that evolved. The missed phone call—maybe you're right, there would have been something else—did change the dynamic at a time that was critical in the process, and, therefore, I think was very important.

William Carrick: Ron, I think the critical thing that Paul Brountas is saying is that Jesse Jackson made a decision to continue his candidacy after he was mathematically an impossible nominee. At that point, you were going to have problems; it was going to create tension. And the end result was negative.

Earlier, Frank Fahrenkopf, who is my candidate for the next Democratic Party Rules Committee chairman, made an essential point. Democrats have designed a process that leads to protracted warfare that has nothing to do with the ultimate outcome of the convention, or who the nominee is.

David Gergen: The rules change.

William Carrick: Yes, the rules change. The winner-take-all system on the Republican side allows them to end their process and start moving to the general election stage. Our rules process encourages people to stay in for symbolic, ideological, philosophical, or empowerment reasons, which is a totally different thing, and it's done damage to the Democratic party and its chances to win general elections.

Susan Estrich: And it will be worse this time, you should all know. You should all be aware that the changes we made are going to take a problem and make it worse because we got rid of direct elections and bonus delegates.

David Gergen: What do you think was the idea behind the change?

Susan Estrich: I think that there are counterbalances, David. I think that it's a judgment call. And there are real questions of fairness in our system.

E. J. Dionne: I want to follow up on what Bill is saying because it's really my question to you. Earlier, we talked at great length about the Republicans dropping out and shutting the process down and letting George Bush start to run against the Democrats. What kind of Democrat is Jesse Jackson that he should put his party through all of this? If Jesse Jackson had dropped out like other candidates drop out of the race and early on said, "Yes, Michael Dukakis is the nominee," obviously this process would have been much simpler and this discussion much shorter. Why didn't he do that, and what does that tell us about Jesse?

Ronald Brown: Jesse Jackson did not have a constituency that would permit him to do that. The reason that there was offense with Jack's question is he was not just another second-place finisher. He was a very special, very different second-place finisher. And Jack explained what he meant, and I accept that. But he was a very special kind of candidate in a very special year. And I think that point maybe needs to get across.

E. J. Dionne: Will he always be a special kind of candidate?

Ronald Brown: No. I think less so, less so in the future. Jesse Jackson is a very special person. I don't know that you're going to change him dramatically—there will not be a frontal lobotomy that will change his personality and his way of doing his politics. But I think as a general statement, it's not unlike Kennedy in 1980, where some of the same things were being said, or Hart or Mondale. And this is not so unusual in Democratic politics.

Frank, we can't get away in the Democratic party with a rules change like that. We have a different kind of party constituency. We have a different kind of delegate coming to the convention and participating in the process.

Frank Fahrenkopf: And we appreciate it.

Ronald Brown: Let me just say this because Paul [Taylor] has said a couple of things that need clarification. Bob talked about the meetings between Dukakis and Jackson, and I agree they were good. The fact is though that these two guys really didn't know each other. They had talked, but not really communicated. And we saw that at the end.

Paul [Brountas] and I were communicating, and we understood each other. I think that we understood what each other was talking about. I don't think that Jackson and Dukakis did. When the four of us sat in that room in Atlanta on Monday morning just hours before the convention opened, that became clear. It took us a couple of hours to deal with concepts like partnership.

It seems to me—and Paul might want to contradict this—that Governor Dukakis and maybe Paul were concerned about a word like partnership because they interpreted it as like a partnership in a law firm—a structured, specific, written kind of partnership. I think when Jesse Jackson uses partnership it's like my partner, my buddy, my friend, the guy that I interact with and share things with and talk to and seek his opinion.

We had that kind of conversation during that Monday morning meeting. It became clear for the first time what folks were talking about. It was a relationship definition. And I think that was very important.

The other thing that has been misreported was Bentsen's role. I have seen a lot of reports that indicate that Bentsen came in and saved the day, which is totally untrue. We had already come to agreement.

Paul Brountas: We had written our statement.

Ronald Brown: Yes, we had written our statement when I think I said to Governor Dukakis, "Don't you think that it would be a good idea to find Senator Bentsen and have him join us." And he agreed right away, with no hesitation, and had him called. Bentsen came over as soon as he was located.

I guess what really brought it together, what was the most significant event, was the three of them—Bentsen, Jackson, and Dukakis—walking out on that press conference stage barely six hours before the convention was to open. And they were holding up each others' hands—it was a love-in. That's what set the stage for a unified convention.

I wasn't sure when we walked into the Monday morning meeting whether it was going to happen. I don't know if Paul had more confidence than I did, but I wasn't sure that it was going to happen because we hadn't had these two guys in the same room. Paul and I had sat in the same room, but we hadn't had Dukakis and Jackson in the same room.

David Gergen: Thank you. We have very little time and a lot of ground still to cover. Maybe we can circle back, and I'm not sure to whom to direct this, but maybe to you, Jack.

You said you broke off and started planning your vice presidential selection early, essentially in May or June. And why did you not also break off and plan your national campaign at that time? In particular, why didn't you reach out? There were a lot of reports that John Sasso was coming back at that point. Why didn't you go forward with Sasso back then?

John Corrigan: I don't know because I wasn't privy to those discussions about bringing John back, but we did go forward and planned a great many things for the fall campaign. We started a process of state campaign manager selection and a process of planning our schedule. We started polling, in May I believe, for the fall election. So we did do a great deal of planning, but we clearly could have done a better job of reaching out and bringing other people in the party.

We eventually did succeed in getting a lot of people to come up and join us for the fall campaign—Mike Berman, Ted Sorenson, people like that. And I think that worked to our advantage. We were definitely slow in moving to do that.

E. J. Dionne: Bill Carrick, I would like to ask you about the whole process of bringing outsiders into the campaign. What's your perspective as to how slow or fast they were?

William Carrick: I think that some of what's been said is a bad rap on the Dukakis campaign. I thought there was an effort to bring people in and consult with them at various levels. There certainly was from the rival campaign managers' standpoint.

Susan and I met as early as the New York primary and had discussions. And from there we had some group encounters with other campaign managers. Tim Ridley was involved in one of those sessions. Fred Martin was involved in another. I think there was an opportunity to consult and contribute and tell people what you thought.

You know, whether we were listened to is one question, whether we should have been listened to is another question. But I think that there was a process established to do that.

E. J. Dionne: But were you listened to? Why weren't people like Bob Shrum or Bob Squier brought in earlier in this process?

William Carrick: I really can't answer why they weren't brought in earlier. I can only speak to my relationship with Susan. I had every opportunity to tell her anything I had on my mind, however inflammatory or radical my ideas were. I had the opportunity to present them. In terms of Bob Shrum's part, I worked with Susan to get him involved at various points. He ended up producing the five-minute spot at the end. I think that Tom Donilon and Susan and John ultimately brought Squier in.

David Gergen: One of the points that came out during the campaign was that the Bush campaign did have about two dozen people on the top of that campaign who had previous national campaign experience. Were you not concerned earlier about having so few people with similar experience in your campaign?

E. J. Dionne: With real roles as opposed to being consulted.

Susan Estrich: To some extent. I think that it's a balance. I said yesterday we brought some of these people in. Maybe we should have brought them in earlier. I'm not going to get into why an individual person wasn't brought in earlier. Some very good people have complicated histories, complicated relationships, and I don't think a review of that serves anybody's interest very well.

I do think there are a couple of issues we started talking about earlier. We have a lot of talented people who worked for Michael Dukakis for President who would be a real asset to whoever the nominee is four years from now. There is no payroll I know of to put those people on, to be involved in politics, for the next four years to ensure that four years from now they are in a position to be involved again. We are simply not in an equivalent situation with the Republicans. I think that it's a much larger question than whether we were early or late in bringing on Bob Shrum, who I happen to think enormously of. We are simply not in an equivalent position.

Most of the Democrats around this table, with one or two exceptions, will be going on to careers other than politics for the next four years, some by choice and some because that is the reality of being a Democrat when you lose. The Democratic National Committee, unlike the RNC, does not have a national campaign staff waiting when you snap your fingers and say you need some help.

I will say that yes, there were people who I would have liked to have gotten sooner, but there were relatively few people of the sort you described who I could snap my fingers and get to Boston. There were many who had complexities in their life. There were lots of people who said to me in June, "I'll give you Labor Day to the election, I cannot give you more, I'm a lawyer now, I'm a this now, I'm a that now."

And there is the additional point that George Bush himself had personal relationships with these 12 or 15 or 20 people who came into his campaign. We brought in almost everybody with whom Michael Dukakis had that kind of personal relationship.

E. J. Dionne: Which is not a large group.

Susan Estrich: Which is not a large group, right, and was one of the reasons why I felt the return of John Sasso was so important. Of that whole group of people with national campaign experience and the like, he was one of very few who had a relationship with Michael Dukakis to build on.

David Gergen: Recognizing that, was there a consideration given as to why he didn't come back earlier?

Susan Estrich: I don't know.

David Gergen: If you both don't know, who does know?

Susan Estrich: Michael Dukakis. I'll be very honest. My only conversation with Michael Dukakis about John Sasso—and I can't even remember the date of this—was when I told him that I would welcome John's return to the campaign, that in no way would I ever stand in the way of John's return to the campaign, that I had nothing but respect for John's ability. John Sasso happens to be a very close friend of mine, and he brought me into the Dukakis campaign early on. Ultimately, that was the governor's choice and decision to make, not mine. And that was my only discussion about it.

E. J. Dionne: So you don't know anything about the discussion of bringing him back, before the convention, or any talk about letting him work on a fall plan?

Jack, you were, according to a number of accounts, involved in helping bring John back and you and Nick Mitropoulos had conversations about organizing this. Why did you think it was important to bring him back?

John Corrigan: Let me set the record straight. There was an account in *The Boston Globe* that said that. The reporter never spoke to me.

You know, John Sasso is one of my best friends. I told Michael Dukakis I did not think that he should resign or be allowed to resign back in October or September of 1987. My position on that remains unchanged to this day.

E. J. Dionne: Did he have to quit?

John Corrigan: I didn't ever think that Michael Dukakis would think that it was a surprising revelation that I thought he should come back to the campaign.

E. J. Dionne: Then in your view, did Sasso have to quit?

John Corrigan: It's not a surprise that I thought Sasso should be in the campaign; that's not news. The only conversations I ever witnessed around the two, Dukakis was speaking Greek, and I don't speak Greek.

David Gergen: Did you ever consider bringing John Sasso back with the governor earlier?

Paul Brountas: Yes.

David Gergen: And what were the considerations?

Paul Brountas: Well, we discussed timing considerations, like when the right time would be and also how he would come back. It wasn't envisioned at that time that he would come back in a full-time role, rather that he would volunteer on a part-time basis and assist in strategic planning and advertising as a senior adviser.

E.J. Dionne: When was this?

Paul Brountas: We probably discussed that preliminarily in April or May, and then later it was decided that John should return just before Labor Day if he could arrange a leave of absence from his employer.

E.J. Dionne: What was the state of the campaign when he came back, and why did he come back, Susan, Jack?

Susan Estrich: We were in the process of bringing in new people, perhaps belatedly, but Michael and I had been talking throughout July and August about who we needed to bring on.

The first round of people we brought on were people Michael knew. The second round of people we were talking about bringing on were people he didn't know, but I felt strongly that I needed a lot more help than I had. So I raised with him at that point the names of a fair number of people, none of whom I'm going to mention in this room, people who he didn't know at all but whose help I felt was important.

I can't speak for Michael, but he did say to me at one point that those people may be fine, but John Sasso was somebody who could do the same jobs that I was talking about. I had thought we needed additional help on the communications and message side. Kirk and I had talked about this at some length. He was feeling over-whelmed with just the burden of managing this process. And we had talked about a number of people who might help us. And I think the governor felt very strongly, and I agreed once the issue was raised, that as talented as some of these other people might have been—and some of them did come aboard as well—there was one person who was worth three of them because he knew the governor and knew how he liked to do things.

Paul and I had talked about it as well. As we were bringing on other people from outside the family, why not bring on somebody who had the governor's confidence, who understood him, who knew how to help him go through the process and make decisions, and who had worked with him for six years? And the governor's reaction was, "Look, if you are going to bring on X and Y and Z, or whomever, John Sasso is worth three of them in terms of my relationship with him." And I agreed.

E. J. Dionne: How difficult was it to get Michael Dukakis to listen to anything you said in the August period when he was being president of western Massachusetts?

John Corrigan: Want to know something, E.J.? We are running to the end of this session, and we have spent a lot of time talking about this tactic, that tactic, and this commercial, that commercial. These presidential elections are decided on very big things, yet we spent very little time talking about Ronald Reagan.

David Gergen: We'll come to Ronald Reagan.

John Corrigan: I don't know when we'll come to Reagan because this session is supposed to end in a half an hour. But we have spent a lot of time talking about John Sasso. And earlier I said what John Sasso did was tell the truth and the Dukakis campaign paid the price for it.

In the general election there were lies told about Michael Dukakis. First there was a rumor spread, according to CBS by people in the White House with ties to the Bush campaign, that Michael Dukakis had been to a psychiatrist and might, in fact, be nuts. Then a Republican senator said that Kitty Dukakis had burned the flag. And that was put on the national news.

There was never an inquiry into how those stories got out into the public domain, into who did it. And the most fundamental thing in this business is the truth, the difference between the truth and a lie, and we have never debated that in this whole conference. And it's coming to a close, and I think that that's what we ought to be debating, not who called Bob Shrum and when. It's just not important compared to the larger issues at stake in the election.

David Gergen: With all due respect, Jack, I agree with you. We'll get to that. There are some though who feel that had the Dukakis campaign reached out earlier and had it built a different kind of campaign staff, it would have been able to respond more easily.

John Corrigan: That's a legitimate issue for inquiry, but it's been debated at great length in the course of the election and it got covered in the national news publications and covered on the networks.

David Gergen: If you can give us two minutes, we'll come back to that.

Howard Fineman: Let's talk about big things for a second. You said that some planning had been done concerning field organization and state strategies and so forth for the fall campaign; some focus groups were done.

Susan Estrich: A lot of focus groups and so forth, Howard.

Howard Fineman: Was there put together, and who did it, a fall campaign strategy plan that said: "These are the five or six things we're going to try to key on?" Now I don't want to commit the historical fallacy that Fred Martin was complaining about earlier. I don't want to cite the Bush campaign as the model of organization just because they won. Had you guys pulled it out, we would have been describing the folly of their plan. But they did have a plan.

It's been said that you guys didn't. Is that an unfair criticism? What was that memo? Is there one around?

Susan Estrich: There were a series of memos, Howard. Tubby did a series of memos throughout the summer which we gave to Dukakis, along with Tom Kiley and myself, on message, themes, issues, and agenda. In addition, there were a series of memos done by Charlie Baker, along with Chuck Campion and others, on a political strategy that looked at the country, looked at the electoral college, that targeted numbers of persuadable voters. There was a media plan done which looked at where we would spend our money and how, based on three different sets of assumptions, the campaign would go forward. And John and I sat down again the first week of September, and given what we had, given what had transpired to date, and given some of our problems, did a second memo or a second longer memo.

Howard Fineman: Excuse me. Your answer so far means that I have to ask my question again. Was there an agreed strategy that could be reduced to one of Lee Atwater's note cards.

Susan Estrich: Yes, yes.

Howard Fineman: When did that come about, May, June, July, August?

Susan Estrich: I would say it was shortly after the California primary. And you know, Howard, we get a little silly here. When you are winning a campaign, you stick with the strategy; but when you are losing a campaign, you're constantly looking for opportunities to do things differently. You are constantly rearguing what you agreed to in June because it doesn't seem to be working.

What we decided in June and basically stuck with throughout was a strategy that emphasized, one, that Michael Dukakis cares about people like you; two, that we had to make the case for change, particularly around the international economic agenda, with the focus on the future and America's place in the world; and, three, we had to stress character and leadership as issues going into not only the acceptance speech but throughout the convention.

If I told you that religiously, notwithstanding seeing ourselves drop and going through whatever, we said we'd continue what we agreed to do when we sat around in June in my office or up in the statehouse in early June in our first media meeting, you would call me a fool, Howard, because you would say it wasn't working and the dynamics had shifted. There was certainly a continuing debate about how to respond to Bush. And I happened to agree with Jack that for all the time and energy we spent discussing it, it was probably less important than Ronald Reagan, the economy, and world peace.

Let me just finish this one sentence, and Jack asked the question a few times. There was a continuing debate as to how to respond to the Bush attacks. It was particularly a debate that took place in September when those attacks emerged on television, but it was also a debate in August.

And you asked me about the governor's receptivity in August. Different positions were taken and decisions were made which have been much criticized in the press.

E. J. Dionne: What are you saying about the governor's receptivity in August? Was he listening?

Susan Estrich: I've got to be honest here. You know, I really feel very strongly that my job as a campaign manager—and I think that I have talked to each of the campaign managers about this—is to give our best advice to the candidate and then defend what decisions are made and not to turn around either publicly or privately, E.J., and say well, don't blame Susan Estrich. You see, I have this memo in June that shows what I said. So that is a question peculiarly that I am not going to answer. I really believe we have gone a little too far.

If I could talk about the press coverage for a second—out onto the extreme of did John Sasso say he should go positive or negative? Was Fred Martin single-handedly responsible for the Gore campaign? Was Gephardt listening to Carrick when he did X, Y, and Z? Governor Dukakis has taken responsibility for the campaign, and I take responsibility for the campaign. But the one thing I think any of us, or certainly I, won't do is sit here and say don't blame me, because I was sitting in August with the magical, brilliant plan that could have saved it single-handedly.

E.J. Dionne: Let's go directly to that question. But I want to throw out a question and then go to Bob Beckel, and Susan and Jack can take this up, and Fred. The question is: One of the mystifying events of this campaign was the second debate. The Michael Dukakis in the second debate was very different from the Michael Dukakis in either the first debate or any of the other debates that we saw. Michael Dukakis on Ted Koppel was so laid back, if you will, that people started speculating that he didn't really want to be President. What happened to Michael Dukakis between that first and second debate? Bob.

Robert Beckel: Well, I've been getting a little frustrated by listening to a lot of this myself. I feel some obligation as the last campaign manager of this party to say a couple of things, one, because I don't think it's fair for Susan and Jack, and they and Paul probably won't like what I'm about to say, but so be it.

The Republicans have gotten an enormous amount of credit for 3-by-5 cards or very smart media strategy. And I walked out of here with a lot more respect for Ailes than I ever imagined I would. But look, in June this campaign had good, solid ideas on how to take on George Bush. You not only have to talk about the big problematic questions of lying—Jack, let's face it, these guys do that all the time. There's nothing new about that. These guys have been running campaigns where they lie, cheat, and steal, and they win; we know that. We can't bitch about it.

I'll tell you fundamentally what is a problem here. And that is that there was a problem with the candidate. And these guys gave you the best campaign situation you could want. George Bush in the final analysis turned out to be a better candidate than people thought, and Michael Dukakis turned out not to be as good a candidate.

You fed all the best stuff you could possibly want to the candidate, but maybe the karma wasn't right or something else, but it was not that he didn't know these attacks were coming. There were a number of people in his campaign and outside who let him know they were coming as early as June. He knew full well what the Lee Atwater strategy was at the end of June; he was told it over and over again. And for some reason constitutionally—it may be because of what he believed was important to tell the country—he did not respond.

And we can't lay the blame at the feet of the Republicans. The Republicans are going to lie about us; we learn to lie right back about them. And I don't mean that in the serious sense—but you know what I mean.

Edward Rollins: As the man who stole 8,000 votes from me in Minnesota, I certainly do.

David Gergen: I agree. Bob has raised this essential question. Let's get back to the Republicans. The question that is on the table is the level of the campaign.

John Corrigan: I believe that we did make a miscalculation, and I believe that Michael Dukakis participated in this miscalculation: that we underestimated or rather we overestimated the political price that would be paid for the lying.

The year 1987, and much of 1988, was a debate about character. And essentially what you saw was a candidate on the Republican side who allowed his campaign to lie in his name and allowed the Republican party to lie in his name. And they paid no political price for this until the end of the campaign. That's a strategic miscalculation, and as a campaign we can collectively accept responsibility for it. But you can't argue that it's smarter to lie, cheat, and steal.

E. J. Dionne: But, Jack, he didn't lose the election because of lies necessarily. He also lost the election because of that second debate, because of the way he as a candidate was behaving.

John Corrigan: I think that given peace and prosperity and given Ronald Reagan's popularity and given what we could all assume was going to be a very effective political campaign, we had no alternative; we had to do everything perfectly.

You raised the Ted Koppel interview. I think Tubby will corroborate this. Everybody in the press and a lot of people in our campaign who talked to the press certainly wanted a much more dramatic confrontation than the one Michael Dukakis engaged in with Ted Koppel. But in terms of the voters, we started to go up during the Ted Koppel interview. And I think the reason for that is that the Republicans had painted Dukakis as a very risky liberal extremist, but what people saw was someone who was not a risky liberal extremist.

Frederick Martin: You can't allege that you were pleased with his performance!

John Corrigan: Well, I like to hit home runs too, but I think that—and Tubby can speak to this—we saw improvements. Much the way that everybody misread the Republican Convention and what the public's reaction would be to Dan Quayle, the voters have a different idea than all of us in the echo chamber—the phrase that someone else used earlier—of what people are looking for. The only reason that Bush/Rather confrontation worked was that Dan Rather had two-to-one negative ratings from Republican primary voters.

E. J. Dionne: I want to move into the broader subject, but I still want a simple, quick answer to the question: Why did Michael Dukakis perform the way he did in that second debate? What happened? What was the briefing like? Was he brutalized by the briefers?

Susan Estrich: No, no, he wasn't. Paul might want to add to this. I don't know the answer to that, E.J. Obviously, it was a disappointment.

It is true that he wasn't feeling that well going into the debate, but he was running for President and he never tried to use that as an excuse nor to whine. But he was physically not well that day, not himself. I'll be honest, I was a little nervous because when he was going into the first debate we were sitting around the table in his suite at 4 o'clock that afternoon with everybody on the edge of the chair playing it out one last time. And going in with that kind of energy is going in strong.

On the second debate I met with him and Paul and a few others early in the morning. But that was the last briefing. After that he saw a doctor and took a nap; he was ill. That was part of it.

Regarding that first question—I have no idea, he hasn't said this to me—I can't imagine any human being going through that first question and answer. I'm not saying it was unfair because when you are running for President, anything can come hitting in your direction. It was clear that it was an opportunity that we missed. Whether it was fair or unfair, I thought we could have won the debate in the first five minutes. We didn't. Maybe we lost the debate in the first five minutes. But I don't know what impact that had on the next hour and 55 minutes.

Remember, he was trying to do two things in that debate which aren't easy to do at the same time, but he had to; the first was to be Mike Dukakis, a human being having a conversation with the voters at home, who deals at least in some way, shape, or form with this question of who are you as a man. And, second, he had to make the case against George Bush, and that meant taking it to George Bush on what in our best judgment—and we had polled fairly carefully—were his vulnerabilities. It's difficult to do those two things at the same time.

Beyond that I just don't know. I think I went through—God

knows, everybody in this room will remember—50 odd debates with Michael Dukakis. And he was very good in most of them; he wasn't good in every single one of them. Unfortunately, this was the most important one of the season, and it was a disappointment.

Paul Brountas: I agree with Susan.

David Gergen: Jack was obviously quite exercised about what he calls the lies of the Republican side. Could you all explain if what they were saying was so outrageous, why didn't you respond earlier?

Susan Estrich: We did, but let me clarify that a little bit. There were some we didn't respond to. We did not respond to the mental health rumor. I think it was Paul Taylor who last night said that I, like everybody in this campaign, seems to have a fixation with these mental health rumors. If so, it's only because we saw our polls drop 8 points in a 24-hour period, which is enough, if you are in my shoes, to give you a fixation. But we didn't respond to the mental health rumors because we thought it would just exacerbate a story we wanted to go away. The governor did not respond to the Steve Simms attack on his wife. And I'm not sure why.

He did respond in East Texas the Friday after Labor Day to the tenor of the first week. I mean in a real way, Labor Day was when America woke up. And the last 10 days in August had been Quayleland. So he responded that Friday. If you remember, he was at the Sam Rayburn College or Library and he did his garbage speech. What he didn't do was give the same speech Saturday, Sunday, Monday, Tuesday, Wednesday, Thursday. He responded that Friday.

And then he moved back to making his affirmative case. He came back to Boston, and I use this as an example, and met with foreign policy experts and Sam Nunn et al., and went out and started giving speeches on foreign policy. So the garbage response, if you happened to miss that 60 seconds of the evening news, didn't exist.

What George Bush did every single day from May until November 8 was attack Michael Dukakis.

David Gergen: Susan, you said earlier that you knew you were vulnerable on the furlough issue, that you could see that coming down the road like a Mack truck. Did you prepare a response?

Susan Estrich: Sure. It was a threefold response. Look, furloughs hit us much earlier, David, not with the impact the Bush campaign had—and I don't want to redo the debate about Willie Horton and how much of the impact of furloughs was race. The first time we saw furloughs was in New Hampshire, in the New Hampshire primary. *The Lawrence Eagle-Tribune* was pumping it. And our response was very simple at that time: It was a mistake, it was a tragedy, mea culpa, we changed the policy.

In my judgment at least, for Michael Dukakis there was no winning a debate about that furlough policy. What are you going to say—it wasn't a mistake to have a policy that allowed somebody to get out of jail and rape a woman? It was an isolated incident, but it was a mistake and a tragedy, and we changed the policy.

The additional elements to that response on furloughs were the objective elements, and by that I mean a distinction between the subjective racial and fear issues, the objective elements being it was a mistake and it was changed—look at the overall record on crime. It was a debate we couldn't win, but we didn't want to lose as badly as we could. And, finally, Dukakis is a person who has been touched by crime, who understands, has a strong anti-crime record, has changed the policy and understands what it means.

Now, I think the more effective response might have been a counterattack on something else, on a different topic. My own view was that the best you could do on furloughs was respond to it effectively. Ultimately, if the debate was a debate about furloughs, we weren't going to win that. We had to be debating something else, whether it was Iran-Contra or Noriega or Dan Quayle or the cost of George Bush's house in Kennebunkport.

David Gergen: There was very little sign of anger on the governor's part to come out and, in effect, punch the guy in the nose and say, "Look, you're attacking my integrity, you're attacking my patriotism," and counterpunch back. Why did he not just go straight at it early?

E. J. Dionne: Like he did against Ed King in 1982?

Susan Estrich: I'm not a psychologist. I can't tell you how he reacted emotionally. Maybe Paul wants to speak to it. I wasn't involved in that earlier fight. He's a very disciplined man and a hands-on candidate. That was a great strength of his in certain circumstances and maybe a liability in others.

Paul Brountas: I think—and, again, going back to the strategy—the governor had in mind spending four to five weeks right after Labor Day laying out positive proposals for health care, health insurance, college loans, child care, foreign policy, defense, armaments, et cetera. Several comprehensive substantive speeches were made over that four- or five-week period. Dukakis felt it was very important to establish that substantive base and create the building blocks so that in the last three or four weeks of the campaign, when he said, "I'm on your side, I am the person who really cares about people like you," he would have credibility.

If this were done in the primaries, it would have lost its impact because most voters weren't listening to the issues at that time. They certainly weren't listening in the summer. Post-Labor Day was the time to do it.

So the issue was whether to abandon our plan and respond to Bush's negative campaign by descending into the mud and start slinging mud. We asked, Who's going to win that battle? And I think we believed that if he didn't create the building blocks and propose positive substantive programs during the month of September and early into October, but instead started slinging mud, then we would lose. That was our judgment.

E. J. Dionne: Ed Rollins wants to defend lying, cheating, stealing Republicans.

Edward Rollins: First of all, I don't believe we lie, cheat, or steal. If both candidates had the opportunity to run the kinds of campaigns they wanted to run, it would have been a great debate on national issues. And I think the fortunate thing is these two men probably reflect where their parties are today as well as anybody coming out.

George Bush began with a very false empathy. Normally, a candidate who has negatives as high as he had, or at least was perceived to have at the convention, is a polarizing figure, someone you love or you hate. Jesse Jackson obviously is a polarizing figure, and you either love him or hate him. Barry Goldwater on our side was a similar type of a candidate. I think these artificially high numbers for George Bush created among the Democrats such a disdain for the man and such an underestimation of the man that he probably got sucked into a false premise.

You had two opportunities in this campaign. You had to make a case against Ronald Reagan, which obviously was tried before and had been unsuccessful, or you had to make a case against George Bush not being Ronald Reagan and not being up to the job. And there was some credibility. There were some serious questions coming out of your convention about George Bush and you did begin a theme.

But I think that to a certain extent there was a little naiveté. Maybe it's because in Boston when you win the primary, you just coast on to the election. I think that to say that George Bush and his people lied and cheated and stole is false—I mean, they came out and they basically made a case against your candidate. And you were arguing intellectually on certain points, and we were arguing on emotional issues. The truth of the matter is you got right on our turf. We went out and raised your negatives, and you jumped right in there saying, "No we didn't, no, we didn't, no, we didn't, no, we didn't."

And to think that Mike Dukakis was ever going to make the case that he was going to be tougher on defense than George Bush and this administration, whether he was tougher on law and order with his history of the furloughs and what have you, is absurd. But the American public didn't necessarily want more defense. They weren't electing sheriffs.

I think that you just missed the opportunity of going out and making a very tough, hardball case against George Bush. He got right on the defensive early on. The truth of the matter is this campaign was over in four weeks.

David Gergen: What four weeks?

Edward Rollins: The first four weeks of September. Once George Bush got back up and went on the offensive, he put enough holes in the side of Mike Dukakis that it didn't matter whether he won both debates. Dukakis had not made his case; he had not raised doubts; and the American public was going to elect George Bush President.

David Gergen: Ed, can you or Frank Fahrenkopf speak to the question raised by the Dukakis campaign: Clearly, they feel very strongly that the rumors about his mental health were a major turning point in the campaign. In particular, they feel President Reagan's comment about the invalid was extremely important and was inspired by the Bush campaign.

Edward Rollins: First of all, anybody who knows Ronald Reagan knows that he is not the controllable entity that everybody thinks he is. Obviously, someone was talking about it in the course of the White House that day, and probably everyone was laughing about it, and Ronald Reagan tried to be humorous. It was a bad joke, but obviously, it gave the networks the opportunity to go public with it. It wasn't Ronald Reagan's comment as much as everybody out and running with it.

Jack, I don't mean to be offensive in any way, shape, or form because this has to be a very painful process for you people. I've always come here as a winner. It's got to be a very painful process to come here and try to explain, but you all have done it with great class and grace. But if you go look at polls today nobody raises the issue about Mike Dukakis being a psycho, nobody raises the issue about Kitty Dukakis burning the flag. What they say about Mike Dukakis is this guy is going to furlough prisoners, he's the guy who's soft on crime, he's going to spend money, he's going to raise our taxes, which obviously were the effective things that Ailes and others did.

But I think also that you never put any dents in Bush. You basically let him get right up off the deck. I mean he was a wounded puppy, and you let him get right up off the deck. And because Iran-Contra and Noriega didn't work in a Republican primary, doesn't mean, if you want to hammer away on those kinds of issues, that they may have enforced the American public's already perceived notion that George Bush wasn't quite up for the job.

The sad part in this election is you had an excellent opportunity, unlike old Beckel over there. You know, all we are is campaign managers. If there's one thing that comes out of this it's we can only make a very slight difference.

What this campaign really came down to is there is not a person who knows George Bush privately who didn't say, "Why can't the private George Bush be shown out there in the public?" I don't think there's anybody, except maybe you who were intimates of Mike Dukakis, who doesn't say Mike Dukakis is a very cold, calculating man. I don't mean to be derogatory, but he's very cold, he's not warm.

The American public got a hard look at both these guys for 10 weeks. Our issues obviously stuck more effectively than yours did. You didn't make any issues. And I think the fact that we can sit here and discuss what the Dukakis fall strategy was after already having been run through really shows that, for whatever reason, the Bush campaign worked very, very well.

Frank Fahrenkopf: It's simplistic to make it good and evil, because that's what Jack is trying to do—that this was good versus evil and evil won. Come on, this is the big leagues. We're talking about a presidential race. And, as Ed has said, you've got issues out there. Have more faith in the American people; they looked at the issues. The people in this room who are reporters worked on it. So it's not a question of who lied or who didn't lie.

David Gergen: But the dynamics did change with some of those rumors.

Frank Fahrenkopf: The assumption that Jack makes is that Ronald Reagan was programmed going into that press conference or Symms was programmed, that it was all part of a master strategy. That's not the way it works.

Robert Beckel: In fact, I've got a tear here in the corner of my eye, I feel so badly for how grieved you feel about Jack Corrigan. Wait one second now, pal. You guys have been very good;

we've talked about this a lot. I talked about that in a positive sense as a former campaign manager.

Frank Fahrenkopf: Where were you four years ago? You weren't here.

Robert Beckel: I was raising taxes, my lasting legacy to Democratic politics.

But the truth is that you all effectively gave facts on that furlough program that were just flat out wrong. But we can't sit here and complain about what happens all the time. We do that. That's true. You did that. And Reagan may have stumbled on that imbecile thing. But let's face it, it hurt and it slowed their momentum down a lot as did the Kitty Dukakis thing from that right-winger Symms.

But the reality is you are right, Frank. It's a big world, and it is played in a tough way. And it requires not a campaign to come up with answers, but a candidate who has got to come back and take it on. And that didn't happen.

John Corrigan: I don't disagree with that. And I think that we were not effective in many ways. You know, we attacked on Noriega a lot. By the end of the campaign I think most people thought that Noriega played second base for the San Diego Padres. They don't know who he is; it didn't get through.

The reason it didn't get through, in our view—and I think our research corroborates this—is that Ronald Reagan was held responsible for that and the American public already made a judgment for that and internalized the concept of what the vice president does. And they basically said so what? So the attacks didn't move votes.

David Gergen: It was your position that Reagan in effect protected Bush on almost every issue except Quayle?

John Corrigan: I think Reagan made the prospect of a Democrat winning very difficult.

E. J. Dionne: Do you think you could have won?

John Corrigan: Yes, I think we could have won, but I think it was very difficult for us. Let me say our task as a campaign was to change the nature of the debate from a debate about the past eight years. A referendum on Ronald Reagan was going to be a vote for the Republican candidate. I think in the CBS exit poll, 56 percent had a high opinion of Ronald Reagan and 84 percent of those voted for George Bush. That's a broad undercurrent in the nation. That's much more important than anything we do.

E. J. Dionne: Something we haven't talked about is something that underlies this whole race, and that is that between May and the end of the race, Ronald Reagan's popularity rose substantially. Confidence in the economy rose substantially. Why did that happen? What did the Republicans do to help make that come about, and could the Dukakis campaign have done something to stop that trend from happening?

Edward Rollins: Personally, I think part of the reason Reagan's popularity really moved from September through November was because of the caliber of this campaign. I think the American public saw what the future was. And, obviously, they didn't like either of these candidates to the same extent that they liked Ronald Reagan. Ronald Reagan's numbers started getting stronger.

I think that if Ronald Reagan had been on the ballot again, he would have won very easily. But I think that this was the Jesse Helms–Jim Hunt race at the presidential level in which two candidates went out there and absolutely destroyed each other or tried to destroy each other. It's not what the American public likes.

Susan Estrich: I have two quickies. One is it may have been the Jesse Helms–Jim Hunt race, but I talked to Jim Hunt two weeks before election day and he was very sympathetic because, in fact, one guy went out and effectively destroyed the other guy.

And I think, Ed, your point yesterday has to be reiterated. Whatever criticisms there may be of Mike Dukakis or his campaign, the standards did change in this campaign. We became like a Senate campaign in ways that presidential races had somehow purported or attempted to be at a different level.

But we saw the increases in Ronald Reagan's popularity beginning with the summit in Moscow and continuing from then. So I think the people were seeing a plague on both your houses, and Reagan looked better from September on. But I think the reality we were certainly seeing began much earlier than that, when Iran-Contra faded back and when he went to Moscow and had what I think was a very successful summit. We began seeing steady increases in Reagan's popularity.

We also saw, much to our concern, steady increases in the confidence which Americans and particularly some of the people who were going to decide this election—white male voters of the Reagan Democrat mold—had in our economic future. The numbers continued getting better and better.

Maybe there were things that we could have done right or better, but there wasn't a hell of a lot we could do about the lowest unemployment rate in 20 odd years and, how many, 60 sustained months of economic recovery.

Frank Fahrenkopf: 70.

Susan Estrich: The change that people were looking for was not broad and radical change. It was precisely the kind of change you get not from throwing out the old party and getting a new one, but from change around the edges. And every time we probed the change, it would become clearer and clearer that it was not radical change.

Frank Fahrenkopf: I think if you track Bush's negative ratings during that period and chart that with Ronald Reagan's job approval, there is a remarkable correlation.

E. J. Dionne: It's almost a total correlation.

Robert Beckel: Also, it's important to note that historically there has not been a campaign since Coolidge handed off to Hoover where a sitting President was able to do as much for a vice president as anybody in his party. Obviously, Eisenhower didn't help Nixon. And we've never had a situation like this, certainly not in the television era, of a fall presidential campaign where a sitting President was able to do so much for the nominee of his party.

The one thing that we don't want to forget is that Reagan provided a third media punch against Dukakis. When Bush hit Dukakis, Reagan could come in right behind and take a shot. That was very important for the Bush campaign.

E. J. Dionne: Could I go over that? A saddened Dukakis supporter told me after the election that Ronald Reagan could not only control events in the country but in the whole world for three months, while they couldn't even sit on lousy budget figures for eight days. How did the Reagan White House succeed so well in that period in putting a lid on absolutely everything?

Edward Rollins: First of all, the transformation from Howard Baker to Ken Duberstein made a tremendous difference. Duberstein had been through campaigns before. He was an adviser to me in the 1984 campaign and had been in the White House. He had a very close relationship with Jim Baker, Craig Fuller, and other people in that campaign.

It was a very, very coordinated effort both in where Reagan went and what Reagan said. Reagan felt it was very, very important that George Bush get elected, for the simple reason he was convinced that in the first three weeks of a Dukakis presidency about half of what he had accomplished would be eroded. So he could certainly go out and bring Republicans and conservatives back. I think that he absolutely, totally should be credited with the victory in California. Bill, I think you were out there running it. And I think his two visits there the last week put that state over. And you've got to use every gun you've got. And we shouldn't be handicapped because we used everything.

Shirley Williams: Dave, there's one difference we haven't discussed at all that shouldn't be disregarded. There was an understanding by the main industrial nations, the so-called "Group of 7," that they would sustain the dollar throughout the campaign and that that would be of great assistance in the reelection of the Republicans. It's exactly the same thing that happened in the campaign of the prime minister of Japan in 1984.

E. J. Dionne: Does this mean the bankers control our elections?

Shirley Williams: I wouldn't go that far, but it's a factor.

E.J. Dionne: Why did they do that for a fellow incumbent?

Shirley Williams: I think they wanted the administration to continue.

David Gergen: There was also some feeling that our government might not, as I understand it, be strong enough to deal or be effective enough to deal with a fallen dollar in an election campaign.

Shirley Williams: The other governments accept, I think, that they cannot expect decisive action from the United States in the months before an election.

David Gergen: But there's some evidence that they supported the dollar throughout the year.

Shirley Williams: I agree. This year such support was necessary.

Chapter 7

TOWARD IMPROVEMENT OF THE SYSTEM

Introduction by David Runkel

Although campaign managers as a class tend to be a cynical bunch, nearly all of those attending the Institute of Politics conference joined with many thoughtful Americans in believing the 1988 campaign to be one of the most troubling of recent times. No aspect of the campaign escaped mention. The press was harshly criticized for not being interested in the issues and for devoting less and less time to a serious discussion of the weighty matters before the country. The candidates were accused of avoiding the tough ones. The media advisers were criticized for fudging the facts. The managers were found lacking for playing too tough, or for not being tough enough. The campaigns were accused of skirting the law in raising money and in spending it, using gaping loopholes in the campaign finance laws to return to pre-Watergate days. Even the public did not escape freely. Accused of lacking knowledge and interest, it was found by the campaigns to be a disinterested participant, or in the case of half the eligible voters, a non-participant in the process.

The 1988 campaign made some managers become more cynical, others become reformers. In the final chapter several suggestions are made for changes in the campaign system. Notably, two seasoned practitioners from opposite sides of the political and philosophical fence, Roger Ailes and Jack Corrigan, found common ground when talking about change in the system. Corrigan was more specific in suggesting changes to allow for more public discussion of the issues, but Ailes struck an overriding theme that it will take cooperation among the politicians to force change. Both agreed that since the majority of the public learns about politics from television, particular attention must be paid to the television industry.

One change accepted during the 1988 campaign year, effective the next time around, is worth noting here and watching as we turn to the 1992 election. Changes in Democratic party rules will guarantee proportional division of the primary vote among the competing candidates. Opponents argue that this change will lead to a prolonged primary season, making it more difficult for the Democrats to unite around the nominee for the fall election, while supporters contend that to do otherwise is unfair. The Republicans like their winner-take-all system, which they say better prepares the party for the fall election by ending disputes within the party swiftly. The Democratic changes should be watched in light of the views of some managers that rules changes have no impact, and the opinion of others that rules changes usually have the opposite impact of that intended.

Thus, if it is the campaign manager's role to win within the parameters of the existing laws, regulations, and rules—even when they change day to day—the astute student of politics should be on the lookout for:

- Changes in the finance laws to tighten up the expenditure of "soft money," to liberalize the spending limits, and to raise the ceiling for private contributions.
- Efforts to impose requirements, such as agreeing to a certain number of debates, upon candidates accepting federal funds.
- Proposals to enact uniform poll closing times.
- Political coverage by the networks as they face greater competition from individual stations and cable television.
- Sophisticated use of two-way television in primary campaigns.

During the Institute's conference, it was suggested that many campaign managers tend to follow the rules of the most recent campaign, just as generals have been accused of fighting the last war. It is clear, however, that many of the campaign decision makers don't want a repeat of the last election, and some predict defeat for anyone who designs a campaign based on 1988. Politics being what it is, only time will tell.

The Discussion

David Gergen: Let's turn to the question of the shallowness of this campaign and what it says about the responsibility of campaign managers and to some of the questions about the need to change this system. The degree of public dissatisfaction with this campaign was so high that all of us need to talk it through further. Roger, does it concern you that people have concluded that this was a shallow campaign?

Roger Ailes: I don't think that you are ever going to get improvement in the kind of campaigning or kind of commercials or the kind of coverage or anything else as long as it's up to one person to try to be a crusader and to say that they are going to run on the issues and to hell with everything else. The system won't support that.

When I am hired by a candidate, my job is to help him get elected. I would like to change the system. I would like to spend all of my time on deep issues and talk about the homeless and figure out how to solve it, but it's damn hard to do it in a 10-week campaign when you are getting banged around by the opponent and the press is interested in pictures, mistakes, and attacks.

So if we all take some responsibility for the shallowness of it and we all try to set up some informal guidelines, maybe we could arrive over a period of time with some way of improving this for the American people. But unless we are all willing to admit that we have a stake in it, to admit that we had a part of it, and discuss mistakes we've made, it ain't ever going to change, folks. It's going to get tougher. And next time it's going to be six-second sound bites.

Robert Beckel: These campaigns tend to seek their own level. I think we need to get away from it a little bit more before we draw too many conclusions about how really negative it was. I had an opportunity to review some footage of the Kennedy race in 1960. It too got pretty brutal on the trail. A lot of things were said, and I think a lot of people probably regret it.

David Gergen: But that campaign also talked about the future.

Robert Beckel: I think that's right. Campaign managers are going to find whatever avenues they can to start moving polls; that's what the job is. And I think that that's what Ailes did by doing what he needed to do. Susan did this during the primary campaign, which we don't want to forget about. These guys ran a flawless primary campaign. People said that they didn't say much, but why do you have to say too much when you are beating these guys every week?

What I think has to happen is that we have to take into account the American people. The American people do not demand a hell of a lot; we're in the decade of the eighties. I think they got what they asked for, which was not much. I think a transitional period is going on, and we had two transitional candidates. I think the only specific thing that I would say, to the Democrats, is there has got to be a serious review of the rules because this thing cannot go on the way it is. The system is too long, and they pay a price for it being that long.

David Gergen: Don't you think there's something wrong in an election system whereby the day after the election we face a totally different set of realities? We have the dollar going down and people are preoccupied with the deficit, which was never discussed during the election campaign in a serious way. It's like a light going off on all the issues that were discussed on the campaign. Willie Horton has disappeared; furloughs have disappeared. Isn't there something wrong with a campaign that's conducted that way?

Robert Beckel: Oh, yes there is. I think the most amazing thing about this campaign is how fast it disappeared. If you think about it, within 48 hours it was gone. I think what happened was that Willie Horton and furloughs and the American flag moved votes for Bush, but he is now dealing with issues that everybody, including the Congress of the United States, had been deathly afraid to touch and had been hiding behind.

What it all comes down to ultimately is we cannot underestimate the prosperity issue. Prosperity was a huge engine driving the Bush campaign and the end of the Reagan era. In politics, all the politics that I have been in 20 years, if you can say one thing that's consistent throughout all my experience, it's that the economy overrides everything else that happens in a campaign, particularly a campaign for President.

But I'll tell you, David, I think what Ailes said is right. We should be willing to sit down and say that, at a minimum, we need to change the process structurally. I don't think that you're going to be able to do much by trying to get people to philosophically change their views about campaigns, but somehow we have to structurally move on and try to get a change by shortening the length of time and making some constraints around the money that we give, the federal dollars that we give. I think that the day presidential candidates agree to accept federal taxpayers' dollars, the taxpayers have a right to demand something for that. And what they have failed to do—and I might add Congress is particularly a villain in this—is to demand anything for that. We're given, say, $45 million. We have the most wonderful day when we get that check. And we go off and deposit it, and all of a sudden we can do whatever you want with it and there are absolutely no constraints.

Edward Rollins: The first rule of governing is to get yourself elected. And I think that in this particular case it's unfortunate that George Bush got to a point where by the time he became the nominee, for whatever reasons, whether it was Reagan's approval drops, or whatever, he was not positioned to be a good defender of what it was that he wanted to lay out. And a kinder, gentler nation wasn't going to be something that was going to cut it and get him elected, because he was a guy sitting there with high disapproval ratings.

So I think the scenario of going out and knocking down Dukakis was a very acceptable alternative, at least by polls. I know Bush very well, and I know Jim Baker very well; this was not the kind of campaign they would have wanted to run. They don't like negative campaigns. But I think they felt that was what they had to have. They had a false impression out there, and they had to go knock Dukakis down. I'm sure that they never thought they could knock him down as easily as they did.

And then when you came back and started arguing on his issues, obviously they weren't going to move away from them. On furloughs, it might have been different if Dukakis had stood up and said, "I made a serious mistake and to the day I die I'll always regret it." But he didn't. He went out and he tried to intellectually argue the case for that. The same way on the flag; he tried to intellectually make the argument. It was an emotional issue that was grabbing folks out there and moving people and creating an image of what a Mike Dukakis was. Mike Dukakis was running for city manager, and George Bush was running for sheriff, and this was a time when the sheriff won.

David Gergen: Let me extend this. Do you think that if the first responsibility of campaign managers is to win, there's also some responsibility to make sure that Americans have a clear sense about the future if they vote for your candidate? You didn't look for a mandate in 1984. And in this campaign a lot of people said George Bush didn't look for a mandate.

Edward Rollins: The mistake we made in 1984 is the same mistake that George Bush will be hobbled with. It's not a mandate; it's an agenda. Ronald Reagan in 1984 had an agenda. A lot of people will argue that he won because of his agenda.

E. J. Dionne: 1980?

Edward Rollins: In 1980 he won because he was an acceptable alternative to Jimmy Carter and the American public had
decided they didn't want him. Fortunately for Ronald Reagan, he
had an agenda that he wanted to implement. He had sufficient
members in the Senate and enough House members that he could
be a successful leader by getting his agenda passed in that first
year. By the end of the first year he had very high marks as a leader
because he was making his agenda work and the Congress was
accepting his agenda.

The difficulty that I think George Bush has is there is not an
agenda here today and there is nothing that he ran on that he can
basically say, "This is what I'm all about." The Democrats in Congress obviously are going to say they have an agenda, their legislative agenda, and they're going to put it forth. You're going to see an
absolute impasse unless Bush can survive by being a nice man, by
having a nice family.

David Gergen: But if you believe that, if you really believe
that he is at least going to be haunted by that, does his campaign
manager have a responsibility to say you're going to need an agenda
to govern when you're elected?

Frank Fahrenkopf: Come on now, this was a status quo
election.

Edward Rollins: I don't think the American public demands
the agenda. And I think until such a time as they reject the negative commercials and reject the characters and say what is it that
you're all about and what is it that you're going to do when you are
leading this country, the campaign manager is going to continue to
do what he has to do to win.

Frederick Martin: When we started this conference, E.J., I
expressed my concern that we were going to commit the historical
fallacy of interpreting the events in the light of the conclusion.
We seem to have avoided that and have instead run the greater
risk of whining. I have never seen more whining by grown-ups
over a 24-hour period than here. The Democrats whine about the
mean attacks on them by the Republicans. The Republicans
whine about poor Marty Plissner and CBS News. And others
whine about Jackson.

We are indeed big boys and girls. We know what we're in for in
these campaigns; we know what our jobs are. I've been surprised
by all the complaining. I agree with Bob Beckel that it's amazing
that we Democrats pretend we didn't expect to have a tough campaign on our hands; we should have. We have seen the Republicans do it time and again.

Now, the one piece of historical interpretation which bothers me is what emerges from the whining and also the press accounts of the last two weeks is the proposition that the Republicans won because they were negative and because they were mean. I don't know when we haven't had a campaign that was negative. In the 19th century, candidates were lucky if they weren't called treasonous by their opposition. We surely could have expected that.

The more shocking thing to me was not that the Republicans were so good at being negative; it was the admission by Lee Atwater on the first night that he positioned his candidate on important matters of ideology purely for political tactics. That's something we haven't discussed. That's not the same as attacking. That's taking what should be the candidate's important views about the future of the country and about himself and converting them into something different for political advantage. If you recall, he said, "Our job was to start out by going to the right and reduce the universe on that side and avoid any candidate coming at us from the right, and then switch back to the middle."

Now, rather than whine about that after the campaign is over—and we haven't even talked about it—that should have been, it seems to me, an essential part of the Democratic campaign during the course of the campaign—to try to pin Bush down for the very cynicism with which he conducted his campaign.

The only thing more striking than the cynicism is the openness with which the Republicans, including Ed Rollins, my good friend here, but particularly Lee Atwater and Roger Ailes, discussed their very tactics. We tend to talk privately among ourselves about calculations that we make in campaigns. To publicly expound on the success of changing positions and to do so without any hint of shame or remorse concerns me a great deal about these campaigns.

Frank Fahrenkopf: I think this election validated a book written about 14 or 15 years ago by two Democrats, Dick Scammon and Ben Wattenberg, called *The Real Majority*. The bottom line in that book fundamentally is that when Americans go into the voting booth, regardless of their party affiliation, and we're at a time of peace, that the driving issue is the domestic economic question. If the economy is healthy, the party that is identified as being the one responsible for that healthy situation is going to benefit.

We went into this campaign year with 62 consecutive months of economic expansion. I think Susan is right; when Ronald Reagan then capped it by taking away the nuclear disarmament issues, by going to Moscow, you had peace and prosperity that were locked in. That was a tremendous obstacle for them to overcome.

And then with all this discussion about negative or positive, the real decision had to be made by the American people as to these two men. And both of them were to some extent blank slates. It was amazing how little everyone knew about George Bush after seven and a half years of being vice president of the United States. They were blank slates out there, and they were filled in. And the American people saw them in debates—whether the debates were enough or not, they did see them in debates—and they developed hard impressions about them and voted it.

I think that Susan and Paul and Jack and the campaign had some tough problems to overcome. Whether they could have done something different—anytime you lose, you can always do something different, but it was tough sledding. We can sit here and talk forever, but it was a status quo election all the way down.

David Runkel: I just wanted to ask Fred: What's the difference between the tactics Lee Atwater described and the obvious Dukakis effort of going to the center and then moving back to the liberal side at the end of the campaign? Everyone has different tactics at different parts of the campaign. And you pick up votes that you need to win.

Frederick Martin: I didn't get the impression that Governor Dukakis ever took a position contrary to his own past views. I did get that sense from Mr. Bush. Whether it was about abortion or about other issues, one did have the feeling that the Bush campaign was moving rather easily across the ideological landscape without any moorings.

William Lacy: Let me take exception to that, Fred. I don't think that there is necessarily any issue that came out in the 1988 campaign where George Bush absolutely changed his position fundamentally. All campaign managers look to points of emphasis: What do you talk about? What are the issues that are going to give me the electorate? But I don't think that George Bush fundamentally changed his point of view on those issues.

Frederick Martin: Well, I thought Bush changed position on abortion, off-shore oil, and a few other issues. He didn't have the same position on abortion for the last 10 years of his career. And Dukakis had a position from the time that he was 15, probably, and stuck with it.

Susan Casey: I want to respond to Bob, basically. He talked about the process, and Frank talked about *The Real Majority* and the economy. There are all these things, and I do not deny them, but the fundamental thing that I think changed this time was the role of the press. Increasingly over time it has become more and more that of a participant.

Jack was making the point about the lies. I don't think what he was saying was so much that they affected him but the press determined whether there was a political price that the Republicans would pay for them. How they covered those lies or distortions, as they did with the Sasso thing, and as they did with the Biden thing, and as they did with the Hart thing, as they did with Jackson, is the issue.

The reason Jackson can have the kind of role he has is because the communications media allows that. The medium that we are playing in is the communications media, and you do what you have to do to win. That's your job. And if what it takes to win is to do the attacks or to do the character thing or to do whatever it takes, that's what you do.

So campaign managers are limited in what they can do to change the process. The rules are limited in what they can do to change the process, regardless if there were more money or less money or if we ended it early or late. We talked earlier about how we should, like the Republicans, end the process early. Well, for Democrats, it's always late in the process when we decide to make up our mind differently. Look at all the elections. We got Carter nominated, but it was like we didn't want this guy; we need a chance at the end to change our mind.

So ending the process early is not necessarily the answer. So we don't necessarily get the best. I think that we fundamentally have to accept the notion, which the Republicans did better than us, that the press is now the major participant in the process. Then, understanding that, go where they are going.

If there is a responsibility that we haven't addressed this week—and I know others have addressed it again and again—its how the communications process around elections controls the process, our role in keeping with it or trying to diverge from it, and the role that the press as an entity has.

Timothy Ridley: I guess, like Fred, I want to whine about the whining a little bit. But I do think Paul [Brountas] really framed what the central strategic question was for Dukakis: Were they going to conduct a classic campaign and lay out the positives and then react, or were they going to live by at least rule one in an aldermanic race, and that is never let your opponent score on you?

Ed [Rollins] made the point yesterday that we have crossed a threshold where now our presidential races can have more the flavor and feel of aldermanic races where very parochial issues become the issues on which the election turns. That's what's new about this presidential election.

I think a lesson for Democrats is we can't sit there and let our opponents score on us the way that George Bush scored against Mike Dukakis. The question is: What can we do about negative campaigning? I don't think there's a lot that we can do about it. Eventually only the American people are going to do something about it. And, in fact, we haven't talked about it yet, but the American people did do something about it this election.

There was clearly a point about the third week in October when the electorate just said, "We've had enough." I saw this happen in both the New Jersey and Minnesota senate races. Senator Frank Lautenberg's lead went from 14 points down to 3 points in five days because he stayed negative too long. He then closed the campaign positively and recovered his lead.

But ultimately the only curb on this thing is the attitude of the American people. I think at the end of this campaign they had enough. In some states voters were willing to be punitive toward excessive negative campaigns. I think come the next presidential cycle somebody may make the mistake of trying to rerun this one, and I think the electorate may have grown more sophisticated and media conscious by that time and it could be a disastrous strategy.

Having offered this hopeful note, I'd still have to close by saying the mistake we Democrats made was permitting George Bush to paint the picture of who Mike Dukakis was, and we let this go on for four weeks and didn't respond.

William Lacy: I think that this is interesting, and you may disagree, but I am in a position of being very empathetic toward the Dukakis campaign. In working for Bob Dole—I think that no one in this room would doubt his ability or his credentials to be President—we thought we had an individual who would be, and I still think he would have been, an excellent President of the United States. And I think the campaign was very difficult. Bob Dole was a good candidate in many ways, but in some ways he wasn't a good candidate. He was poorly served in many cases by his campaign.

I think that it's very simplistic for us to say in retrospect that Bob Dole lost because of one simple reason or two or three simple reasons. I think there are many reasons. It's a very complex case and very complex situation ranging all the way from what we've been talking about for the last two or three days, from Ronald Reagan, the political environment, and lots of other factors.

Clearly in my mind, and it has been discussed over the last two days, there are some changes that we have to make. We ought to be looking at fund-raising and how monies are spent. We ought to be looking at something that I saw first-hand: the impact out in California of poll closing times. There are lots of things we should look at.

But I just thought I should finish off with one comment, coming from a very similar point of view: There is not one specific reason why George Bush won and Mike Dukakis lost; there are lots.

John Corrigan: Well, the question was what we would do to reform the process. We don't have any official position on this, but I think that there are a couple of things that are clear. One is that to govern the country it's probably a good idea that you be smart, that you have some values that the American people share, and that you have some political skills.

There was some talk earlier that we are going to change the Democratic party nominating process. Usually we change the Democratic party nominating process and we get exactly the opposite result than what we intended to get. Obviously, Super Tuesday really wasn't designed to help Michael Dukakis and Jesse Jackson, the two people who won the most delegates on that day.

But in the early part of the process candidates face questions from voters, any question the voters want, and the candidates have to answer them. They are seen up close and personal. They get tested in terms of what kind of people they are. There's a pretty clear analysis of their character, and phonies are spotted early. That's not to cast any aspersions on the candidates who didn't do well, but the process is one that allows for close scrutiny of the kind of people that these candidates are.

As we move to the general election, we are basically in a system where limited access is rewarded. And the sound bite shrunk from 14 seconds to 9 seconds in the national news this year. Polls are covered more than anything else. There is no discussion of the deficit. There is no serious attempt to have a discussion of the issues. There is no serious push or testing in campaign skills or of the individual qualities of these candidates, particularly this year.

If I wanted to make some off-the-cuff suggestions for reform of the process, it would be that in some European countries the networks are required to give air time to the candidates in equal amounts. That would be a good reform as a replacement for paid advertising. Then if there was less money spent on paid advertising, the amount of money you get from the federal government would be substantial and you could do a lot of things to increase participation, build a strong grass-roots organization, and get more people involved in the process.

And I think that it's a worthwhile idea to consider requiring the two major party candidates to debate more often, and debate in a format that's less structured and allows more candidate give-and-take so that you actually see how these people perform under pressure. There was a lot of press commentary about these things being joint press conferences. I think that Lincoln-Douglas formats worked pretty well in the 19th century and they would probably work pretty well again. And more would be better than less.

I don't think in terms of what's good for democracy that you can argue against more information about the candidates and broader exposure of the candidates themselves. And I think that would have served our interests as well as serving the country.

Daniel Mariaschin: I just have a comment on the process as it relates to our specific campaign and that is whether or not today a nontraditional politician can enter the process and have an equal shot at the prize. For the nontraditional politician, the fund-raising and organizational obstacles are immense.

In our case, I think we had the ultimate insider and the ultimate outsider. And he was faced with one front-runner who had an inside track on the party structure with its fund-raising potential and a couple of front-runners who by virtue of their having run for President before or being members of Congress had the option, whether or not they used it, to roll over campaign funds into a presidential campaign. They also had the advantage of having run before and all the public relations and "comfortability" that comes with having been around the track, not to mention the opportunity to build national political organizations. The outsider had to really start from scratch.

Notwithstanding our own mistakes, I think this is an issue which we have to consider since we may be denying ourselves top-notch, substantive, quality leaders from the outside that simply in this day and age may not be able to make it in a presidential sweekstakes.

Terry Michael: As somebody who sat at a national party committee for about five years and answered thousand of questions about process, I don't think our loss had anything to do with the process. I think that's the last refuge some Democrats use every four years to try to explain why we lost.

I think we lost because our party has been on the defensive for the last 20 years, and we had an issue environment in which people weren't interested in any big things. Given that we had only one choice, we had to engage not in lies but in at least a little gentle demagoguery. We had to paint an unpretty picture of the Republicans for those Reagan Democrats. That was our mission. We didn't come up with our own symbolic issues comparable to the power of Willie Horton, the Pledge, or the ACLU. I'm not sure that our candidate was constitutionally able to do that.

Saying that I don't think the loss had anything to do with process, I will turn right around and make a suggestion for changing the process. But this change is for a different reason. It's not something I think is necessarily going to help us win. There is a perception out there that we didn't have the first stringers running: that the Cuomos and the Nunns wouldn't go through the exhausting and humiliating process of Iowa and New Hampshire. Whether that's true or not, it's kind of silly to let one little state go first by itself. I would like one little state from each region to go first, four on the same date. I would propose a "first state, four-state, mini-national-primary." But they should be small states so that the candidates have to talk to people in living rooms and town halls, and so that candidates without much money but with big ideas have a chance to compete.

I think we ought to force candidates to run a national strategy from the first date, and that would happen if you took one state from each region. I think Iowa and New Hampshire probably will have to represent the Midwest and Northeast, or they wouldn't play along with such a change.

Paul Brountas: If I were going to be a campaign manager or political consultant in the future, I would look very hard at what Roger Ailes said. Many people around this table have listened to him and praised him for his results. And, therefore, what he did and how he did it, if it contributed to the results, and I believe it did, is an important message. He talked about the importance of images and attacks, and I think that he used the words "issues don't mean a hill of beans."

That's a sad state of affairs in this country when talking about issues is suicide. As someone said, the media, the press, the networks are participants. If they are participants, then I think that we have to make them real participants.

I haven't discussed it with Jack, but I appreciate what Jack has said. I think of what I had to go through to try to get three debates which were nothing more than joint press conferences because essentially we were told, "This is the way it is, take it or leave it." I think Roger said that he wanted to get away with only one debate. We wanted three presidential debates and we got two plus one vice presidential debate. And we got a format that we didn't really want. We wanted an open format where subjects could be discussed freely and openly without 60-second time limitations.

So I think that we have got to go to the networks for help. Maybe we should establish a condition of federal funding in the future to the effect that if you want $46 million of federal funds, then you will have to agree to debates on each of the networks so that there will be four debates for an hour and a half or two hours each. And there would be a format which would permit open, free discussion with a moderator solely to assure that there's a proper mix of subjects. Some of the debates should be subject-specific. And then to supplement the nightly news maybe there should be an occasional half-hour discussion on specific issues by the candidates, 15 minutes for each candidate.

As Jack said, you get terrific exposure during the primaries and people see the candidates in their living rooms and in their towns, and they talk to them, they get to determine what their character is and what they stand for. And then after New Hampshire this kind of personal campaigning disappears.

It seems to me the emphasis in the general election campaign should be on the issues, and making the time available for each candidate to discuss the issues. Maybe people will switch it off, but I suspect if you do it for a couple of years, it may become a valuable part of our political system.

Frederick DuVal: I guess I'll begin by saying I'm not sure that it was ever a winnable race for a lot of the reasons that have been said. And I subscribe to the cyclical theory. I'm not sure that it's our turn yet. I think that there are some things that we can do to reach up and grab it, but I don't think the conservative cycle has yet run its full course.

I think there were also some candidate-related facts which limited our ability to reach up and grab some of the economic issues and foreign policy issues. Having managed a governor's campaign and finding that it was very difficult to get credibility on foreign affairs, I think that is something that hasn't been discussed here a lot. We never really got over the credibility threshold on foreign affairs.

Third, I think clearly that on economics and prosperity, I'm not sure I prescribe to the notion that the facts of prosperity were so overwhelming that we couldn't have made the case that in fact the economy does require change and therefore a change in the White House.

I think that we never quite carried the ball on the big issues: the economy and the managing of Soviet and foreign affairs. Because we failed to make a case for change on the big issues, the campaign was conducted on a tactical level, and on, if you will, the smaller issues—to use Ed's phrase, the sheriff level.

What I would hope we would do is figure out how to reform the process in two ways; one is to narrow the gap between the nominating process and winning a general election. And I think that's a problem more for the Democrats than for the Republicans. We proceed to destroy ourselves in the nomination process and pay the price in the general.

And, second, as a first-time campaign manager I'm resisting the temptation from this weekend to leave extremely cynical because I would hope that we would find a way to use our obligation as campaign managers and with our candidates to draw a closer connection between campaigning and governing.

When Ed said the first obligation of governing is to get elected, I appreciate that. But I would hope that we could reform the system in a way which rewards a style of campaigning which attempts to build a constituency around agenda items which bring people together rather than tear them apart. I think the entire process needs to be reviewed, and most of us here have an overriding obligation to do that.

Ronald Brown: Tim Ridley has said that maybe the invisible hand, Lee Atwater's term, is going to help us all and that the invisible hand is that the American public is tired of what happened this time. I hope he's right. I'm not sure he's right. I think that's the only hope that assuages our cynicism. I think that these matters end up being pretty simple and that we probably make a difference only at the margins and that nobody would have done much better than Beckel did in 1984 with Walter Mondale as a candidate and that nobody would have done better than Paul, Jack, and Susan in 1988 with Mike Dukakis as a candidate.

I think the American public makes a fairly simple and fairly early determination. Just as in 1980, I thought we grossly overreacted to the Reagan victory as some kind of radical move to the right. I think the American public made a pretty simple decision that they liked Ronald Reagan better than they liked Jimmy Carter. After the election, polling was done on the great social issues of the day. It was expected to show a great shift to the right, but it turned out not to show any great shift at all.

I think the same thing happened this time. Michael Dukakis was not a good candidate in the general election until it was too late. The last two or three weeks he was a terrific candidate; before that he wasn't. He said to me, and I assume that he said to other people who were closer to him than I, that he didn't like the feel of the general election. He felt as if he was in a time capsule being hurled through space. He was much more comfortable in the primary election. He thought he could feel the pulse better and touch people more, and he was more at ease.

George Bush was a much better candidate than many of us, including those who supported him, thought he would be. Obviously, the negative stuff made a big difference. I wish it hadn't.

I think our talking about changing outcomes by changing the nominating rules, Bob, is completely wrong. I don't think that it's going to make any difference at all. I think that we are deluding ourselves if we think that we're going to change the kind of nominee we get by changing nominating rules. I must admit that Jack Corrigan came up with two very good suggestions that could make a difference in the general election campaign: the debate suggestion and the free time suggestion, which I think do have some impact on the process and can make a difference.

I think that this was winnable as far as we on the Democratic side are concerned, but it was really a terrific uphilll struggle, and it would have taken a perfect campaign and taken a perfect scenario of putting together the right group of electoral victories in various states.

And, you know, we weren't, if you really examine it, as far off as some people are saying now. You take a look at the Midwest and take a look at the Farwest, including California, and there were some things that could have happened that could have made it doable. This was not 1984; this wasn't even 1980. You are not happy when you lose, but the defeat in a lot of terms was not as devastating as it is now being painted. I think the pendulum is now beginning to swing back. And I look forward to 1992.

Susan Casey: Two quick things. I think Gary Hart was as prepared to govern this country as any of the other candidates. I think his personal mistakes should have been included in the mix of information that voters have to make their decision, not the way reporters reported it. And I thought the mix was way too overwhelming.

And I think that we—we meaning all the participants, the press, the candidates, and the campaigns—have got to find a way to make issues as sexy as sex. I think that we have got to take the Aileses and the Shrums and the Doaks and the Squiers and everybody and we . have got to figure out how to sell things that are important, because the things that sell now aren't so important, but that's what sells. And those unimportant things have become much too big a part of of the mix—the ads and the negative stuff and the phone calls have become too great a part of that mix.

The things that we read about and that seem to take our energy, and took our energy here for two days, were really not the important things in this country that one would think ought to be a part of what the process of getting elected is. I think that rather than complain about it, which is what we all like to do, we ought to have a session, not just a session but days, on how to make issues work in this communications environment. Because if we don't come up with some creative solutions, I just don't see how it's ever going to happen.

William Carrick: I think that anyone who tried to sit down objectively in November 1987 to analyze a hypothetical race between the vice president of the United States, George Bush, and Michael Dukakis, a liberal governor from Massachusetts, would have quickly concluded that it would be a very, very tough race. And during the course of the campaign we had various events that occurred. Obviously, Iran-Contra was a major event, and Democrats concluded that we had an excellent opportunity to win in November.

However, I believe Dukakis had very little chance against Bush. But what chance he had was hurt by our failure to articulate a reason for change. Democrats never came up with a rationale the voters could understand and appreciate and use to replace the Republican crowd with the Democratic crowd. We never did that.

I think the failure of that is not Susan's failure or Paul's or Jack's or John Sasso's. The failure is Michael Dukakis's. He was not comfortable doing the things that the political process, no matter how much we condemn it, demands right now. He was not comfortable doing those things and he didn't do them. Dukakis refused to respond to the demands of the political process.

George Bush, in contrast, had been around the track, as we described the first night here. One of the biggest advantages of any candidate is having the experience of having run before. And he was able to grow in terms of the context of this process and become a very, very attractive candidate by general election day.

I think that was the whole campaign. And all of this about missed phone calls and the rest of it—and even I make process arguments along with every other rules junkie in the world—doesn't really matter. And the bottom line is the thing was not to be won unless we could have articulated a very reasoned and rational approach to change.

Robert Beckel: I just have one thing I want to say because I think that these campaigns are a reflection of the people and the times. And I don't think that's an excuse not to change them, but I just want to say one thing.

If you haven't managed one of these before, I don't think that you can appreciate it. I have an enormous amount of respect for the people who sat here. Most people sitting around this table had an opportunity to manage a presidential race. Very few people ever get a chance to do it. The thing that would be very dangerous to do is to leave here too cynical, because there's not enough people who are willing to do it. It's an important occupation. I enjoyed it. I have made some of my best friends—one of my best friends [Rollins] who is sitting across the table looking at me right now ran a campaign against me.

But I also want to say one last thing, having managed a whopping loss in 1984. It's not as difficult to come in here as a winner as it is to come in here a loser. And there are a lot of people in here who lost a primary campaign, but it's very tough and very personal to lose a general election campaign. And I applaud the grace and dignity that Susan, particularly, showed in coming here and being willing to talk this thing through; and, Jack, I didn't agree with a lot of what you said, but I understand how much it hurts; and, Paul, as usual, you showed your dignity. These are not easy things to take.

And, believe me, this campaign may have ended quickly for a lot of us, but if you have been through a lot of them, this is a very short time and the pain ain't gone away. So you are to be congratulated. I think that you've got a lot to be proud of.

David Runkel: I think we can all second that. (Applause).

CAMPAIGN CALENDAR HIGHLIGHTS

1984

December 19   Vice President George Bush meets with Lee Atwater in VP office to begin planning for the 1988 presidential campaign.

1986

January 1   Senator Edward M. Kennedy of Massachusetts announces he will not seek the Democratic nomination for President.

March 9   Democratic National Committee approves 1988 Presidential nominating rules.

May 20   Mario Cuomo declares re-election candidacy for New York gubernatorial election, but does not commit to serving full term; speculation increases about his interest in a Presidential bid.

June 7   Willie Horton is furloughed from a Massachusetts prison and is later arrested in Prince Georges County, Maryland, for rape.

August 5   Michigan GOP precinct delegate elections kick off 1988 campaign; Bush, Kemp, and Robertson compete; results unclear.

September 16   Former Delaware Governor Pete du Pont announces that he will run for the Republican nomination; first candidate to formally announce.

August 17   Television evangelist Pat Robertson says he will seek GOP nomination if he can collect three million signatures in next year.

November 4   MIDTERM ELECTIONS: Democrats regain Senate, but their large majority of governorships is diminished.

	Michael Dukakis re-elected Massachusetts Governor with 69% of the vote.
Christmas holidays	Dukakis aide John Sasso sends a memorandum to Governor Dukakis outlining plans for Presidential campaign.

1987

January 23	Republicans select New Orleans as 1988 National Convention site.
February 11	Democrats choose Atlanta for 1988 National Convention site.
February 20	Cuomo announces he will not seek the Democratic nomination.
February 26	Tower report on Iran-Contra affair released.
March 10	Former Arizona Governor Bruce Babbitt announces he will seek the Democratic nomination.
March 17	Governor Michael Dukakis announces.
March 20	Senator Dale Bumpers of Arkansas says he will not seek the Democratic nomination.
March 24	Former Secretary of State Alexander Haig announces.
April 7	Congressman Jack Kemp of New York announces.
April 10	Senator Paul Simon of Illinois announces.
April 14	Former Senator Gary Hart of Colorado announces.
May 4	*Miami Herald* publishes article about Hart spending time with model Donna Rice.
May 9	Hart withdraws from campaign after failing to defuse charges of womanizing.
May 17	U.S.S. *Stark* hit by Iraqi missile; 37 American servicemen killed.
June 10	Senator Joseph Biden of Delaware announces.
June 26	Justice Lewis F. Powell retires from Supreme Court; Reagan nominates Robert Bork to fill slot.
June 30	Senator Albert Gore of Tennessee announces.
July 1	On "Firing Line" the seven announced Democratic candidates debate for the first time on national television.
July 10	Iran-Contra hearings begin in Congress.
August 26	After testing the waters, former Senator Paul Laxalt of Nevada announces he will not run for GOP nomination.

August 27	Senator Sam Nunn of Georgia says no to Democratic presidential bid.
September 12	In surprise, Robertson wins Iowa straw poll sponsored by state GOP.
September 16	Front-page story in *The New York Times* reports that Biden delivered a speech in Iowa using words very similar to those of British Labor Party leader Neil Kinnock without attribution.
September 23	Biden withdraws from Democratic race after failing to defuse charges of plagiarism in speeches and in law school, and of exaggerating his academic accomplishments.
September 28	Congressman Patricia Schroeder of Colorado announces she will not run for the Democratic nomination.
September 30	Dukakis admits his campaign aides gave reporters the damaging Biden/Kinnock videotape; John Sasso and Paul Tully resign from Dukakis campaign.
October 1	Pat Robertson announces.
October 10	Jackson formally enters Democratic race; leads other Democrats in polls, but behind "undecided."
October 13	Bush announces.
October 19	Black Monday on stock market; Dow Jones industrial average plunges 508 points, a 22.6% drop.
October 23	Bork nomination rejected by Senate.
October 26	Former United Nations Ambassador Jeanne Kirkpatrick officially declines to be considered for GOP nomination.
October 28	On "Firing Line" all six Republican candidates debate for the first time on national television; five of them take jabs at front-runner Bush.
November 7	Douglas Ginsburg withdraws his name from consideration for Supreme Court after admitting having smoked marijuana. Ginsburg's admission encourages Babbitt and Gore to admit past marijuana use.
November 10	Senator Robert Dole of Kansas announces.
November 11	Anthony M. Kennedy is nominated to fill Supreme Court spot; later confirmed by Senate.
December 1	All Democratic and Republican candidates hold a two-hour television debate sponsored by NBC and moderated by Tom Brokaw.

December 1	Manchester *Union Leader* endorses Du Pont.
December 8–10	Gorbachev-Reagan summit in Washington, D.C.; the two sign INF Treaty, agreeing to scrap intermediate-range nuclear weapons.
December 13	All three networks announce plans to modify reporting approach to be new, lean, and more analytic in order to cover large number of candidates.
December 15	Hart re-enters race, vowing to "let the people decide."

1988

January 4	Matching funds distributed to candidates by FEC; over $25 million given out initially, including more than $5 million to Bush.
January 8	*Des Moines Register* debate for GOP contenders; Bush defends INF Treaty and his role in Iran-Contra.
January 14	Bush apparent winner over Kemp-Robertson coalition in first GOP vote of 1988, the confusing and bitterly contested Michigan county conventions.
January 15	*Des Moines Register* debate for Democratic candidates; Hart is focus of attention, but his performance is subdued.
January 25	Bush and Dan Rather spar in live interview on "CBS Evening News."
January 31	*Des Moines Register* endorses Simon among Democrats and Dole among Republicans, making its first endorsements in history of Iowa caucuses.
February 3	House of Representatives defeats Reagan's Nicaraguan Contra-aid package, 211–219.
February 5	Dole angrily confronts Bush on floor of U.S. Senate over Bush press release in Iowa; Robertson landslide winner in Hawaii GOP caucuses.
February 5	General Manuel Noriega of Panama indicted by Florida grand juries on drug-trafficking charges.
February 8	IOWA CAUCUSES: Dole wins GOP straw vote, with Robertson second and Bush third; close Democratic finish, with Gephardt, Simon, and Dukakis in 1–2–3 order.
February 13	Haig withdraws and endorses Dole.
February 15	In New Hampshire Bush attacks Dole on taxes.

February 16	NEW HAMPSHIRE PRIMARY: Bush rebounds, beating Dole by 9 points; Kemp third and Robertson fifth. Among Democrats, Dukakis the big winner, as expected, and Gephardt narrowly places second ahead of Simon. Dole responds tartly to defeat in TV interview, telling Bush to "stop lying about my record."
February 18	Babbitt and Du Pont withdraw.
February 21	Televangelist Jimmy Swaggart confesses to moral sin on TV and steps down temporarily from his Baton Rouge-based ministry; two days later Robertson complains Bush may have some role in the timing of Swaggart's revelations.
February 23	Dole sweeps Minnesota and South Dakota, and Robertson wins strong second place showings; for Democrats, winners are Dukakis in Minnesota and Gephardt in South Dakota.
February 24	Simon, impoverished financially, says he will bypass Super Tuesday.
February 25	Dole campaign chairman Bill Brock fires two top consultants in shake-up.
March 3	Former Virginia Governor Charles Robb endorses Gore; former U.N. Representative Kirkpatrick endorses Dole.
March 5	Bush wins nearly half the vote in critical pre-Super Tuesday GOP primary in South Carolina; Dole, Robertson far behind.
March 8	SUPER TUESDAY: Bush sweeps all sixteen GOP primaries; Robertson wins Washington caucuses; Dole shut out. Democrat results muddled: Jackson wins most votes; Dukakis wins most states and delegates; Gore exceeds expectations; Gephardt's only win is his home state of Missouri.
March 10	Kemp withdraws; Jackson wins Alaska caucuses.
March 11	Hart withdraws again.
March 15	ILLINOIS PRIMARY. Bush wins big in GOP contest; Simon further muddles Democrat race with decisive win.
March 22	Congress overrides President Reagan's veto of Grove City civil rights bill.

March 26	Jackson wins upset landslide with 47% of the vote in Michigan.
March 28	Kemp endorses Bush; after third place Michigan finish, Gephardt withdraws.
March 29	Dole withdraws.
April 5	WISCONSIN PRIMARY: Dukakis scores breakthrough victory over Jackson, with surprisingly large 48–28% win.
April 7	Simon suspends campaign after distant fourth place finish in Wisconsin.
April 15	Pakistan, Afghanistan, Soviet Union, and United States sign agreements in Geneva providing for the withdrawal of Soviet forces from Afghanistan.
April 19	NEW YORK PRIMARY: Dukakis breaks open race with decisive win; Jackson strength limited to New York City, which he wins narrowly in spite of Mayor Koch's strident support of Gore; Jackson wins Vermont caucuses by small margin.
April 19–20	Senate and House superdelegates selected; begin breaking for Dukakis.
April 21	Gore suspends campaign after distant third-place finish in New York.
April 26	PENNSYLVANIA PRIMARY: In first one-on-one test, Dukakis beats Jackson by margin of more than 2-to-1; Bush wins enough delegates to clinch GOP nomination.
May 5	*Newsweek* publishes Regan book's claim that Nancy Reagan and astrology guide the President's schedule.
May 11	President Reagan endorses Bush; Robertson announces he will suspend campaign on May 16 and endorse Bush.
May 17	OREGON PRIMARY: Dukakis wins, but Jackson's 38% share is his best in a state with virtually no black base. *New York Times*/CBS poll puts Dukakis at 49%, Bush at 39%.
May 19	New Jersey focus groups review "issues" for the Bush campaign.
May 25	Reagan vetoes Omnibus Trade Bill because of plant-closing notification section.
May 27	Senate ratifies INF Treaty.
May 29–June 2	Reagan-Gorbachev summit in Moscow.

June 7	Dukakis clinches delegates needed for Democratic nomination with four-state sweep, including California and New Jersey; Jackson later pledges to continue campaigning until the convention.
June 8	Dukakis receives endorsements from Gephardt, Simon, Babbitt, and Cuomo.
June 16	Gore endorses Dukakis on swing through South.
June 25	Democratic platform and rules conclude pre-convention work; Jackson files minority reports to platform, which he considers too bland, but wins concessions from Dukakis camp on rules changes for 1992.
July 3	U.S.S. *Vincennes* mistakenly shoots down civilian Iranian airliner over the Persian gulf, killing all 290 aboard.
July 4	Dukakis hosts Jackson for dinner at his home in Brookline, Mass.
July 5	Embattled Attorney General Edwin Meese III announces he will resign his post in several weeks.
July 8	Labor Department announces unemployment rate has fallen to 5.2%, lowest since 1974.
July 12	Dukakis announces Senator Lloyd Bentsen of Texas as his VP choice; Jackson refuses to condemn or endorse ticket, and Jackson supporters say he was slighted by lack of prior notification.
July 13	House passes plant-closing notification bill by 286–136 margin, large enough to override a potential presidential veto; President Reagan allows the bill to become law without his signature.
July 18	Democratic National Convention opens in Atlanta; Dukakis and Jackson announce healing of rift; Texas State Treasurer Ann Richards delivers withering personal attack on Bush in keynote speech.
July 19	Jackson urges crowd to "keep hope alive" in stirring convention address; Democrats adopt 4,500-word platform after Dukakis supporters defeat two minority planks; Senator Kennedy of Massachusetts, in a speech questioning Bush's role in the Reagan administration, asks "Where was George?"
July 20	Dukakis receives Democratic nomination on first ballot, with 2,876.25 votes to 1,218.5 for Jackson.

July 21	Dukakis accepts nomination with speech touted as most effective of his career; Dukakis says the election is "not about ideology" but "about competence"; Bentsen nominated for VP by acclamation.
July 27	Commerce Department announces that the gross national product (GNP) grew at a rate of 3.1% during the second quarter of 1988, following a 3.4% growth in the first quarter.
July 28	Polls taken after the close of the Democratic convention show Dukakis with a 17-point lead over Bush; Gallup Poll gives Dukakis a 55–38% lead, and an NBC/*Wall Street Journal* poll puts him ahead 51–34%.
July 30	Dukakis implicitly criticizes Reagan and his administration for the handling of the Pentagon procurement scandal, saying, "a fish rots from the head first."
August 3	Reagan vetoes a $299.6 billion defense authorization bill, saying it would lead back to the "weakness and accommodation of the 1970s"; suggestions are made that the veto is an attempt to boost Bush's campaign.
August 3	Asked at a press conference about rumors concerning Dukakis's mental health, Reagan says, "I'm not going to pick on an invalid"; he later apologizes for the remark.
August 4	Bush continues to assail Dukakis' foreign policy views, claiming they would make the world a "more dangerous" place.
August 4	Dukakis visits Philadelphia, Miss., where three civil rights activists were found slain in 1964, but makes no mention of civil rights while addressing a predominantly white audience. Later Jackson says Dukakis missed an opportunity to send a "profound message."
August 6	James A. Baker resigns as Secretary of the Treasury to join Bush campaign.
August 8	Bush addresses Republican Platform Committee and calls Dukakis "the stealth candidate," whose policies "can be neither seen nor heard."
August 10	Dukakis appears at ground-breaking ceremony for a $6 billion sewage-treatment plant designed to clean up Boston Harbor, a project he had once said the state could not afford.

August 12   GOP Platform Committee completes 40,000-word platform, which calls for a cut in the capital gains tax, supports "rapid and certain deployment" of the Strategic Defense Initiative, and declares that the rights of the fetus "cannot be infringed" under any circumstances.

August 15   Republican National Convention opens in New Orleans; President Reagan in farewell address defends his administration's accomplishments, says "George was there" when important decisions were made, and urges Bush to "win one for the Gipper."

August 16   Bush introduces Senator Dan Quayle of Indiana as his VP choice, calling him a "dynamic young leader"; pick pleases conservatives; New Jersey Governor Thomas H. Kean gives keynote speech and strongly attacks Dukakis.

August 17   Bush nominated without opposition, but caught in controversy over the selection of Quayle; reporters chase rumors that Quayle received preferential treatment in gaining admission to an Indiana National Guard unit in 1969, at the height of the Vietnam War.

August 18   Bush accepts nomination in speech acclaimed as his best ever, calling for a "kinder and gentler nation" and vowing "I mean to win." Quayle accepts VP spot with a speech stressing small-town values.

August 19   At a press conference in Quayle's home town of Huntington, Ind., a partisan crowd jeers at some press questions directed at Quayle.

August 24   Bush's poll standing surges after the convention; an NBC News/*Wall Street Journal* poll taken Aug. 20–22 puts him ahead of Dukakis 44–39%; a CBS News poll released Aug. 22 gives him a 46–40% lead.

August 24   AFL-CIO endorses Dukakis.

August 26   In Texas Bush says Dukakis opposes gun ownership and the Pledge of Allegiance, and he attacks the Massachusetts prison furlough program.

September 1   Bush takes a boat ride in Boston Harbor, criticizing Dukakis' record on the environment; a *Boston Herald* poll shows Bush even with Dukakis in Massachusetts.

September 2   Longtime Dukakis confidant John Sasso rejoins the campaign; the move is seen as a sign that Dukakis is concerned with the campaign's progress.

September 7 | Bush, in a break with the GOP platform, says he supports "some adjustment" in the $3.35 per hour minimum wage.

September 7 | Dukakis unveils a sweeping student-loan program to aid college students; loans would be repaid through a payroll deduction, similar to the Social Security program.

September 8 | Dukakis' campaign, making concessions to the Bush camp, agrees to two presidential debates and one VP debate; Dukakis' representatives had proposed four presidential debates.

September 8 | National Education Association endorses Dukakis.

September 9 | Cleveland *Plain Dealer* reports Quayle was accepted into law school under a program designed in part to aid minorities and the poor.

September 11 | Bush adviser Frederick V. Malek resigns after *The Washington Post* reports that in 1971, as an assistant to President Richard M. Nixon, Malek compiled a list of Jews working at the Bureau of Labor Statistics; two Jewish employees of the agency were subsequently reassigned.

September 13 | Dukakis rides in an M-1 tank to show support for defense; the photo is later featured in a Bush TV ad.

September 20 | Dukakis proposes mandatory employer-provided health insurance; Bush visits New Jersey flag factory.

September 22 | Bush in Boston picks up the endorsement of the Boston Police Patrolman's Association; Dukakis counters with a hastily arranged counter-rally with law-enforcement officers.

September 25 | First Bush-Dukakis debate held in Winston-Salem, N.C.; Dukakis given high marks for substance, Bush for likability.

September 26 | Bush and Quayle attend a rally in Jackson, Tenn., their first appearance together since Aug. 19.

October 3 | League of Women Voters bows out of sponsorship of second presidential debates, saying candidates gave them no role in developing format. Bipartisan Commission on Presidential Debates, which was sponsoring the other two debates, takes over.

October 5 | Bentsen-Quayle VP debate held in Omaha, Neb.; Bentsen tells Quayle during debate, "You're no Jack Kennedy." Media declares Bentsen the debate winner.

October 5	Labor Department releases unemployment figures; civilian rate announced as 5.4%, 2 points lower than on election eve in 1984.
October 13	Second and final Bush-Dukakis debate, held at UCLA; media widely hail Bush as the winner; Dukakis seen as showing no emotional range in his answer to a hypothetical question on what he would do if his wife were raped and murdered.
October 17	NBC News/*Wall Street Journal* poll finds Bush ahead 55–38%; Dukakis camp disputes accuracy of poll.
October 17	Teamster's Union endorses Bush.
October 19	Dukakis in Quincy, Ill., rips into GOP campaign literature on Massachusetts' prison-furlough program, calling the material "political garbage."
October 19	With rumors rife that *The Washington Post* is about to print a story about Bush's private life, Dow Jones industrial average drops 43 points; the *Post* denies it is printing such a story.
October 26	GNP growth for the third quarter of 1988 slows to 2.2%; drought and trade deficit are cited as contributing factors.
October 30	After dodging the "L" word throughout the fall campaign, Dukakis, campaigning in California's Central Valley, says he is a "liberal in the tradition of Franklin Roosevelt and Harry Truman and John Kennedy."
November 2	Polls give Bush a 12-point lead over Dukakis; a *Washington Post*/ABC News survey taken Oct. 26–31 shows a 55–42% margin; CBS News poll gives Bush a 53–41% edge.
November 8	ELECTION DAY.

Sources: Congressional Quarterly, various newspapers, and the campaign managers themselves.

INDEX